Leading Systemic School Improvement Series

...helping change leaders transform entire school systems

This Rowman & Littlefield Education series provides change leaders in school districts with a collection of books written by prominent authors with an interest in creating and sustaining whole-district school improvement. It features young, relatively unpublished authors with brilliant ideas, as well as authors who are cross-disciplinary thinkers.

Whether an author is prominent or relatively unpublished, the key criterion for a book's inclusion in this series is that it must address an aspect of creating and sustaining systemic school improvement. For example, books from members of the business world, developmental psychology, and organizational development are good candidates as long as they focus on creating and sustaining whole-system change in school district settings; books about building-level curriculum reform, instructional methodologies, and team communication, although interesting and helpful, are not appropriate for the series unless they discuss how these ideas can be used to create whole-district improvement.

Since the series is for practitioners, highly theoretical or research-reporting books aren't included. Instead, the series provides an artful blend of theory and practice—in other words, books based on theory and research but written in plain, easy-to-read language. Ideally, theory and research are artfully woven into practical descriptions of how to create and sustain systemic school improvement. The series is subdivided into three categories:

Why Systemic School Improvement Is Needed and Why It's Important. This is the *why*. Possible topics within this category include the history of systemic school improvement; the underlying philosophy of systemic school improvement; how systemic school improvement is different from school-based improvement; and the driving forces of standards, assessments, and accountability and why systemic improvement can respond effectively to these forces.

The Desirable Outcomes of Systemic School Improvement. This is the *what*. Possible topics within this category include comprehensive school reform models scaled up to create whole-district improvement; strategic alignment; creating a high-performance school system; redesigning a school system as a learning organization; unlearning and learning mental models; and creating an organization design flexible and agile enough to respond quickly to unanticipated events in the outside world.

How to Create and Sustain Systemic School Improvement. This is the *how*. Possible topics within this category include methods for redesigning entire school systems; tools for navigating complex change; ideas from the "new sciences" for creating systemic change; leadership methods for creating systemic change; evaluating the process and outcomes of systemic school improvement; and financing systemic school improvement.

The series editor, Dr. Francis M. Duffy, can be reached at 301-854-9800 or fmduffy@earthlink.net.

Leading Systemic School Improvement Series
Edited by Francis M. Duffy

SYSTEMS THINKERS IN ACTION

A Field Guide for Effective Change Leadership in Education

Edited by
Blane Després

Leading Systemic School Improvement,
No. 10

Rowman & Littlefield Education
Lanham, Maryland • Toronto • Plymouth, UK
2008

Published in the United States of America
by Rowman & Littlefield Education
A Division of Rowman & Littlefield Publishers, Inc.
A wholly owned subsidary of The Rowman & Littlefield Publishing Group,
Inc.
4501 Forbes Boulevard, Suite 200, Lanham, Maryland 20706
www.rowmaneducation.com

Estover Road
Plymouth PL6 7PY
United Kingdom

British Library Cataloguing in Publication Information Available

Library of Congress Cataloging-in-Publication Data

Systems thinkers in action : a field guide for effective change leadership in
education / edited by Blane Després.
    p. cm.
  ISBN-13: 978-1-57886-659-5 (cloth : alk. paper)
  ISBN-10: 1-57886-659-6 (cloth : alk. paper)
  ISBN-13: 978-1-57886-660-1 (pbk. : alk. paper)
  ISBN-10: 1-57886-660-X (pbk. : alk. paper)
  1. Educational leadership. 2. Educational change. 3. School improvement
programs. I. Després, Blane, 1954–
LB2831.6.S96 2006
371.2–dc22   2007025246

∞™ The paper used in this publication meets the minimum requirements of
American National Standard for Information Sciences—Permanence of
Paper for Printed Library Materials, ANSI/NISO Z39.48-1992.
Manufactured in the United States of America.

CONTENTS

FOREWORD

Michael Fullan

SYSTEM THINKERS IN ACTION

Applied complexity theory or what I call "system thinkers in action" has enormous potential for contributing to transforming whole school systems for the better. Yet there are few practical, comprehensive treatments of the topic. Blane Després and his colleagues have addressed this gap by assembling an array of chapters that systematically covers just about every aspect of leadership and change that will be essential for bringing about systemwide improvement.

All the key complexity theory concepts are pursued: complex adaptive systems, chaos theory, strange attractors, feedback loops, self-organizing properties, and so on. The particular contribution of this book, however, is that these powerful ideas are linked to all aspects of the field of education improvement including: school improvement, school and system leadership, shared accountability, moral purpose, student achievement, cultures of learning, and expanding the reach of education strategies to transform systems.

This is complex terrain and each of the twelve chapters furnishes insightful and interesting analysis and grounds for action. As a whole, this systems-oriented field guide is the best, most comprehensive book available on the topic of applying complexity theory. What is also exciting is that *System Thinkers in Action* makes it clear that this is just the beginning of opening up a whole new, rich vein of potentially powerful ideas and strategies for change. The last chapter captures this spirit precisely because it formulates "conclusions and continued beginnings." This is a book that will provide immediate payoff for those looking for something more powerful to inform approaches to school and system improvement. And it should spawn many more ideas and expanded possibilities as others take up the numerous implications of the areas identified across the chapters. As someone deeply interested in how to make system thinking of practical use, I applaud the efforts of the authors to advance the field in such a significant way.

INTRODUCTION

Blane Després

λέγει που Ἡράκλειτος, ὅτι πάντα χωρεῖ, καὶ οὐδὲν μένει· καὶ ποταμοῦ ῥοῇ ἀπεικάζων τὰ ὄντα λέγει, ὡς δὶς ἐς τὸν αὐτὸν ποταμὸν οὐκ ἂν ἐμβαίης

> Socrates: Heracleitus is supposed to say that all things are in motion and nothing at rest; he compares them to the stream of a river and says that you cannot go into the same water twice.
>
> —Plato Cratylus, 402A1[1]

How do you develop and sustain a greater number of "system thinkers in action"? I call this breed of leader "the new theoretician." These are leaders at all levels of the system who proactively and naturally take into account and interact with larger parts of the system as they bring about deeper reform and help produce other leaders working on the same issues. They are theoreticians, but they are practitioners whose theories are lived in action every day. In fact, that is what makes their impact so powerful. Their ideas are woven into daily interactions that make a difference.[2]

Leaders at all levels in the education system who are, or who wish to be, involved in change in education will appreciate the practical applications and discussions in this field guide. Change and reform in education at a systemic level have become near meaningless, fashion buzz words. The challenge to leaders—from teachers to administrators—is properly interpreting what such change or reform means in practice in the inherently complex theater of education. One of the distinguishing characteristics of this field guide is in the underlying thread of systemic thinking in education. Throughout the book, the essays and ideas will enable the neophyte through to the practiced critical systems thinker to grasp not only the complexity of education systems, but also to gain insights about some of the innovative and creative means of improving our understanding of and response to that complexity.

Systems and complexity can be subtle, like the poetic rhythms of a river meandering through a countryside. There is a sense in which I can stick my foot into the river one summer and come back again the next summer, or multiple summers later, to the "same" river. Yet, according to Heracleitus, it is never the same river.[3] Part of the complexity from this metaphor for life is in water and motion, river source, vegetation, weather, erosion, the impact of animals and humans interacting with rivers via transportation, recreation, sanitation, and living. Coming to that water time after time I may not take stock of all these related configurations, oblivious to their relationships or content to remain with the seeming simplicity of water and the moment. Nevertheless, the water is in motion, the river is dynamic, the ecosystem around it is growing and dying, and each of these contributes to life.

Similarly systems and complexity can be strikingly obvious. The organizations that we form, and that contribute to forming us in turn, are complex, sometimes chaotic systems. More than material constructions and people, they are imbued with the chaos of lives working to live. People interact in organizations with sometimes conflicting, sometimes co-synchronous perceptions about purposes of life, work, organizational raisons d'être, and the dynamics of working with and for others. This complexity is compounded by the practices of people, processes, individuals, cultures, bureaucratic procedures, by theories and thoughts of is and ought, and by desire.

Making sense of the chaos of life, perhaps paradoxically organized as it is, has taxed linear thinking about change and challenged our notions of straight line or curved path routes to understanding parts of organizations in relation to the whole organization. In an emergent response, Senge (1990) introduced us to systemic thinking, or moving beyond the reductionist celebration of the parts as pretense for knowing the whole, to cogitating about, acknowledging and tracing the relationships of life events, organizations, systems. In that way only could we begin to comprehend patterns or archetypes, relationships, systems, transdisciplinary and interdisciplinary interplay. But not all organizations or systems—or individuals—have been able to secede the status quo of hierarchies or ambivalence to a new(er) paradigm. In the case of education, the practical absence of systemic thinking in school systems surely is a problem associated with the complexity of education itself. In addition, however, its absence results from lack of understanding of exactly what systemic thinking is and how it could possibly be of any use in education. Add in there a touch of fear of change, or as one teacher educator put it, "I'm just trying to keep the wheels on the bus. And the bus is moving!"

A simple, online search for *systemic thinking* will produce copious resources that have more to do with its applications in business, science, and psychology, especially in therapy (e.g., Byron 1997a, 1997b; Emery, Finchman, and Cummings 1992; Espejo 2002; Fuchs 2003; Harung 1997; Sexton 1994; Ulrich 2000). Education from preschool through to universities and continuing education has its share of systems-thinking proponents and entrepreneurial people capitalizing on marketing techniques, spin-doctoring, and advantageous timing. A challenge is to find solid applications of systemic thinking in education. Sure, there are examples of systems dynamics and instructional design, and plenty of writing about the need for, and some successes in, systemic change in districts, programs or schools (Baker and Richards 2004; Hepp, Hinostroza, and Laval 2004; Horn and Carr 2000).[4] Yet there is a corresponding blandness in what constitutes systemic thinking practice or research in chaos and complexity in education. Why in education? Why, of all institutions, including its unions, is systemic thinking still such a foreign and missed opportunity in education? Systemic thinking, and its siblings, chaos and complexity, and systems dynamics, are rich with experience and research from diverse fields, from business, to therapy, to sciences and philosophy. However, education has been much slower to embrace systemic thinking, whether as a result of resistance, its sheer complexity, or other unfortunate reasons.

As an example of the paucity of representation of systemic thinking in education is the volume of presentations at the 2005 American Education

Research Association (AERA) annual meeting—the largest education conference in North America having over ten thousand in attendance—in Montréal, Québec. The AERA spans topic areas found many times over in the literature, from critical theory, to educational reform, to leadership, and so on. The 278 subject index titles in the conference presentations program along with the hundreds more topics beneath these titles of this AERA meeting[5] clearly corroborate that education is complex. Of those hundreds of topics, systemic thinking and chaos and complexity occupied a mere eight presentations.[6] Unfortunately systemic thinking, representing as it did a mere fraction of the presentations at this conference, demonstrates all the more reason why there is a greater need for this field guide and more.

RATIONALE FOR THIS FIELD GUIDE

As a unique contribution to education, organizational dynamics, and systemic thinking, this field guide, to adapt Michael Fullan's ideas, presents a humble opportunity to forefront "system thinkers in action . . . [these] new theoretician[s]," and to hold up to the world examples of current systemic thinking and action relating to education in a broader social and global context. To outsiders this field guide provides an insightful look into education in relation to a concept that has already been abuzz for a few decades in science and nearly two decades in business and therapy. This is a book that ambitiously sets out to encourage and educate leaders and to excite them about systemic thinking through examples and challenging ideas pertinent to education.

Education is complex, which is no surprise. This book demonstrates through practical applications and research how some educational change agents are responding to that complexity. If practitioners, societies, governments, and even publishers are to develop the best possible understanding of education in the context of other social organizations, a systemic approach ought to be fundamental. Reform is more than the infusion of capital or novel programs and enthusiasm; accountability is more than rising test scores and teacher attitudes; increased funding is more than building corporate relationships or increasing taxes; and preparing students for living and coping in a growing, global context is more than curricular tampering. As one might expect from this collection of authors in this field guide, ranging from the seasoned and established to the emerging next generation, the variety of topics penned under particular headings provide the reader with a much broader perspective of current systems thinking in education, which also aids in understanding education in general.

The selection of authors was for their work in the field of education and especially their practical consideration of systemic thinking. Systems thinking is concerned about systems—plural—in general. Systemic thinking focuses on a particular system. And a system is any composition of factors (variables, elements, parts) whose function in combination produces a complete and complex unity that would not otherwise exist. What compounds the complexity of a system is that there are attending subsystems or microsystems that also figure in the study of a system. Formal education is a system. On a direct or immediate macrolevel—the big picture—it comprises kindergarten through twelfth grade schooling, alternative learning approaches, adult education, and colleges and university education. Each of these is a microsystem of education. Each one functions as a complete unity independent of the others while remaining related. Other systems that influence education both at the macrolevels and microlevels include government systems, service provider systems (from electricity to textbooks, to cleaning, to whatever is deemed necessary to the sustainable functioning of that system), local cultural systems, and even economic systems. A systems thinker, then, is one who contemplates and considers the factors at a systemic level.

But this tends to be problematic for at least two main reasons. The first is the lack of understanding the *what* and the *why* of systemic thinking. Educators might not have a sufficient enough understanding of what constitutes systemic thinking. The second reason is that they do not appreciate why systemic thinking is probably the most important practice they could engage in for the total improvement of education. However, systemwide improvement to any system or organization demands challenges to the hegemonic paradigm, by which I mean the reigning or accepted model for practice. For example, schooling is the reigning paradigm in formal education beginning at kindergarten and continuing through to university despite more successful, alternative models, or paradigms, that exist. Change leaders must be mindful of these two problems.

Mindfulness, however, is not enough. Educators might be alert to these two problems but remain inert, unable to effect changes that are operationally at a higher level of order in the best interest of children and adolescents in their learning. Change leaders will be creative in both their exposure and the revolution to change them. This book is an attempt to provide these systems thinkers in action with additional details in making systemwide change happen. It will not occur overnight. Suggesting a change of paradigms is not like suggesting a change of eating venues. It is much deeper than that. People are particularly phobic about competing paradigms. After all, these models of behavior and practice find root at a heart depth, intricately bound with core beliefs. Suggested change of one shakes up the other, and that is a discomfort that does not enjoy a facile following. Just the opposite is true. Thus will creative change leaders need to become critical system thinkers in action who are also compassionate in their efforts.

FIELD GUIDE OVERVIEW

In Frank Duffy's opening chapter, an overview of systemic thinking and its usefulness to change leaders in education serves as a backdrop to the field guide. It provides the reader, especially the uninitiated in systemic thinking or chaos and complexity theories, an introduction to pertinent terms and concepts used.

Charles Reigeluth examines ways that chaos and complexity study could assist change leaders in the transformation of K–12 education, he says, "to correct the dangerous evolutionary imbalance that currently exists."

Bill Thornton and George Perreault collaborate to bring us a discussion of sustained change in schools. They present a practical tool for diagnosing organizational structure and the possibilities.

Howard Adelman and Linda Taylor draw attention to the limited view and certain failure of the No Child Left Behind (NCLB) advocacy. Beginning with an overview of current practices in schools regarding learning, behavior, and emotional problems, they then move on to discuss impediments in educational learning followed by alternative systemic changes possibilities geared for sustainable success.

In a related vein, Thomas L. Alsbury presents findings from an empirical study of change leadership in one school district that challenges the linear progression of all-too-common management techniques.

In his chapter, David Bower focuses on holistic practices and principles of self-organization to better equip change leaders in education for sustainable change. His study of those practices and principles in one school district informs the reader about change possibilities.

Sarah Smitherman and Angelle Stringer capitalize on aspects of chaos and complexity theory to examine education leadership, particularly in the school setting. Their research into education leaders as a "strange attractor" affords the reader an alternative understanding and approach to leadership.

Part of the challenges of leaders in educational change has to do with accountability. Carlos Torre and Charlene Voyce examine this timely topic in the light of complexity science with the goal in mind of providing education leaders with alternative ideas and practices.

The ongoing work in systemic thinking by Lees Stuntz, Jeffrey Potash, and John Heinbokel reads both as a resource section for education leaders and as a discussion forum for change leaders who want to know more about change.

As an example of systemic thinking in practice, Ray Barnhardt and Anagayuqaq Oscar Kawagley team up to discuss the impact of chaoplexity science in indigenous education in Alaska. The positive results of the educational reform practices of the Alaska Rural Systemic Initiative demonstrate to change leaders in education what is both possible and necessary.

In another example of systemic thinking application, this time from experiences in a teacher education program, Brent Davis weaves between theoretical principles and education practices in math.

Finally, in an effort to understand as best as possible the complex nature of education—or any organizational structure—and change, I present a model that helps to collect and categorize all the systemic elements of any given event so that change leaders could quickly see where problems lie, what works, and where attention must be focused for successful change to be sustained. Using that model, I categorize the contributors' works in this guide as a means to demonstrate not only the variety of foci in the vast field of K–12 education, but also the strength of the SyFIA to expose how systemic one is in one's thinking or research, where incongruities lie and the degree of alignment between factors. In this way the change leader in education (or any organization) could be better equipped to speak to change.

The flow of this field guide deliberately moves the reader through a range of applications and ideas, from an introduction to, or review of, the crucial concepts in systems thinking pertaining to education, to some case studies of systemic thinking in educational practice, to a systems tool that allows organizational leaders to ascertain the positive and negative interconnections of their organization. The addition of the systemic factors inventory analysis (SyFIA) matrix (see table 12-2) provides a reference grid that indicates how the contributions fit together, where researchers could continue on with further explorations, and where the reader could determine areas in need of further consideration before attempting implementation. In this way, the field guide demonstrates current practices, research, and ideas across multiple disciplines and interests and paves the way for new directions by educating the reader about possibilities regarding systemic or holistic improvements in K–12 education and beyond.

REFERENCES

Baker, B. D., and C. E. Richards. 2004. *The ecology of educational systems: Data, models, and tools for improvisational leading and learning.* Columbus, OH: Pearson.

Byron, M. 1997a. Crisis-driven evolutionary learning: A procedural mechanism for systemic learning. *Journal of Social and Evolutionary Systems* 20 (2): 179–84.

———. 1997b. Systemic learning and the trajectory of the world system. *Journal of Social and Evolutionary Systems* 20 (3): 281–309.

Cuban, L. 1984. How teachers taught: Constancy and change in American classrooms, 1890–1980. New York: Grove.

Emery, R. E., F. .D. Finchman, and E. M. Cummings. 1992. Parenting in context: Systemic thinking about parental conflict and its influence on children. *Journal of Consulting and Clinical Psychology* 60 (6): 909–12.

Espejo, R. 2002. Self-construction and restricted conversations. *Systems Research and Behavioral Science* 19 (6): 517–29.

Fuchs, C. 2003. Structuration theory and self-organization. *Systemic Practice and Action Research* 16 (2): 133–67.

Fullan, M. 2005. *Leadership and sustainability: System thinkers in action.* Thousand Oaks, CA: Corwin Press.

Harung, H. S. 1997. Enhanced learning and performance through a synergy of objective and subjective modes of change. *The Learning Organization* 4 (5): 193–210.

Hepp, P., J. H. Hinostroza, and E. Laval. 2004. A systemic approach to educational renewal with new technologies: Empowering learning communities in Chile. In *World yearbook of education 2004: Digital technology, communities and education*, ed. A. Brown and N. Davis, 299–311. London: Routledge.

Horn, R. A., and A. A. Carr. 2000. Providing systemic change for schools: Towards professional development through moral conversation. *Systems Research and Behavioral Science* 17: 252–72.

Senge, P. M. (1990). *The fifth discipline: The art & practice of the learning organization*. New York: Doubleday-Currency.

Ulrich, W. 2000. Reflective practice in the civil society: The contribution of critically systemic thinking. *Reflective Practice* 1 (2): 247–69.

NOTES

1. Plato, http://www.mlahanas.de/Greeks/Heraclit.htm Retrieved June 13, 2005.

2. Michael Fullan, *Leadership and Sustainability: System Thinkers in Action* (Thousand Oaks, CA: Corwin Press, 2005), ix.

3. Actually it is the water passing through that conduit called river that is different moment by moment.

4. The contributors in this book provide us with a variety of examples.

5. *Demography and Democracy in the Era of Accountability* (American Educational Research Association annual meeting program, Montréal, Canada, April 11–15, 2005).

6. Although more presentations are listed for the Systems Thinking category (AERA program, p. 428), the titles of the actual presentations themselves (and attended by the author) indicate either a hopeful connection to systemic thinking or misapplication of the concept.

❶

OPEN SYSTEMS THEORY AND SYSTEM DYNAMICS: THE TWIN PILLARS OF TRANSFORMATIONAL CHANGE IN SCHOOL DISTRICTS

Francis M. Duffy

When whole school systems are transformed, unparalleled opportunities to improve student, faculty and staff, and whole-system learning can be created. To transform an entire school system, leaders advocating change in that system must understand how their school district functions as an open system; they must understand the influence of deep-seated and invisible system dynamics called *system archetypes*; they must comprehend what it means to be a systems thinker; and they must be skillful in using a set of systems-thinking tools. This chapter addresses the first two competency sets.

SCHOOL DISTRICTS AS OPEN SYSTEMS

Before getting into a presentation on how a school district functions as an open system, it is important to be clear that this section of the chapter is not an in-depth exploration and discussion of all the concepts and principles related to open systems theory. Instead, a few of the crucial concepts from open systems theory that are relevant to transforming school systems are presented.

To transform an entire school system from what it was and what it is into what it ought to be, change leaders in school districts must have a solid grounding in open systems theory (which is derived from the biological and life sciences as an explanatory metaphor for how organizations function as systems). Open systems theory is an important foundation for leading whole-system change because it explains how organizations, such as school districts, are affected by, and how they affect, their external environments. These effects can have a significant impact on a school system's performance (e.g., consider the influence of the "No Child Left Behind [NCLB]" federal legislation in the United States).

OPEN SYSTEMS THEORY

A simple figure depicting a school system is shown in figure 1.1. The system in that figure has the following components: an environment, inputs, a conversion process (which is classroom teaching and learning and other supporting work processes), an internal social infrastructure that supports the conversion process, outputs, and a feedback loop. The system to be improved is everything inside the dotted line (Emery and Purser 1995). The environment is everything outside the dotted line.

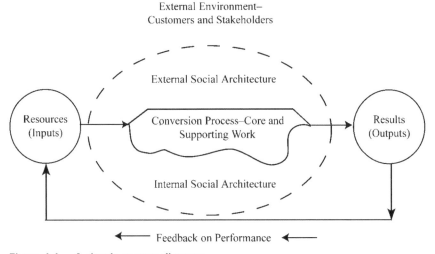

Figure 1.1.   A simple system diagram

An open system depends on its external environment for its life energy. In the case of school systems, life energy is composed of human, technical, and financial resources. In return for these resources, school systems are expected to provide a valuable service to their community; that is, they are expected to educate their community's children. The school system also continually interacts with its environment to resupply its resources and to provide educational services. It is this symbiotic relationship with an environment that makes a school system an open system.

A school system takes in required resources from its environment and converts those resources into a valued service for its community; that is, it uses the resources to educate a community's children. The quality of that education is then evaluated by the consumers of those services (e.g., parents, community organizations, businesses that hire graduates of the school system, colleges and universities that enroll graduates of the school system, and other stakeholders). The evaluation results are fed back into the system. The evaluation data influence the availability of future resources for a school system.

A school system has internal components that are easy to identify. There are two broad categories of components: the core and supporting work processes (which together are called the *technical subsystem*) and the internal social infrastructure (which is often called the *social subsystem* and includes organization design, power and political dynamics, organization culture, job descriptions, reward systems, spans of control, and the number of departments or divisions). "All of these parts compose a whole, a total organization that represents an entity different from the simple sum of its elements and dimensions, which is a basic tenet of Gestalt psychology" (Burke 2002, 44).

CHARACTERISTICS OF OPEN SYSTEMS

Von Bertalanffy (1950) and Katz and Kahn (1978) described ten characteristics that define an open system. Each one is summarized here and interpreted to fit school systems so that readers can better understand how open systems theory influences efforts to improve entire school systems.

Importation of Energy

All school systems need energy from their external environments. This energy is derived from human, technical, and financial resources that districts need to educate children. Declining resources threaten the performance of a school system, therefore system leaders invest a lot of their personal energy in identifying and securing the resources their school systems need to perform.

Throughput

For a school system, throughputs are processes by which external resources are converted into a valued service; that is, human, technical, and financial resources are converted student learning, using a two-part core work process (a linear and sequential instructional program conjoined with nonlinear classroom teaching and learning) and a set of varied supporting work processes (e.g., administration, supervision, busing, cafeteria services, custodial services, and other pupil personnel services).

The conversion process (the core and supporting work processes) is tightly entwined with the system's internal social infrastructure. This infrastructure creates an internal environment within which educators do their work, and it is composed of organization design, organization culture, power and political dynamics, communication processes, evaluation processes, reward systems, and other related components. The core and supporting work processes and the internal social infrastructure are significantly intertwined and inseparable; therefore, both must be improved simultaneously for sustainable, systemwide changes to occur.

Output

School districts educate students. Teachers organize the best information they can learn about their subject area, and they present that information to students using a teaching method. Students take that information and transform it into personal knowledge. This teaching-learning process frequently occurs across fourteen plus years (pre-kindergarten through twelfth grade); therefore a student's education is not what he or she learns in the third grade or in a middle school. His or her learning is the cumulative effect of his or her learning career in a school district (in the case of highly mobile students who go in and out of school districts, this learning is still a function of their learning career and not what they learn in a particular grade or at a specific level of schooling).

Systems Are Cycles of Events

For every graduating class of high school seniors, there is a beginning class of preschoolers or kindergarteners. For every sixth grade class moving into seventh grade, there is a class of fifth graders replacing that graduating sixth grade class. School systems are organized using cycles of learning. In this way, this cycle of events is a vital feature that marks the identity of a school system.

Negative Entropy

Entropy, according to Katz and Kahn (1978), is defined as follows:

> [The] entropic process is a universal law of nature in which all forms of organization move toward disorganization or death . . . [but] by importing more energy from its environment than it expends, the open system can store energy and acquire negative entropy. (25)

If a school district is not getting the resources it needs to perform well, district leaders do not ask, "What can we do to stop this entropy?" However, they do realize that if they do not take positive steps to increase the quality and quantity of needed resources that their district will suffer terribly. For school districts, resources include not only money and top-notch teachers, but also the goodwill of their community, good relations with stakeholder groups, and a reputation for providing excellent learning opportunities for students. These intangible resources also have to be replenished and "stored" for future use. The replenishment of needed resources is called *negative entropy (negentropy)*.

Information Input, Negative Feedback, and the Coding Process

School districts as systems need information from their stakeholders about how their services are perceived and valued. This information often takes the form of positive and negative feedback. Negative feedback, in particular, has a way of helping school districts improve their services because of its potential to trigger people's motivation to change.

School districts cannot possibly respond to all the feedback they receive—positive or negative. So leaders in the district select which feedback to pay attention to and which to ignore. This selection process results in feedback being sorted into broad categories that leaders think are relevant to their particular system. This sorting process is called *coding*.

Steady-State and Dynamic Homeostasis

Homeostasis can be steady or dynamic. Homeostasis is also called *equilibrium*. Steady-state homeostasis is often called *balancing equilibrium* (i.e., the system dynamics in a school district that keep it in a steady or stable state). Dynamic homeostasis is sometimes called *reinforcing equilibrium* (i.e., system dynamics that drive a school district out of its steady-state equilibrium toward a new level of equilibrium). A third kind of equilibrium that is sometimes discussed in systems theory is neutral equilibrium. Neutral equilibrium is like having a car in neutral with the engine running. Then the driver steps on the gas, the engine revolutions increase, but the car does not move. When a change is introduced to a school system, if change activities increase but nothing changes, the district is in a state of neutral equilibrium.

Differentiation

Entropy is a natural process of energy depletion. Negative entropy is when energy (human, technical, and financial resources) is replenished. As a school district replenishes and stores resources it often grows in size. As it grows in size, bureaucracy often increases hierarchical levels and departmentalization. Hierarchy and departmentalization is a managerial attempt to divide up the work of a district to make it easier to be effective. Dividing up the work is called *differentiation* (Lawrence and Lorsch 1967). Uncontrolled differentiation creates what is frequently referred to as organization silos; that is, discrete, relatively autonomous departments, programs, or divisions.

Not only does differentiation occur as school districts grow in size, but also a fascinating process called *internal elaboration* emerges. Internal elaboration is organization complexity in full bloom and in rapid propagation. With internal elaboration, there is an explosion of policies and procedures to control human behavior in a growing school district.

Integration and Coordination

To counterbalance unchecked differentiation and internal elaboration, managers use integration and coordination. Integration is when units or organization levels that must collaborate to produce a service or product are naturally clustered so they can do that. Integration occurs in a school district when a high school and all the middle and elementary schools that feed into it are clustered because they must collaborate to provide students with a "total" education.

The internal social infrastructure of a school district (which includes organization culture, organization design, policies, procedures, reward systems, and so on) is the primary vehicle for achieving integration and coordination. This is true because although differentiation can be created on paper by redrawing the organization chart and can be facilitated by reassigning people or by rewriting job descriptions, integration and coordination are quintessential interpersonal activities requiring trust, commitment, and collaboration.

Equifinality

Von Bertalanffy (1950) first espoused this principle. He said a system can achieve a single goal from different starting points and by following a variety of paths. However, this principle is not often enacted in school systems. Frequently, district administrators require everyone in a school district to pursue district goals in *exactly* the same way, on *exactly* the same time line, and with *exactly* the same resources. This brand of forced uniformity of means is assumed to result in uniform results; however, experience demonstrates that it seldom does.

Unity of purpose does not require uniformity of action. Unity of purpose does not preclude equifinality. People in a school district can walk arm-in-arm without seeing eye-to-eye. People in a district can pursue districtwide goals in a variety of different, yet acceptable ways. But all this interaction must be strategically aligned with the district's grand strategy and future vision and must be done "for the good of the whole" (Duffy 2003; 2004).

Ackoff (1999, 6–8) added to our understanding of organizations as open systems. He said a system is a whole entity consisting of several parts with the following properties, which were edited to fit school systems:

- The whole school system has one or more defining properties or functions; for example, a defining function of a school district is to educate students;
- Each component of a school system can affect the behavior or properties of the whole; for example, several low-performing schools in a district can drag an entire district into low-performing status;
- There is a subset of school system components that are essential for carrying out the main purpose of the whole district but they cannot, by themselves, fulfill the main purpose of a school system; for example, teachers, classrooms, and individual school buildings are essential elements of a school system, and they are necessary for helping a school system fulfill its purpose, but these elements alone cannot and never will be able to do what the whole system does;
- There is also a subset of components that are important but nonessential elements that are intended to support a school district's main purpose (which is educating students using classroom teaching and learning that is guided by an instructional program). Although these elements are nonessential, they are still important for the success of a school system, and they must be effective in support of the district's main purpose. These nonessential, but important, elements include administration, supervision, school public relations, and pupil personnel services;
- A school system depends on its environment for the importation of energy (i.e., human, technical, and financial resources); therefore it is an open system. A school district's external environment consists of individuals and groups in its community and the state and federal departments of education (collectively called *stakeholders*). At a broader level, society is also part of a school system's environment;

- The way in which an essential element of a school system affects the whole system depends on its interaction with at least one other element; for example, the effect a single school's performance has on the whole district depends on the interaction that the school has with at least one other school in the system;
- The effect that any subset of essential school district elements has on the whole system depends on the behavior of at least one other subset of elements; for example, let us say that a school district is organized pre-kindergarten through twelfth grade (thus, the work process for that district is fourteen steps long) and that the district has several high schools.

Now, let us say that district leaders are concerned about the performance of their high schools (which represent an essential subset of the system). These high schools contain ninth through twelfth grades. It would be a mistake to focus improvement efforts only on those high schools because their performance is affected by at least two other subsets of schools (i.e., the elementary and middle schools that feed into those high schools).

Because all essential elements of a school system interact, a systemic approach to improving the performance of the high schools would be to cluster each high school with the middle and elementary schools that feed into it. Then, improvement efforts would focus on the entire pre-K–12 grade instructional program within each cluster. Alternatively, focusing improvement only on the high schools would be a nonsystemic, and therefore, piecemeal approach to improvement.

- A school system is a whole entity that cannot be divided into individual components without losing its essential properties or functions. For example, the dominant approach to school district improvement is called *school-based management* or *site-based improvement*. This approach divides school systems into their aggregate parts; that is, individual schools. Then, it is assumed that improving these individual schools will somehow improve the whole system. Further, this improvement assumption is extended to presume that each individual school somehow has the ability to fulfill the essential purpose of a school system; that is, providing children with a total education. But individual schools do not, and never will, provide children with a total education, they only provide children with a partial education represented by the curriculum for the grades embedded in a particular school. When a school system is managed in this way—by disaggregating it into individual schools—its effectiveness as a system deteriorates rapidly;

• Because a school system derives its effectiveness from the interaction of its components rather than from what the components do independent of the system, when efforts are taken to improve the individual components as if they were not part of a whole system (as in school-based improvement), the performance of the whole system, according to Ackoff (1999, 9), deteriorates and the system involved will be significantly weakened.

UNDERLYING SYSTEM STRUCTURES THAT DRIVE SYSTEM PERFORMANCE

Another set of important concepts for understanding how school systems perform the way they do is collectively called *systems archetypes*. These deep system structures have profound influence on human behavior in organizations. A few examples of archetypes that operate within school systems are described here.

Often, what educators observe and experience as a problem in a school district is really a symptom of invisible and powerful system dynamics. Many of these dynamics are driven by system structures called *archetypes*. The observable and "felt" symptoms of these archetypes can be painful and disturbing, but if the symptoms are responded to as if they were the real problems, educators will repeatedly experience the same symptoms in the future because the underlying problems caused by the archetypes were not dissolved.

In the language of systems dynamics experiencing this kind of symptomatic "pain" is an event. Kim says, "We live in the world of events. Things happen and we respond. . . . Each event creates another event, in an endless stream of cause-and-effect relationships" (2000, 2). If observed carefully, these painful events in school systems can be clumped into patterns. A pattern is any event (or set of related events) that is repeated. The more times seemingly related events are repeated, the stronger the pattern is. If educators can identify patterns of painful events then they can take action to create and implement high-leverage interventions to improve their system's performance.

If change leaders in a school district assess their district's performance problems at a deeper level, they can begin to identify what is causing the troublesome symptoms that are manifested in the overall performance of their district. Given the location of the "real" cause of troublesome symptoms (symptoms such as the achievement gap between certain groups of students, low-performing schools, the inability to rise up to the challenges of the NCLB legislation, low teacher morale, lack of commitment to the district's goals, the inability to sustain changes, the inability to recruit and keep top quality teachers, and frequent turnover in senior leadership positions), these leaders can then take steps to dissolve the problems causing these symptoms rather than just react to the symptoms in a piecemeal fashion. It is at this deep level of understanding—at the level of system dynamics and system structures—that the greatest leverage for improving the overall performance of a school system exists.

SYSTEM ARCHETYPES—A SPECIAL SET OF SYSTEM STRUCTURES

The term *system archetype* was created in the mid-1980s to describe invisible, but powerful, system dynamics that have a significant influence on human performance in organizations.[1] Since that time, these archetypes have influenced the way systems thinkers in organizations work to create and sustain transformational change in their systems. Although descriptions of these archetypes have primarily focused on business organizations, several of the archetypes are particularly relevant to school systems. All eight archetypes are particularly helpful for assessing seemingly unsolvable long-term problems in organizations.

All eight system archetypes are not discussed in this chapter (all eight are described in Kim 2000). Instead, three archetypes that seem to be prevalent in school systems are presented. Figures illustrating these archetypes are provided as is a brief hypothetical description of how each archetype functions. Before describing the three selected archetypes, key systems terms must be defined. These terms are used to explain the dynamics portrayed in the archetypes.

Causal Loops and Links

In drawings of system archetypes links between events, let's say event x and event y, are depicted. These links are drawn as curvilinear arrow lines in the archetype diagrams.

There are two kinds of links used to illustrate system behavior in the diagrams shown. The first kind of link represents a positive correlation whereby a change in event x causes a change in event y, which moves in the same direction as x. When this happens, this link is drawn as a curvilinear arrow with an *s* on it (the *s* means moving in the same direction). Or, if x adds to or increases y, this is also a positive correlation, and the curvilinear arrow is marked with a plus sign (+).

The other kind of link represents a negative correlation whereby a change in event x causes a change in event y, but it is in the opposite direction. This curvilinear arrow is marked with an *o* (the *o* means moving in the opposite direction). And, if x subtracts from y, then the line is marked with a minus sign (–).

Feedback Loops

These loops are the building blocks of all systems (Senge, Kleiner, Roberts, Ross, and Smith 1994, 114). There are two kinds of feedback loops portrayed in the archetype figures shown: reinforcing feedback loops, which stimulate and reinforce either positive or negative change, and balancing feedback loops, which stabilize a system and maintain its status quo (Forrester 1968; Goodman 1974; Randers 1980).

Reinforcing feedback loops create either exponential growth or exponential collapse; in other words, when there is a reinforcing feedback loop at work in a school system, things are changing either for the better or changing for the worse, and changing rapidly. With these loops, change occurs at ever-increasing rates of acceleration because the changes (negative or positive) are being positively reinforced. In archetype diagrams, reinforcing feedback loops are marked with the letter R. If there is more than one reinforcing loop, then a number is added as in R_1 and R_2.

Balancing feedback loops are systemic forces that create stability and equilibrium in a school system. Sometimes these loops are good for a system because all systems occasionally need stability and equilibrium. Equilibrium is especially important after periods of great change because a constant state of change consumes resources (an organization's source of energy), which is known as *entropy*. Uncontrolled entropy results in the debilitation or death of a system.

However, when system change is desired, balancing feedback loops can resist change by creating forces that strive to keep a system in its status quo or balanced equilibrium state (Burchill and Kim 1993). If educators in a district characterize change in their school system as "the more things change, the more they stay the same" they are probably in the throes of a wicked balancing loop. In archetype diagrams, balancing feedback loops are marked with the letter *B*. If there is more than one balancing feedback loop, then a number is added as in B_1 and B_2.

THREE SYSTEM ARCHETYPES AT WORK IN SCHOOL SYSTEMS

System Archetype I—Organizational Addictions

This archetype[2] is illustrated in figure 1.2. Here is a description of how the organizational addictions archetype might manifest itself in school systems (see Kim 2000, 8–9 for a detailed description of this archetype). Refer to figure 1.2 as this description is read.

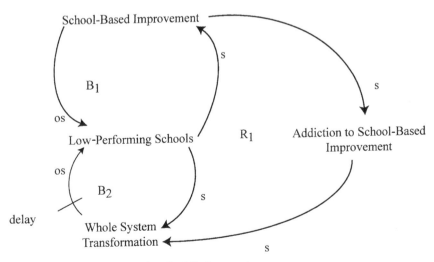

Figure I.2.   The organizational addictions archetype

A school system experiences a persistent and recurring problem identified as low-performing schools. School district administrators address that problem by using school-based improvement. The initial use of school-based improvement strategies produces a few visible improvements in some of the low-performing schools. These improvements are represented by the arrow marked with an *s* leading out from low-performing schools to school-based improvement. However, other schools do not improve and in some cases schools that started to improve revert back to their low performance. This lack of improvement or reverting back to low performance is represented by the arrow marked with an *o* leading out from school-based improvement to low-performing schools. As the system applies the school-based improvement process balancing equilibrium is created to keep that process in place (the balancing feedback loop is designated as B_1).

The repeated use of the school-based improvement methods creates an unintended side-effect; that is, an addiction to school-based improvement. The creation of this addiction is represented by the arrow marked with an *s* leading out from school-based improvement to addiction to school-based improvement. Because the school system becomes addicted to this approach, a more effective approach (whole-system transformation) for dissolving deep-seated system dynamics remains unknown or is ignored. In other words, the addiction blocks movement toward using whole-system transformation strategies, which is represented by the arrow marked with an *o* leading out from addiction to school-based improvement to whole-system transformation. The growth and strengthening of this addiction is fed by a reinforcing feedback loop designated as R_1.

Instead of the school-based improvement strategy, school district administrators could implement a whole-system transformation strategy, which is identified by the arrow marked with an *s* leading out from low-performing schools to whole-system transformation. Over time (which is represented by the word *delay*), the whole-system transformation strategy could dissolve deep-seated system dynamics causing the low-performing schools symptom. The shrinkage or dissolution of the low-performing schools symptom through whole-system transformation is represented by the arrow marked with an *o* leading out from whole-system transformation to low-performing schools. As the whole-system transformation process is used repeatedly, balancing equilibrium is created (this balancing feedback loop is designated by B_2).

One of the most insidious consequences of this organizational addiction (and, in fact, of all organizational addictions) is that the addiction ultimately becomes more "painful" to the system than the original low-performing schools symptom because the addiction prevents district leaders from changing their improvement efforts to create and sustain whole-system transformation. And the inability or unwillingness to engage in whole-system transformation almost guarantees that the system will continue to create low-performing schools.

System Archetype 2—Drifting Goals

An invented example of how this archetype might play out in a school system is displayed in figure 1.3 (see Kim 2000, 12–13 for a detailed description of this archetype). Refer to figure 1.3 as this description is read.

Educators in a school system are experiencing external pressure to improve the performance of their school system. The pressure is coming from stakeholder expectations for school district quality. Additionally, the quality of neighboring school districts and private schools influences the stakeholder expectations because the stakeholders see and hear about what those other school systems are doing. The influence of the neighboring school systems on the stakeholders is represented by the arrow marked with a plus sign (+) connecting both events, which means that the stakeholders' expectations are being increased.

The stakeholder expectations and the quality of neighboring school systems and private schools create pressure for improving the school system's performance. This pressure results in district leaders setting district improvement goals. Because the improvement goals are influenced by external stakeholder expectations for their school district's quality and by the quality of neighboring school districts, this influence is represented by the arrows marked with an s leading out from stakeholder expectations and quality of neighboring school districts to district transformation goals.

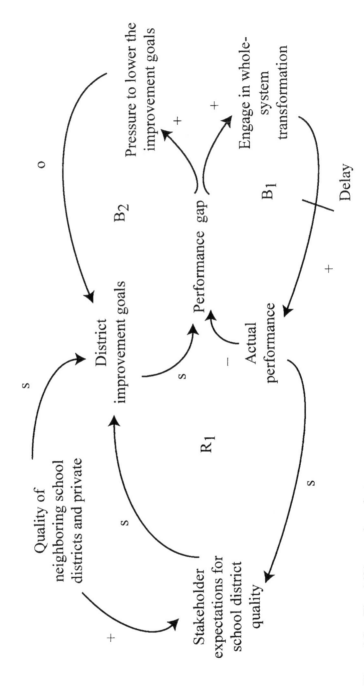

Figure I.3. The drifting goals archetype

The pressure for improvement is fueled by a reinforcing feedback loop (R_1). Because this feedback is in the form of a loop, the pressure for change cycles through the school district on regular intervals (e.g., yearly, every three years, and so on).

Next, given the new district improvement goals, change leaders collect data about their system's actual performance levels. They compare these data to the district improvement goals for their school system, which represents the future. They and their colleagues see a performance gap between where they are and where they want to be. The performance gap creates psychological pressure to close the gap. There are two options available to close the performance gap.

Option One: Engage in Whole-System Transformation   This option is represented by the arrow leading out of performance gap toward engage in whole-system transformation. This arrow is marked with a plus sign (+) because the decision to engage in whole-system change increases whole-system improvement activities.

The whole-system improvement activities eventually improve the actual performance of the district. This improvement is represented by the arrow marked with a plus sign (+) leading out from whole-system transformation to actual performance. Because whole-system transformation takes time to improve the actual performance of a school district, the passage of time is marked on the figure with the word *delay*.

As the system begins to improve through whole-system transformation, activities the existing performance gap between the district improvement goals and actual performance begins to close. The closing of this gap is represented by the arrow leading out of actual performance to performance gap and marked with a minus sign (−), which means that the activities decrease the size of the performance gap. Over time, the transformation activities will produce real improvements in the district's performance that will be sustained by a balancing feedback loop (B_1).

Option Two: Lower District Improvement Goals   This alternate course of action is represented by the arrow leading out of performance gap toward pressure to lower the improvement goals. This line is marked with a plus sign (+) because actions are taken to increase the pressure to lower improvement goals.

Given the pressure to lower improvement goals, change leaders water down the original district improvement goals to make them easier to achieve or avoid making the difficult and challenging changes that the original goals proposed. This diluting of the improvement goals is represented by the arrow leading out from pressure to lower the performance goals to district transformation goals. This line is marked with an o to represent the lowering of the improvement goals, which is the opposite of the original desire to improve the district's performance.

If option two is chosen, people cry out for easier or more acceptable improvement goals. People want to scale-back the district's movement toward these goals because of the costs. As the original improvement goals are diminished, people start to observe that not much has changed and that the district is performing much like what it was before the improvement process was started. The district is basically back to where it started, thereby leading people to think "the more things change, the more they stay the same." Finally, if this option is chosen, the pressure to lower the improvement goals enters a state of balancing equilibrium (B_2) that will keep the pressure to lower the goals in place.

System Archetype 3—Fixes that Fail

An example of how the "fixes that fail" archetype might play itself out in a school district is depicted in figure 1.4 (see Kim 2000, 16–17 for a detailed description of this archetype). Here is how this archetype might work in a school system.

A school district's state department of education declares that students are doing poorly on state assessments in several schools in the district. District leaders quickly develop and hurriedly implement a solution to this problem, which is really a symptom of deep-seated system dynamics, to assuage the state department of education because they want to demonstrate that they have the problem under control and that they are doing something about it. The quick fix they choose is send in heroic principals to turn around those low-performing schools. Implementing the send in heroic principals strategy creates a balancing feedback loop (B_1) to keep that strategy in place.

The send in heroic principals quick fix temporarily reduces the problem of the students are doing poorly on state assessments in the affected schools identified by the state department of education. The temporary

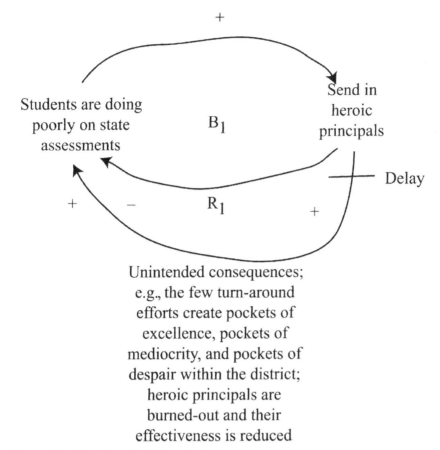

Figure 1.4. **The fixes-that-fail archetype**

improvement in test scores in the affected schools is represented by the arrow leading out from send in a turn around specialist to students are doing poorly on state assessments. That line is marked with a minus sign (–) to denote the temporary reduction of the original symptom (low test scores). Everyone in the district feels good about this.

Quick fixes, however, almost always have unintended consequences that cause the original symptoms to return or to become worse. As time passes (represented by the word *delay* in the figure) unintended consequences emerge, such as the ones illustrated in the figure. The emergence of unintended consequences is empowered by a reinforcing feedback loop (R_1).

The three archetypes described here are prevalent in school systems, and they have a powerful influence on system performance. In the absence of courageous, passionate and visionary change leadership to uncover and correct these dynamics, educators can become addicted to particular ineffective improvement strategies, can be lured into a downward spiral that leads them away from ambitious change goals, or can be enticed into using quick fixes to solve difficult problems. Of course, as the literature on open systems theory and systems dynamics shows, none of these responses are effective over time. They are all terrible traps disguised as attractive options that lock school districts in the jaws of inescapable inferior system performance.

Nonsystemic, piecemeal approaches to improving student, faculty and staff, and whole-system learning often fail, and they never work if educators want to dissolve "wicked problems" in their school district. *Wicked problems* is a term coined by Horst Rittel (Rittel and Webber 1973). A wicked problem is one for which each proposed solution changes the problem. The wicked problems associated with efforts to improve school systems cannot be solved using traditional school district improvement techniques because contemporary school districts are systems, not confederations of semiautonomous schools. School districts also exist within complex and unstable environments that create constant pressure for school districts to improve.

The complexity of systems combined with external pressure to change creates wicked problems that cannot be dissolved using traditional linear problem-solving techniques because the ways in which the problems are perceived and understood evolves with each new proposed solution. Wicked problems also always occur in a social context because various individuals and groups with a stake in a school district's performance problems offer their views and propose possible solutions. The degree of "wickedness" increases as the diversity of stakeholders increases. Some specific aspects of problem wickedness are offered by the CogNexus Institute (n.d.). These are:

- You do not understand the problem until you have developed a solution. Indeed, there is no definitive statement of the "problem." The problem is ill-structured, an evolving set of interlocking issues and constraints.

- Wicked problems have no stopping rule. Because there is no definitive problem, there is also no definitive "solution." The problem-solving process ends when you run out of resources.
- Solutions to wicked problems are not right or wrong, simply better, worse, good enough, or not good enough.
- Every wicked problem is essentially unique and novel. There are so many factors and conditions, all embedded in a dynamic social context, that no two wicked problems are alike, and the solutions to them will always be custom designed and fitted.
- Every solution to a wicked problem is a "one-shot operation"; every attempt has consequences. . . . This is the catch-22 about wicked problems: you can not learn about the problem without trying solutions, but every solution you try is expensive and has lasting unintended consequences which are likely to spawn new wicked problems.
- Wicked problems have no given alternative solutions. There may be no solutions, or there may be a host of potential solutions that are devised, and another host that are never even thought of.

To manage wicked problems educators need to use a whole-system transformation methodology (e.g., Duffy 2002; 2003; Duffy and Chance 2006; Reigeluth and Garfinkle 1994) that helps them create and sustain whole-system change in their districts. These methodologies must be built on a foundation composed of open system theory, systems-thinking skills, and systems-thinking tools (e.g., brainstorming tools, dynamic thinking skills, structural thinking skills, and computer-based tools) that can be applied to uncover underlying system dynamics such as the archetypes described in this chapter.

CONCLUSION

In this chapter, an overview of how a school district functions as an open system was provided. Three underlying system structures known as system archetypes were also explained. These ideas are important for leading entire school systems toward higher levels of performance. Efforts to improve entire school systems will surely fail if these concepts and principles are not learned and applied.

REFERENCES

Ackoff, R. L. 1999. *Re-creating the corporation: A design of organizations for the 21st century*. New York: Oxford University Press.

Burchill, G., and D. H. Kim. 1993. System archetypes as a diagnostic tool: A field-based study of TQM implementations. *Center for Quality of Management Journal* 2 (3): 15–22.

Burke, W. W. 2002. *Organization change: Theory and practice*. Thousand Oaks, CA: Sage Publications.

CogNexus Institute (n.d.). *Wicked problems*. Retrieved from www.cognexus .org/id42.htm, June 7, 2006.

Duffy, F. M. 2002. Step-Up-To-Excellence: An innovative approach to managing and rewarding performance in school systems. Lanham, MD: Scarecrow Education.

———. 2003. *Courage, passion and vision: A guide to leading systemic school improvement*. Lanham, MD: Scarecrow Education and the American Association of School Administrators.

———. 2004. Moving upward together: Creating strategic alignment to sustain systemic school improvement. Lanham, MD: Rowman & Littlefield Education.

Duffy, F. M., and P. L. Chance. (2006). Strategic communication during whole-system change: Advice and guidance for school district leaders and PR specialists. Lanham, MD: Rowman & Littlefield Education.

Emery, M., and R. E. Purser. 1995. *The search conference: A comprehensive guide to theory and practice*. San Francisco: Jossey-Bass.

Forrester, J. 1968. *Principle of systems*. Cambridge, MA: Productivity Press.

Goodman, M. 1974. *Study notes in system dynamics*. Cambridge, MA: Massachusetts Institute of Technology Press.

Katz, D., and R. L. Kahn. 1978. *The social psychology of organizations*, 2nd ed. New York: John Wiley & Sons.

Kim, D. H. 2000. *Systems archetypes I: Diagnosing systemic issues and designing high-leverage interventions*. Williston, VT: Pegasus Communications, Inc.

Lawrence, P. R., and J. W. Lorsch. 1967. *Organization and environment: Managing differentiation and integration*. Cambridge, MA: Harvard Business School Publications, Harvard University Press.

Randers, J. 1980. *Elements of the system dynamics method*. Cambridge, MA: Massachusetts Institute of Technology Press.

Reigeluth, C. M., and R. J. Garfinkle, eds. 1994. *Systemic change in education*. Englewood Cliffs, NJ: Educational Technology Publications.

Rittel, H., and M. Webber. 1973. Dilemmas in a general theory of planning. *Policy Sciences* 4: 155–59.

Senge, P. M. 1990. *The fifth discipline: The art and practice of the learning organization.* New York: Doubleday.

Senge, P. M., A. Kleiner, C. Roberts, R. B. Ross, and B. J. Smith. 1994. *The fifth discipline fieldbook: Strategies and tools for building a learning organization.* New York: Doubleday.

von Bertalanffy, L. 1950. An outline of general systems theory. *British Journal of the Philosophy of Science* 1: 139–64.

NOTES

1. Under the auspices of *Innovation Associates*, Jennifer Kemeny developedeight diagrams to illustrate system dynamics. Peter Senge and Michael Goodman helped her create these diagrams. Some of these diagrams were influenced by the thinking of John Sterman. Some of the archetypes were also derived from the "generic structures" described by Jay Forrester in the 1960s and 1970s. Peter Senge's 1990 book, *The fifth discipline: The art and practice of the learning organization* brought the eight archetypes into the management lexicon.

2. These figures have been significantly simplified to convey a quick understanding of how the selected archetypes influence human behavior and system performance. For a more detailed description of these archetypes, please refer to Kim (2000).

2

CHAOS THEORY AND THE SCIENCES OF COMPLEXITY: FOUNDATIONS FOR TRANSFORMING EDUCATION

Charles M. Reigeluth

Public education in the United States is an array of highly complex systems whose behavior, or causal dynamics, has proven difficult to understand. Similarly, the process of transforming a school system is highly complex and difficult to predict or control. Chaos theory and the sciences of complexity (Gleick 1988; Holden 1986; Kellert 1993; Lorenz 1995; Nowotny 2005; Wheatley 1999) are branches of systems theory that were developed to help understand highly complex systems. They recognize that beneath the apparently chaotic or unpredictable behavior of a complex system lie certain patterns that can help one to both understand, and especially in the context of the theme of this book, influence the behavior of the system. This chapter begins with a summary of some of the key features of chaos theory and the sciences of complexity and then explores the ways that these theories can inform systemic transformation (paradigm change) in K–12 education in the United States and other parts of the world.

WHAT ARE CHAOS THEORY AND THE SCIENCES OF COMPLEXITY?

Some of the key features of chaos theory and the sciences of complexity include coevolution, disequilibrium, positive feedback, perturbation, transformation, fractals, strange attractors, self-organization, and dynamic complexity. Each of these is briefly discussed and related to school systems.

COEVOLUTION

For a system to be healthy, it must coevolve with its environment: It changes in response to changes in its environment, and its environment changes in response to its changes. Wheatley says, "We inhabit a world that co-evolves as we interact with it. This world is impossible to pin down, constantly changing . . . " (1999, 9). A K–12 educational system exists in a community and larger society that are constantly evolving. But how are they evolving? Toffler (1980) has identified three major waves of societal evolution. Each has been accompanied by a fundamental change of paradigm in all of our society's systems, and they provide us with examples of coevolution between educational systems and their respective environments. During the agrarian age, the one-room schoolhouse was the predominant paradigm of education, with its focus on tutoring and apprenticeship. During the industrial age, the factory model of schools became the predominant paradigm of education, with its focus on standardization and teacher-centered learning. Now, as we evolve ever deeper into the information age, society is undergoing just as dramatic a change as during the industrial revolution, and this is putting greater pressure on our educational systems to coevolve through a similarly fundamental shift in paradigm.

As our communities and society evolve deeper into the information age in which knowledge work is rapidly replacing manual labor and more and more children are being raised in poverty and single-parent or dual-income households, the need for coevolution in education has become ever more urgent (Reigeluth 1994). Banathy (1991) has pointed to a large coevolutionary imbalance between education and society, which places our society in ill-health and peril. Schlechty (1990), Caine and Caine (1997), and others have pointed out that our educational systems are doing a better job than ever at what they were designed to do, but that our society is increasingly calling on them to do things they were not designed to do. Therefore, our educational systems must coevolve to meet the changing educational needs of society.

To identify how an educational system should coevolve, there are two issues we must look at. One is how its environment has changed. This includes changes in the community's educational needs, in the tools it offers to educators, and in other community (and societal) conditions that impact education, such as drugs, violence, teen pregnancy, and latch-key children. However, an educational system is not just shaped by its community; it also helps shape its community. Thus, the second issue for identifying how an educational system should coevolve is the ways the community would like its educational system to change to better reflect the values of the community and thereby to help make the community more consistent with its values. Therefore, an educational system should coevolve based on the evolving values, beliefs, and visions of the community and on the evolving educational needs of the community. This brings us to the all-important question: How can coevolution be fostered in our educational systems?

DISEQUILIBRIUM AND POSITIVE FEEDBACK

According to chaos theory and the sciences of complexity, coevolution is fostered by disequilibrium and positive feedback. Equilibrium is defined as "a condition in which all acting influences are canceled by others, resulting in a stable, balanced, or unchanging system" (American Heritage Dictionary, as quoted by Wheatley 1999, 76). Systems can be in a state of equilibrium, in which case, minor changes or adjustments to the system are all that is necessary; or systems can be in a state of disequilibrium, in which case, they approach the edge of chaos. This might lead one to believe that disequilibrium is a bad thing. However, Wheatley (1999) makes the following points:

> "I observed the search for organizational equilibrium as a sure path to institutional death." (76)
>
> "In venerating equilibrium, we have blinded ourselves to the processes that foster life." (77)
>
> "To stay viable, open systems maintain a state of non-equilibrium. . . . They participate in an open exchange with their world, using what is there for their own growth." (78)

"Prigogine's work demonstrated that disequilibrium is the necessary condition for a system's growth." (79)

Hence, disequilibrium is one important condition for coevolution. The other is positive feedback, which has a particular meaning in systems theory.

Systems may receive both negative and positive feedback. Negative feedback provides information about deficiencies in attaining a system's goals, so that the system can adjust its processes to overcome those deficiencies. In contrast, positive feedback provides information about opportunities for a system to change the goals that it pursues. Thus, positive feedback is information from the environment that helps a system to coevolve with its environment. Often, it takes the form of perturbations (or disturbances) that cause disequilibrium in a system.

PERTURBATION

A perturbation is any change in a system's environment that causes disequilibrium in a system. For example, as our society in the United States has evolved into the information age, a new educational need that has arisen is the need for lifelong learning. Rapid change in the workplace and the new reality of multiple careers during one's life require people to be lifelong learners. To help people become lifelong learners, schools must cultivate both the desire to learn (a love of learning) and the skills to learn (self-directed learning). However, our typical industrial-age school systems do the opposite on both counts, placing stress on the environment (coevolutionary imbalance) and causing the environment to put pressure (perturbation) on the educational system to undergo fundamental change or transformation.

TRANSFORMATION

Disequilibrium creates a state in which the system is ripe for transformation, which is reorganization on a higher level of complexity. Transformation occurs through a process called *emergence*, by which new processes and structures emerge to replace old ones in a system. Transformation is paradigm change and stands in contrast to piecemeal change, which leaves the structure of a system unchanged. Piecemeal change often involves finding better ways to meet the same needs, whereas transformation entails modifying the structure of a system, usually in response to new needs. Piecemeal change usually changes one part of a system (albeit perhaps a part that exists in all schools within a district) in a way that is still compatible with the rest of the system, whereas transformation (or paradigm change) entails such a fundamental change that it requires changes in other parts of the system because the other parts are not compatible with the change.

According to Duffy, Rogerson, and Blick (2000), transformation of an educational system requires simultaneous changes in the core work processes (teaching and learning), the social architecture of the system (culture and communications), and the system's relationships with its environment.

FRACTALS AND "STRANGE ATTRACTORS"

Transformation is strongly influenced by strange attractors, which are a kind of fractal (Wheatley 1999). Fractals are patterns that recur at all levels of a system, called *self-similarity*. In educational systems, they can be considered core ideas and values or beliefs (Banathy 1991; 1996) that guide or characterize the design of the new (transformed) system. These recurring patterns can be structural or behavioral—that is, they can be patterns of form or function, and they strongly influence, and are influenced by, complex system dynamics (Senge 1990). One example of a fractal in education is top-down, autocratic control. On the district level of an educational system, the school board typically controls the superintendent, who controls the principals. On the building level, the principals control their teachers. And on the classroom level the teachers control their students.

Another example of a fractal in education is uniformity or standardization. On the district level, all elementary schools are typically supposed to be the same (equal) in such key features as policies, curriculum, methods, and assessments. On the building level, all teachers at the same grade level are supposed to teach the same content at the same time with the same textbooks, again to provide equality. On the classroom level, all students in a classroom are typically supposed to learn the same thing at the same time in the same way. And even for professional development, all teachers typically engage in the same professional development activities at the same time. Top-down control and uniformity are but two of many fractals that characterize our factory model of schools. Although we are beginning to see changes in some of these patterns, few would argue that they were not typical of our industrial-age educational systems, and they are still the predominant paradigm in educational systems today.

A strange attractor is a kind of fractal that has a powerful influence over the processes and structures that emerge in a system undergoing transformation. Fractals are similar to what Dawkins called "memes," which are ideas or cultural beliefs that are "the social counterpoints to genes in the physical organism" and have the power to organize a system in a specific way (Caine and Caine 1997, 33). One example of a strange attractor, or meme, in education is stakeholder empowerment or ownership, which entails providing both the freedom to make decisions and support for making and acting on those decisions. On the district level, this takes the form of the school board and superintendent empowering each building principal to experiment with and adopt new approaches to better meet students' needs and to make other important decisions (hiring, budgeting, and so on). On the building level, the principal empowers each teacher to experiment with and adopt new approaches to better meet students' needs and to participate in school policymaking and decision making. On the classroom level, the teacher empowers each student to make decisions about how to best meet her or his needs. This form of leadership at all levels entails providing guidance and support to cultivate the ability to make good decisions and act effectively on them.

A second example of a strange attractor is customization or differentiation (or diversity). On the district level, each school has the freedom to be different from other schools. On the school level, each teacher has the freedom to be different from other teachers. And on the classroom level, each student has the freedom to be different from other students (with respect to both what to learn and how to learn it). A third example is shared decision making or collaboration. On the district level, the school board and superintendent involve community members, teachers, and staff in policymaking and decision making. On the school level, the principal involves parents, teachers, and staff in policymaking and decision making. And on the classroom level, the teacher involves the child and parents in decisions and activities to promote the child's learning and development.

To become an effective strange attractor for the transformation of a school system, the core ideas and values (or beliefs) must become fairly widespread cultural norms among the stakeholders most involved with making the changes. Once that status is reached, little planning needs to be done for the transformation to take place. Appropriate behaviors and structures will emerge spontaneously through a process called *self-organization*.

SELF-ORGANIZATION

Self-organizing systems are adaptive; they evolve themselves; they are agile (McCarthy 2003). They require two major characteristics: openness and self-reference (Wheatley 1999). To be open with its environment, a system must actively seek information from its environment and make it widely available within the system.

The intent of this new information is to keep the system off balance, alert to how it might need to change. An open organization does not look for information that makes it feel good or that verifies its past and validates its present. It is deliberately looking for information that might threaten its stability, knock it off balance, and open it to growth (Wheatley 1999, 83).

But the system must go beyond seeking and circulating information from its environment; it must also partner with its environment. As Wheatley (1999) notes: "Because it partners with its environment, the system develops increasing autonomy from the environment and also develops new capacities that make it increasingly resourceful" (84).

A second characteristic of self-organizing systems is the ability to self-reference on the core ideas, values, or beliefs that give the organization an identity. In this way, "When the environment shifts and the system notices that it needs to change, it always changes in such a way that it remains consistent with itself. . . . Change is never random; the system will not take off in bizarre new directions" (Wheatley 1999, 85).

A third characteristic is freedom for people to make their own decisions about changes. Jantsch (1980) has noted a paradoxical, but profound, systems dynamic: "The more freedom in self-organization, the more order" (40, as cited by Wheatley 1999, 87). As long as the freedom is guided by sufficient self-reference, it will allow changes to occur before a crisis point is reached in the system, thereby creating greater stability and order. Paradoxically, the system is "less controlling, but more orderly" by being self-organizing (Wheatley 1999, 87). Typically, coevolution occurs through self-organization, but complex system dynamics have a powerful influence on self-organization and any resulting systemic transformation.

DYNAMIC COMPLEXITY

According to Peter Senge, social systems have detail complexity and dynamic complexity, "When the same action has dramatically different effects in the short run and the long, there is dynamic complexity. When an action has one set of consequences locally and a very different set of consequences in another part of the system, there is dynamic complexity. When obvious interventions produce nonobvious consequences, there is dynamic complexity" (1990, 71). System dynamics are the web of causal relationships that influence the behavior of a system at all its various levels. They help us to understand how a change in one part of an educational system is likely to impact the other parts and the outputs of the system and to understand how a change in one part of an educational system is likely to be impacted by the other parts of the system. Dynamic complexity is captured to some extent by Senge's "11 laws of the fifth discipline" and his "system archetypes." The laws include such general dynamics as:

The harder you push, the harder the system pushes back.
The easy way out usually leads back in.
The cure can be worse than the disease.
Faster is slower.
Cause and effect are not closely related in time and space.

Small changes can produce big results—but the areas of highest leverage are often the least obvious (see chapter 4)

Senge's (1990) system archetypes include:

"Limits to growth" in which an amplifying process that is put in motion to
create a certain result has a secondary effect (a balancing process) that
counters the desired result.

"Shifting the burden" in which the underlying problem is difficult to
address, so people address the symptoms with easier "fixes," leaving the
underlying problem to grow worse unnoticed until it is much more difficult, if not impossible, to fix.

"Tragedy of the commons" in which a commonly available but limited
resource is used to the extent that it becomes more difficult to obtain,
which causes intensification of efforts until the resource is significantly or
entirely depleted.

"Growth and underinvestment" in which growth approaches a limit that
can be raised with additional investment, but if the investment is not rapid
nor aggressive enough, growth will be stalled and the investment will become unnecessary.

"Fixes that fail" in which a fix that is effective in the short run has un-
foreseen long-term effects that reduce their effectiveness and require
more of the same fix (see chapter 6.)

Senge's laws and archetypes identify high-level or general system dynamics, but it is also important to identify the complex system dynamics at play in a particular educational system. Those dynamics are complex causal relationships that govern patterns of behavior, explain why
piecemeal solutions are failing, and predict what kinds of solutions
may offer higher leverage in transforming a system to better meet students' needs.

HOW CAN CHAOS THEORY AND
THE SCIENCES OF COMPLEXITY INFORM
THE TRANSFORMATION OF EDUCATION?

The remainder of this chapter explores the ways that chaos theory and
the sciences of complexity can inform the systemic transformation of ed-

ucation. They can do so in two fundamental ways. First, they can help us to understand the present system of education and how it is likely to respond to changes that we try to make. Second, they can help us to understand and improve the transformation process, which is itself a complex system that educational systems use to transform themselves.

UNDERSTANDING THE PRESENT SYSTEM

Chaos theory and the sciences of complexity can help us to understand our present systems of education, including (a) when each is ready for transformation and (b) the system dynamics that are likely to influence individual changes we try to make and the effects of those changes.

READINESS FOR TRANSFORMATION

Chaos theory and the sciences of complexity tell us that readiness for transformation is influenced by several factors. First, there must be sufficient impetus for transformation, which is created by perturbations from outside the system that produce a state of disequilibrium in the system. That disequilibrium may be caused by either of two kinds of changes in the environment (a school system's community): 1) ones that create problems for the system (such as dysfunctional home environments and lack of discipline in the home), or 2) ones that present opportunities to the system (such as the Internet or other powerful technologies to support learning). Second, there must also be sufficient enablers of transformation, which are created by factors inside the system, such as "participatory" (Schlechty 1990) or "transformational" leadership (Duffy et al. 2000), as opposed to the industrial-age command-and-control form of leadership—or more appropriately, management—and sufficient levels of trust within and among stakeholder groups, such as the teachers association, administration, school board, and parents.

SYSTEM DYNAMICS

System dynamics are complex sets of causes and effects that are largely probabilistic, meaning that a cause increases the chances that an effect will take place but does not require that it must take place. The complex sets of causes and effects are also highly interactive, meaning that the extent of influence of a cause on an effect is strongly influenced by other factors, including other causes. Regarding causes, system dynamics provide us with an understanding of aspects of the current system that will likely influence the viability and durability of any given change. For example, we come to learn that high stake tests that focus on lower levels of learning in Bloom's taxonomy (Bloom, Krathwohl, and Masia 1956) are likely to reduce the viability and durability of attempts by teachers to develop higher-order thinking skills because such efforts will necessarily reduce the amount of time the teachers spend on the lower-level content, causing a decline in the high-stakes test scores. Regarding the effects of any given change, system dynamics provide us with the ability to predict the effects a change is likely to have on the outcomes of the transformed educational system, such as levels of student learning. For example, as the Saturn School of Tomorrow found (Bennett and King 1991), allowing students to be self-directed learners can cause a reduction in "time on task" to learn the important skills and understandings, resulting in a reduction in learning.

UNDERSTANDING THE TRANSFORMATION PROCESS

Chaos theory and the sciences of complexity can also help us to understand and improve the transformation process in which educational systems engage to transform themselves. The transformation process is itself a complex system comprised of many subsystems, processes, and dynamics. With research and experience we can expect to learn much about the dynamics that influence the subsystems and processes that are most likely to foster systemic transformation, but chaos theory and the sciences of complexity tell us that we cannot hope to control the transformation process (Caine and Caine 1997; Wheatley 1999). Caine and Caine state that "the underlying belief is that we are in charge and can control the nature of change. All the reports on how difficult it has been to change education confirm the failure of this logic" (12). Chaos theory and the sciences of complexity also tell us that we can hope to influence the process through the use of such tools as strange attractors and leverage points and that we must constantly adjust and adapt the process to the emerging, ever-changing reality of a particular educational system and its environment (Caine and Caine 1997; Wheatley 1999).

STRANGE ATTRACTORS

The most powerful strange attractors are core ideas and beliefs like those described previously: ownership or empowerment, customization or differentiation, and shared decision making or collaboration. These core ideas stand in stark contrast to those that characterize the industrial-age mindset about "the real school" (Tyack and Cuban 1995): centralization and bureaucracy, standardization (or uniformity), and autocratic (or command-and-control) management. However, to have a powerful influence on the features that emerge in the system undergoing transformation, the core ideas and beliefs must become integral parts of the mindsets or mental models held by a critical mass of participants in the transformation process, and therefore, they must collectively comprise the culture of the transformation process as a system. This means that the major focus of a systemic transformation process in a school district must be on helping all stakeholders to expand their mindsets about education and to develop a set of shared core ideas and beliefs about the ideal kind of educational system they would like to have (Banathy 1991; Caine and Caine 1997; Reigeluth 1993). This entails helping people to uncover the mental models that often unwittingly control their views of education and then deciding whether or not that is the way they really want their educational system to be.

LEVERAGE POINTS

Leverage points can greatly facilitate the systemic transformation of educational systems. An example of a leverage point is student assessment. Our industrial-age schools reflect the belief that the purpose of student assessment is to compare students with each other. Hence we use norm-based tests, we grade on a curve, and students become labeled as winners and losers, successes and failures. In contrast, if we want all children to succeed (no children left behind), then the purpose of assessment should be to compare students with a standard of attainment, so that they may continue to work on a standard until it has been met. The current report card, with its list of courses and comparative grades, could be replaced by an inventory of attainments that are checked off as they are reached by each student. This one change could exert powerful leverage on other parts of the system, most notably the way teaching and learning occur in the classroom—leverage that might be more powerful than the forces that the rest of the system would place on the inventory of attainments to change it back to a sorting-focused assessment system. Furthermore, if appropriate strange attractors have been developed (e.g., enough stakeholders have expanded their mental models to encompass the belief that student assessment should be designed to inform learning rather than to sort students), those strange attractors will create a powerful force in support of such a compatible leverage point and against those aspects of the current system that would otherwise be working to change the assessment system back to what it was.

CONCLUSION

Just as the industrial revolution made the one-room school house obsolete, the information revolution has made our current factory model of schools obsolete. Our educational systems must transform themselves to better meet the dramatically changing needs of our children and communities. An understanding of chaos theory and the sciences of complexity (two recent developments in systems theory) is crucial to successfully navigate such systemic (or paradigmatic) transformation of our educational systems. Helpful concepts include coevolution, disequilibrium, positive feedback, perturbation, transformation, fractals, strange attractors, self-organization, and dynamic complexity. These concepts can help us to understand when a system is ready for transformation and the system dynamics that are likely to influence individual changes we try to make and the effects of those changes. Furthermore, chaos theory and the sciences of complexity can help us to understand and improve the transformation process as a complex system that educational systems use to transform themselves. Strange attractors and leverage points are particularly important to help our educational systems to correct the dangerous evolutionary imbalance that currently exists.

REFERENCES

Banathy, B. H. 1991. *Systems design of education: A journey to create the future.* Englewood Cliffs, NJ: Educational Technology Publications.

———. 1996. *Designing social systems in a changing world.* New York: Plenum Press.

Bennett, D. A., and D. T. King. 1991. The Saturn school of tomorrow. *Educational Leadership* 48 (8): 41.

Bloom, B. S., D. R. Krathwohl, and B. B. Masia, eds. 1956. *Taxonomy of educational objectives, the classification of educational goals.* New York: David McKay.

Caine, R. N., and G. Caine. 1997. *Education on the edge of possibility.* Alexandria, VA: ASCD.

Duffy, F. M., L. G. Rogerson, and C. Blick. 2000. *Redesigning America's schools: A systems approach to improvement.* Norwood, MA: Christopher-Gordon Publishers.

Gleick, J. 1988. *Chaos: Making a new science.* New York: Penguin Books.

Holden, A. 1986. *Chaos.* Princeton, NJ: Princeton University Press.

Jantsch, E. 1980. *The self-organizing universe.* Oxford: Pergamon.

Kellert, S. H. 1993. *In the wake of chaos: Unpredictable order in dynamical systems.* Chicago: University of Chicago Press.

Lorenz, E. N. 1995. *The essence of chaos.* Seattle: University of Washington Press.

McCarthy, M. P. 2003. *Agile business for fragile times: Strategies for enhancing competitive resiliency and stakeholder trust.* New York: McGraw-Hill.

Nowotny, H. 2005. The increase of complexity and its reduction: Emergent interfaces between the natural sciences, humanities and social sciences. *Theory, Culture and Society* 22 (5): 15–31.

Reigeluth, C. M. 1993. Principles of educational systems design. *International Journal of Educational Research* 19 (2): 117–31.

———. 1994. The imperative for systemic change. In *Systemic change in education* ed. C. M. Reigeluth and R. J. Garfinkle, 3–11. Englewood Cliffs, NJ: Educational Technology Publications.

Schlechty, P. C. 1990. *Schools for the twenty-first century: Leadership imperatives for educational reform.* San Francisco: Jossey-Bass Publishers.

Senge, P. M. 1990. *The fifth discipline: The art and practice of the learning organization.* New York: Doubleday.

Toffler, A. 1980. *The third wave.* New York: Bantam Books.

Tyack, D. B., and L. Cuban. 1995. *Tinkering toward utopia: A century of public school reform.* Cambridge, MA: Harvard University Press.

Wheatley, M. J. 1999. *Leadership and the new science: Discovering order in a chaotic world.* San Francisco: Berrett-Koehler Publishers.

3

USING SYSTEMS THINKING TO IMPROVE TWENTY-FIRST CENTURY SCHOOLS

Bill Thornton and George Perreault

As we enter the twenty-first century, schools in North America are faced with demands from governmental mandates to dramatically improve performance, often expressed in the form of assessment of student performance on standardized tests. In the United States, the No Child Left Behind (NCLB) Act is the most obvious example of this movement, but local, state, and provincial governments have all begun to exert increasing pressure. School systems have typically reacted by adopting various "silver bullet" programs without looking carefully at the deep changes that are needed to improve complex organizations like public schools. Significant lasting change is not possible without using systems theory to guide reform.

An analysis of the complexities of the issues facing education leads to the conclusion that change is not a linear function and that each change, no matter how small, can have consequences at many levels within an organization. Practicing education leaders, therefore, must have the tools and skills to envision the impact of proposed changes on various systems and subsystems of schools. At the same time, leaders need to be able to plan changes across the many domains within an organization. Because systems thinking can provide a tool for understanding the structure of an organization and can provide a way to examine the impact of projected changes, the development of systems-thinking skills should be regarded as the key challenge in implementing sustained school reform.

The concept of systems thinking is not new, and many educators have attempted to implement systems thinking (Fullan 2004; Hargreaves and Fink 2003; McTighe and Thomas 2003; Waters Foundation 2006). However, systems paradigms, systems tools, and examples of applications of systems thinking are often complex. The task undertaken in this chapter is to outline a straightforward method of studying and implementing systems change. This is crucial because if, in reality, the process of systems change cannot be understood and applied at all levels within a school district, then school improvements are doomed to fail from the beginning. By design, effective systems thinking leads to procedures that will help schools learn as organizations and will help them avoid and repeat mistakes that prevent continuous improvement of the teaching and learning process.

SCHOOL-IMPROVEMENT PLANS WITHOUT SYSTEMS THINKING

Often, school-improvement plans are deficient because they fail to reflect on the impact of planned improvements on the system. School-improvement plans that fail to apply systems thinking are lacking in at least one of the following crucial areas:

- Plans are linear in nature.
- Plans fail to think about other interactions from and with other domains.
- Plans fail to evaluate the results before moving to the next cycle.
- Plans fail to have alignment between identified needs and planned improvements.
- Plans fail to address root causes of problems.

In many ways, systems thinking is the opposite of linear thinking. Thinking is linear if a neat chain of logic is developed such that A causes B, then B causes C, and so on. Linear thinking fails to look at feedback, complex interactions, and interdependent relationships. A systems-thinking approach would integrate these concepts and relationships into the whole. Because schools are complex organizations and are not linear in nature, linear plans are inappropriate. Yet linear plans are often adopted because the basic structure of schools and school systems promotes the implementation of such plans and reinforces their use. For example, schools operate on a calendar of approximately 180 days. Often, the only criterion for success—some form of high-stakes tests—does not produce data until the end of the school year or even after the close of school. Or if the scores are returned before school is out for the summer, there is no provision for key personnel (such as teachers) to study the data until next year. And at any rate, the students are in the process of moving to another grade level, another school, or possibly to another district, and their issues are transferred to another group of uninformed educators. Fortunately, some schools are beginning to address this concern and have scores that are available much earlier in the school year, but the general prevalence of this phenomenon illustrates a systems failure.

Another contributing factor that contributes to linear planning is the rate of turnover of staff and leadership. Many union contracts and board policies promote ready transfer of teachers for one building to another. If a teacher transfers away from a school, then the chain of accountability for quality teaching has been broken. If the principal provides the replacement teacher with feedback on level of achievement of the past teacher and previous student to the new teacher who has different students, the results will have little meaning. Likewise, if a principal leaves the building, the chain of accountability is broken. In some schools, the principals change every year or two. In some districts, the principals are shifted routinely from building to building by administrative policy and procedures. A school district that took a system approach to student achievement would carefully consider the consequences of such factors in the policy development process. For a school district to practice a system approach to student achievement, it would have to carefully weigh the consequences of such factors in the policy development process.

Another example of the lack of a systems approach to program improvement is that, often, the basic school-improvement plans are self-contained within a building or other administrative unit. For example, an elementary school might develop a plan of action to improve reading skills of the students. The plan would have goals, measurable outcomes, and action plans for the staff and students of the building. However, most plans fail to look at the interactions with the other domains of the district. If staff development is required to implement the school-improvement plan of an elementary school, then the central office has a level of interaction that affects the ability of the elementary school to successfully implement its plan. These interactions could include funding, time, resource, support staff, or conflicting plans of the central office. Without looking across domains, the central office could omit allocation of appropriate resources for appropriate staff development, or the training director could implement a staff development schedule that did not include the needed programs in reading instruction. Systems thinking would require that each domain have at least one planned component related to the goal of improvement of reading instruction in the elementary school.

As another example, if the district operated under a philosophy of independence at the building site level, then the central office would need to develop an approach ensuring the alignment of appropriate resources. Conversely, if the district operated with a top-down philosophy, then the central office goals would drive the school-improvement plans of the individual buildings.

Another common fault of school-improvement plans is weak evaluations that provide limited feedback within a domain and across domains. The failure of a school can be established without any consideration of outside factors. If the evaluation fails to collect information related to barriers created by other domains, then knowledge and deep organizational change are restricted. Education leaders must pay attention to the results of the implementation of the plan within each domain before moving forward to another cycle or year because sometimes the underachievement of an individual unit is impacted by factors that are never acknowledged, and therefore, not addressed.

A basic tenet of school-improvement research is that, if school-improvement plans do not align specific identified needs with specific improvement strategies, then the plan will fail to meet the needs of the students served. On the surface, such situations seem unlikely; however, in a recent review of school-improvement plans of selected schools in a

Western state, we found that many plans lacked this type of alignment. A variety of simple errors appeared in the planning process. For example, some schools failed to conduct a data-based needs assessment. Some schools implemented improvement strategies independent of assessed needs. Other schools failed to implement their plans because of a variety of reasons, both internal and external.

On another level, many school-improvement plans address symptoms of failure within the teaching and learning process but do not address root causes of problems. For example, a school could expend significant resources to ensure that students were present during testing days. The school could have staff assigned to drive students to school, call parents, offer rewards, and use other strategies. However, if the school failed to address the attendance during the balance of the school year, any improvements would be suspect. Some schools have had short-term gains in student scores by focusing on test-taking skills, but these are not sustainable and fail to yield the kind of gains that establish a trend toward actual improvement.

CREATING A NEW PARADIGM OF KNOWLEDGE

Numerous conflicting domains of teaching and learning have been proposed and studied (Bloom, Engelhart, Furst, Hill, and Krathwohl, 1956; Marzano and Pickering 1997; Wiggins and McTighe 1998). In addition, researchers and theorists have proposed and studied various leadership approaches (Deming 1986; Greenleaf 1991; Kotter 1995; Kouzes and Posner 2003; Senge 1990), but as a first step in developing a paradigm for implementing systems thinking, we have adapted a division of the school into the three domains proposed by Cordell and Waters (1993) and modified by Mid-continent Research for Education and Learning (McRel; 2000). This model is shown in table 3.1. The exact nature of theoretically established domains is not as important as the agreement that, within an organization, such domains can be defined and can provide a practical method to illustrate an approach to systems thinking.

McRel (2000) proposed that leaders take three basic steps and repeat the steps across all domains of the organization. These steps were: (1) identify the change initiative, (2) develop specific questions related to the change, and (3) consider possible actions. This linear process would promote thinking about the implications of the proposed change in relationship to each domain, and this is an important first step because systems thinking requires considerations of all dimensions of a system. However, the ultimate goal of systems thinking in education is to lead a school to a state where it becomes a "learning organization" (Senge, Cambron-McCabe, Lucas, Smith, Dutton, and Kleiner 2000), and this cannot happen unless two additional concepts are embedded in the process. First, school leaders need to provide careful feedback mechanisms to ensure that data are collected in an ongoing way and fed back into the system for consideration. Second, school leaders need to be cognizant of the fact that systems thinking is not a linear process and that all human organizations are, to an important degree, nonrational.

This means that no plan, no matter how careful conceived and thoughtfully implemented, will match what was devised beforehand. The best we can hope for is that careful monitoring will allow useful modifications to be made as the process unfolds. Commitment to this tentative, recursive approach is what Fullan (2001) means by "evolutionary planning." It also means that school leaders need to be aware

Table 3.1.   Domain characteristic concerns of the domain

Curriculum	The components which are directly related to teaching and learning in the classroom: • Standards • Curriculum • Instruction • Assessment • Evaluation
Culture	The components which are related to attitudes, capacity, and professional interactions: • Staff development • Leadership • Supervision • Internal communication • Climate
Context	The components which are related to supporting structures of the system: • Formal policies and procedures • External environment • Stakeholders • Resource allocations • Technology • Accountability

that the human elements within an organization are both crucial and to some degree unpredictable. The nature of a service-oriented profession, such as education, is that the effective delivery of services requires flexibility, a range of strategies, and nonroutine judgment in complex situations—and this is being accomplished by people whose professional and personal lives are always in flux. Under these circumstances, perfection is not an option, and systems thinking is a useful tool for dealing with these less than ideal conditions. That said, let us examine the domains proposed for this approach to school improvement.

THE CURRICULUM DOMAIN

The curriculum domain of a school system includes what students are expected to learn, how teachers will ensure that they have the opportunity to learn, and how individual teachers and the system as a whole will assess student learning. Obviously, this constitutes the core technical function of any school. Leaders seeking improvement within this domain might focus on such tasks as developing standards and benchmarks for various grade levels; aligning curricula with those standards; identifying effective classroom instructional strategies; and redesigning assessments to better measure student achievement and progress. The following components of education are part of the curriculum or technical domain:

- Standards
- Curriculum
- Instruction
- Assessment
- Evaluation

THE CULTURE DOMAIN

The culture domain refers to those parts of the system steeped in human capabilities and human relationships. These include school and district leadership, professional development activities, communication, and the personal interactions among students, teachers, and administrators and the organizational ambiance these factors collectively create.

Improvement efforts that focus in this domain include ensuring that students and teachers value the vision and mission of the organization, processes that increase teachers' capacity to support learning, and instructional supervision clearly tied into improving student outcomes. The following aspects of a school would belong to the domain of culture:

- Staff development
- Leadership
- Supervision
- Internal communication
- Climate

THE CONTEXT DOMAIN

The context domain of a school system refers to the larger environment in which any school and its internal teaching and learning occur. Issues related to this domain might include the school's external environment (e.g., Have the student demographics been changing? Has the legislature passed a new mandate?); stakeholders (e.g., Are parents a valuable resource to the school? Are there any especially influential community members whose opinion should be sought?); and such practical issues as the level of resources (both technical and human) and the availability of adequate technology. A further issue in the current political arena is the impact of accountability reporting.

Improvement efforts related to this domain might include such tasks as finding ways to involve stakeholders meaningfully in school-improvement efforts, encouraging teachers to integrate technology effectively into instruction, and evaluating emerging government regulations. Typical focal areas in the context domain include:

- Formal polices and procedures
- External environment
- Stakeholders
- Resource allocations

- Technology
- Accountability

APPLICATION OF SYSTEMS THINKING

Planning in a simple system, the way it is often taught and applied, would include the following steps:

- Development of a plan,
- Implementation of the plan,
- Evaluation of the results, and
- Action taken based on the results.

The flow of the process could be illustrated as in figure 3.1. In the illustration, A leads to B, which leads to C, which leads to D, and then back to A. The system uses feedback to improve the plan. To illustrate the cycle with feedback, assume that an elementary school plans to improve reading by increasing time on task—the plan. The teachers implement the plan by doubling the time spent on reading. Next, they

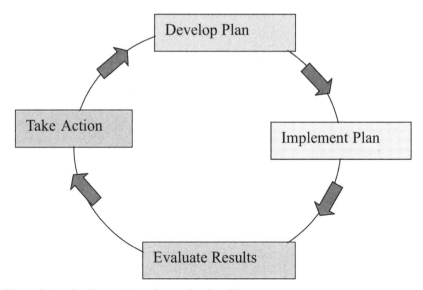

Figure 3.1. An illustration of organizational improvement

assess reading achievement four times a year, disaggregate the reading achievement scores by key concepts, and derived data is shared across the school—they study the results. In addition, they would study impact on other parts of the system such as achievement in the areas that received less instructional time. The final step would occur when the teachers take action based on the information obtained from the data. They could keep the new plan because the data indicated that it was working, adjust the plan because the data indicated that it was working but need improvements, or eliminate the plan because the data indicated that the plan had failed. A key component to effective feedback is that it must occur in a timely fashion to allow adjustment to programs; end of the year feedback is not sufficient by itself. However, if a school operates as indicated previously, it can learn from experience and might be able to promote continuous improvement of a simple process.

Nevertheless, education is not a simple organization but is instead composed of significant and interacting forces. In our model, we have assumed that the system can be subdivided into three domains—curriculum, culture, and context. If a planned organizational improvement is implemented within any of the domains, interactive forces will be set up both within each domain and between the domains. These forces could be illustrated by figure 3.2. Within an organization, each domain would have an internal chain of events triggered by the implementation

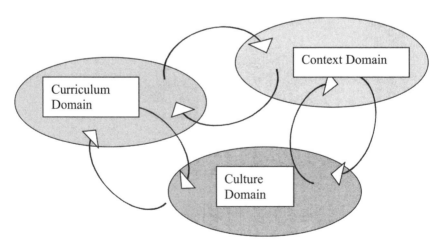

Figure 3.2. An illustration of interactions across domains

of planned improvements; in addition, however, each domain would have interactions from the other two domains.

If the four-step process shown in figure 3.2 were applied to a school and if systems thinking were used, then each step would have an important additional component: What are the implications for interactions across the domains? The four steps would thus read as follows:

Step 1: Develop a plan for improvement for each domain of the organization with consideration for impacts between each of the other domains

Step 2: Implement the plan within each domain with consideration for impacts between each of the other domains

Step 3: Evaluate the results of the implementation with consideration for impacts between each of the other domains

Step 4: Take action based on the results with consideration for impacts between each of the other domains

This additional required process—with consideration for impacts between each of the other domains—may seem unnecessary when planned organization improvements are being discussed. However, many schools fail to apply basic systems thinking when school-improvement plans are developed and significant problems often occur.

To illustrate a more thoughtful approach, the following section presents a hypothetical planning for an effort to implement data-based decision making in a school with the goal of improving the teaching and leaning process. A systems-thinking approach to the stream of necessary questions is illustrated in table 3.2.

At each step, both the intradomain and interdomain implications need to be weighed. For each domain, specific questions about data-based decision making in relationship to the components within each domain must be asked. In addition, barriers and supports from each of the other domains must be integrated at each level. For example, do policies and procedures of the central office prevent the successful implementations of data-based decision making at the building level? Conversely, do the behaviors of the principals prevent the district from meeting specific goals or legal requirements for state accountability?

Table 3.2. A Systems-thinking approach to the stream of necessary questions

	Step 1: Consider impact for each domain	Step 2: Implement plan in each domain	Step 3: Evaluate results of plan	Step 4: Take action based on results
Curriculum domain: What are the implications for teaching and learning	How can we prepare teachers to use data to improve teaching? How can instructional units be planned for students using data? What assessments would support learning? What curriculum changes would be needed?	Set up committees to implement use of data in teaching and learning Standards Curriculum Instruction Assessment Evaluation	Design an evaluation of goals and objectives of plan Impact of data on teaching and learning	The plan is working and will be continued The plan needs adjustments
			Interaction with other domains Provide feedback within and across domains	Barriers caused by other domains Support from other domains
Culture domain: How will the plan impact attitudes and skills of staff?	What types of professional development activities are needed?	Conduct needs assessments	Design an evaluation of goals and objectives of plan	The plan is working and will be continued

How can the principal support staff efforts? What skills are needed to improve school climate in relationship to use of data in classrooms?	Schedule staff development Send staff to conferences Implement a train-the-trainer model	Impact of data on teaching and learning Interaction with other domains Provide feedback within and across domains	The plan needs adjustments Barriers caused by other domains Support from other domains
Context domain: How will the organization support the implementation? How can resources be allocated to support activities in the other domains? What policies support data based decisions? Are teacher evaluations aligned with curriculum domains?	Align budget with requirements in curriculum and culture domains Modify policies as needed	Design an evaluation of goals and objectives of plan Impact of data on teaching and learning Interaction with other domains Provide feedback within and across domains	The plan is working and will be continued The plan needs adjustments Barriers caused by other domains Support from other domains Feedback to other domains

Systems thinking requires leaders to specifically take note of such interactions across the various domains.

DEVELOPMENT OF A PLAN

Most school districts and many states have procedures to design and implement a school-improvement plans. Often, the school-improvement
plan takes the form of a strategic plan with goals, measurable outcomes,
monitoring of progress, and reporting. We will not repeat the concepts
associated with the development of a school-improvement plans or
strategic plans; instead, we ask that school leaders address the requirements imposed by systems thinking when school-improvement plans are
developed, implemented, and evaluated. What crucial components are
often omitted? What steps should be taken to ensure systems thinking
when planning organizational improvements? If the questions are addressed, then both intrarelationships and interrelationships will be revealed.

IMPLEMENTATION OF A PLAN

If a plan is correctly developed, the implementation is straightforward.
Time lines, responsibilities, and desired outcomes are well defined in a
good plan. Measurable goals and reporting functions are clear. Still,
unanticipated barriers can prevent a plan from operating as written. If
the plan lacks the key components, then these components will need to
be defined during the implementation process. Within each domain,
questions must be asked about the impact on other domains, and potential barriers should be explored in a collaborative fashion.

EVALUATION OF A PLAN

Any plan needs to be evaluated based on defined goals and outcomes.
The stated outcomes provide the basis to determine the success of a
plan, and the evaluation provides the feedback for the staff and leader-

ship of the each domain. Unfortunately, evaluation plans often only provide feedback within a specific domain. If evaluations lack an assessment of the level of interactions across domains, the school will not be able to learn effectively from its experiences.

TAKE ACTION BASED ON THE RESULTS

The three fundamental options are available following an effective evaluation: (1) The plan is working and should be continued. (2) The plan has merit, but it needs adjustments and should continue after adjustments. Finally, (3) the plan lacks merit and, therefore, it will be discontinued. The result of such decision making is a continuous improvement of programs and procedures, and it can be shown that the organization has learned from its experience. School-improvement plans can provide continuous incremental improvement if systems thinking is applied.

SUMMARY

This chapter has illustrated an approach for continuous improvement based on systems thinking. Often, the best intended school-improvement plans fail and struggle because they do not reflect such an approach. Planned improvements within a complex system require the holistic consideration of all component parts and a projection of impact on those parts by the balance of the system.

The crucial role of education leaders has become change agent and the role of instructional leaders in the twenty-first century requires a systems thinking perspective. If education change leaders are to solve the complex problems that our schools face, they must study conditions, root causes, and proposed solutions from a systems viewpoint. The skillful ability of leaders to develop systematic solutions underlies the success of effort to reform schools. If the approach discussed in this chapter is applied, it may be possible for education leaders to implement effective school-improvement plans that can sustain continuous incremental improvements over time.

REFERENCES

Bloom, B., M. Englehart, E. Furst, W. Hill, and D. Krathwohl. 1956. *Taxonomy of educational objectives: The classification of educational goals.* New York: Longmans.

Cordell, F., and J. Waters. 1993. *Improving student performance: New strategies for implementing higher standards.* Greeley, CO: The Center for Peak Performing Schools.

Deming, W. 1986. *Out of crisis.* Cambridge, MA: Massachusetts Institute of Technology.

Fullan, M. 2001. *New meaning of educational change,* 3rd ed. Williston, VT: College Teachers Press.

————. 2004. *Leadership and sustainability: System thinkers in action.* Thousand Oaks, CA: Sage Publications.

Greenleaf, R. 1991. *Servant leadership.* New York: Paulist Press.

Hargreaves, A., and D. Fink. (2003). Sustaining leadership. *Phi Delta Kappan* 84 (9): 693–700.

Kotter, J. 1995. *The new rules.* New York; The Free Press.

Kouzes, J., and B. Posner. 2003. *The leadership challenge* 3rd ed. Indianapolis, IN: John Wiley & Sons.

Marzano, R., and D. Pickering. 1997. *Dimensions of learning teacher's manual,* 2nd ed. Alexandria, VA: Association of Curriculum and Supervision.

McTighe, J., and R. Thomas. 2003. Backward design for forward action. *Educational Leadership* 60 (5): 52–55.

Mid-continent Research for Education and Learning (McRel). 2000. *Asking the right questions: A leader's guide to systems thinking about school improvement.* Aurora, CO: McRel.

Senge, P. M. 1990. *The fifth discipline: The art and practice of the learning organization.* New York: Doubleday.

Senge, P. M., N. Cambron-McCabe, T. Lucas, B. Smith, J. Dutton, and A. Kleiner. 2000. *Schools that learn: A fifth discipline fieldbook for educators, parents, and everyone who cares about education.* New York: Doubleday.

Waters Foundation. 2006. *Systems thinking in schools: A Waters Foundation project.* Retrieved from www.watersfoundation.org/index.cfm?fuseaction=materials.main, February 28, 2006.

Wiggins, G., and J. McTighe. 1998. *The understanding by design.* Alexandria, VA: Association of Curriculum and Supervision.

4

SCHOOL IMPROVEMENT: A SYSTEMIC VIEW OF WHAT'S MISSING AND WHAT TO DO ABOUT IT

Howard S. Adelman and Linda Taylor

School systems are not responsible for meeting every need of their students. But when the need directly affects learning, the school must meet the challenge.

Carnegie Task Force on Education, 1989

If we want to bring . . . quality, equity, and new life to our system— we must trust in a vision and a process of change.

Dwight Allen, 1993

Concerns are increasing about the degree to which achievement test score averages are plateauing and the failure of current reforms to make a significant dent in the achievement gap. Yet the call for leaving no child behind continues to stress the same formula for school improvement—higher standards and greater accountability, improved

Support for this work comes in part from the Office of Adolescent Health, Maternal and Child Health Bureau (Title V, Social Security Act), Health Resources and Services Administration (Project #U93 MC 00175) and from the Center for Mental Health Services, Substance Abuse and Mental Health Services Administration. Both are agencies of the U.S. Department of Health and Human Services, Public Health Service.

curricula and instruction, increased discipline, reduced school violence, and on and on. None of it means much if such calls do not result in substantive systemic changes in the many schools where too many students do not have an equitable opportunity to succeed. Moreover, if the intent is to leave no child behind, essential improvements in how schools address barriers to learning and teaching must occur in all schools. And there is growing recognition that effective change on a large scale cannot even be approximated as long as systemwide change continues to be treated as an afterthought. Each of these matters represents fundamental systemic concerns that require greater attention from policy makers, education leaders and staff, and researchers.

In discussing these concerns, our focus first is on highlighting the chaos related to what schools do currently to deal with learning, behavior, and emotional problems. Then from the perspective of addressing barriers to learning and teaching, we clarify what is missing in school-improvement planning. We move on to outline the type of comprehensive, multifaceted, and integrated system designed to fill the gaps. Finally, we briefly highlight considerations related to making systemic changes that are sustainable and that can be implemented throughout a school district.

Before proceeding, however, we should clarify use of the term *systemic change* in the context of this chapter. Our focus is on district and school organization, operations, and the networks that shape decision making about fundamental changes and subsequent implementation. From this perspective, systemic change involves modifications that amount to a cultural shift in institutionalized values (i.e., reculturalization). For interventionists, the problem is that the greater the distance and dissonance between the current culture of schools and intended school improvements, the more difficult it is to successfully accomplish major systemic changes.

WHAT SCHOOLS DO TO ADDRESS STUDENT PROBLEMS: WHY IS IT SO FRAGMENTED?

Over the years, awareness of the many external and internal factors that are barriers to learning and teaching has given rise to legal mandates and a variety of counseling, psychological, and social support programs and to initiatives for school–community collaborations. In the United States, enactment of the No Child Left Behind Act (NCLB) of 2001 accelerated awareness of the need to attend to such matters.

As a result, a cursory look at most school districts finds an extensive range of programs and services oriented to students' needs and problems in schools. Encompassed are efforts to reduce barriers directly and to create buffers against them (i.e., protective factors). Some programs are provided throughout a school district, others are carried out at or linked to targeted schools. Some are owned and operated by schools; some are owned by community agencies. The interventions may be offered to all students in a school, to those in specified grades, to those identified as "at risk," or to those in need of compensatory education. The activities may be implemented in regular or special education classrooms and may be geared to an entire class, groups, or individuals; or they may be designed as "pull out" programs for designated students. They encompass ecological, curricular, and clinically oriented activities designed to reduce problems, such as substance abuse, violence, teen pregnancy, school dropouts, and delinquency.

Although schools can use a wide range of people to help students, most school-owned and operated services are offered as part of what are called *pupil personnel services* or *support services*. Federal and state mandates tend to determine how many pupil services professionals are employed, and states regulate compliance with mandates. Governance of daily practice usually is centralized at the school district level. In large districts, counselors, psychologists, social workers, and other specialists may be organized into separate units. Such units overlap regular, special, and compensatory education.

In general, then, there is considerable activity. There is, however, no well-conceived and cohesive approach. This state of affairs is exacerbated by the specialized focus of the various organizational divisions in a district, such as curriculum and instruction, student support services, activity related to integration and compensatory education, special education, language acquisition, parent involvement, intergroup relations, and adult and career education. It is commonplace for such divisions to operate as relatively independent entities. Thus, although they usually must deal with the same common barriers to learning (e.g., poor instruction, lack of parent involvement, violence and unsafe schools, inadequate support for student transitions), they tend to do so with little or no coordination, and sparse attention to moving toward integrated efforts. Furthermore, in every facet of school district operations, an unproductive separation often is manifested between those units focused on instruction and those concerned with addressing barriers to learning.

In addition, analyses of the situation consistently find that the majority of programs, services, and special projects designed to address barriers to student learning are viewed as supplementary (often referred to as auxiliary services), operate on an ad hoc basis, and are planned, implemented, and evaluated in a fragmented and piecemeal manner (Adelman and Taylor 1997; 2006; Dryfoos 1994; Gardner 2005). As a result, student support staff tend to function in relative isolation of each other and other stakeholders, with a great deal of the work oriented to discrete problems and with an overreliance on specialized individual and small group services. In some schools, a student identified as at risk for grade retention, dropout, and substance abuse may be assigned to three counseling programs operating independently. Such fragmentation and competition for sparse resources not only is costly, it works against developing cohesiveness and maximizing results (Adelman 1996a; Adelman and Taylor 1997; 1999).

Also, it should be stressed that, although a variety of student support activity exists in any school district, it is common knowledge that few schools come close to having enough resources to respond when confronted with a large number of students who are experiencing a wide range of factors interfering with learning and performance. Many schools offer only bare essentials. Too many schools cannot even meet basic needs. Primary prevention often is only a dream. Thus, at many schools, teachers simply do not have the supports they need when they identify students who are not functioning effectively. (For the remainder of this chapter, the term *learning supports* will be used to designate student/learning supports.)

SCHOOL-IMPROVEMENT PLANNING: WHAT'S MISSING?

Given the unsatisfactory status quo related to learning supports, one would expect this arena to be a major emphasis in school-improvement planning guides. Analyses of such planning guides, however, make it clear how little attention is given to using this significant pool of resources more effectively (Center for Mental Health in Schools 2005a; 2005b). In particular, there is widespread failure to plan ways to enhance the ability of teachers and student support staff with respect to addressing barriers to learning and teaching, including better interventions for engaging and reengaging students in classroom learning. As a result, programs, services, and special projects providing learning supports at schools and district wide continue to be conducted in an ad hoc and piecemeal manner and are viewed as nonessential add-ons despite the considerable resources being expended (Adelman and Taylor 2006; Center for Mental Health in Schools 2005c).

Widespread recognition of the piecemeal nature of learning supports has produced some planning to enhance coordination. Better coordination is a good idea. But it does not address the fundamental systemic problem that school-owned student supports are marginalized in policy and practice. Thus, although there is a lot of observable activity in schools, the efforts are not a significant focus when it comes to planning school improvements. This is particularly ironic given the aura of dissatisfaction that surrounds current learning supports.

So, what is missing in school-improvement plans? We find no systemic focus on developing the type of comprehensive, multifaceted, and integrated approaches necessary to address the many overlapping barriers to learning and development. School-improvement planners have ignored the need to use a unifying umbrella concept as a basis for (a) rethinking and restructuring the work of student support professionals, (b) redeploying existing resources for learning supports, and (c) weaving school and community resources together. As a result, they have deemphasized the potential role such improvements can play both in helping teachers enhance student engagement and reengagement in classroom learning and in establishing the type of caring climate in classrooms and schoolwide that promotes progress and well-being.

A related gap in school-improvement planning is how little of on-the-job education focuses on improving classroom and schoolwide approaches for dealing effectively with mild-to-moderate behavior, learning, and emotional problems. This becomes clearly evident in analyses of how resources for inservice are used in building the capacity of

teachers, student support staff, administrators, paraprofessionals, aides, and volunteers.

In short, most school-improvement plans currently pay little attention to substantially enhancing the way schools provide learning supports. At best, most reformers have offered the notions of establishing family resource centers and full-service schools to link community resources to schools and enhance coordination of services (Dryfoos 1994). Connecting school and community resources is another good idea. But community involvement at schools also is a marginalized matter, and when not done properly, it compounds the problems of fragmentation and counterproductive competition. These problems arise when the focus is primarily on coordinating community services and collocating them at schools. Available evidence makes it clear that much more fundamental, systemic changes are needed to braid resources and integrate them with the ongoing efforts of school staff (Gardner 2005).

NEEDED: A POLICY SHIFT AND A CONTINUUM OF INTEGRATED SCHOOL–COMMUNITY INTERVENTION SYSTEMS

Limited efficacy seems inevitable as long as interventions are carried out in a chaotic fashion. Some policy makers have come to appreciate the relationship between limited intervention efficacy and the way learning supports are provided. For the most part, however, reforms have focused on a symptom—fragmentation. This bypasses the underlying systemic issue, namely that addressing barriers to learning and teaching remains a marginalized aspect of policy and practice.

Unfortunately, concern about the marginalization is not even on the radar screen of most policy makers. This is reflected not only in school-improvement planning, but also in consolidated plans and certification reviews and the lack of efforts to map, analyze, and rethink how resources for learning supports are allocated. As long as educational decision makers ignore the need to make fundamental systemic changes that end the marginalization, it is unlikely that the problem of fragmentation will be resolved effectively, and the potential benefits of learning supports for large numbers of children and adolescents will be unfulfilled.

TOWARD ENDING THE MARGINALIZATION
OF LEARNING SUPPORTS

Analyses by our research group indicate that school reform is currently dominated by a two-component systemic model (Adelman 1995; 1996a; 1996b; Adelman and Taylor 1994; 1997; 1998; Center for Mental Health in Schools 1996; 1997). That is, the main interest thrust is on improving instruction and school management. Although these two facets obviously are essential, ending the marginalization of efforts to effectively address barriers to learning and teaching requires establishing a third component as a primary, essential, complementary, and overlapping facet of transforming the educational system (see figure 4.1).

As can be seen in figure 4.1, we designate the component to address barriers to learning as an *enabling component*; others who have adopted it use the term *learning supports component*. This third component not only provides a basis for combating marginalization, it establishes a focal point for developing a comprehensive learning supports framework to guide systemic changes. Its usefulness for these purposes is evidenced in its adoption by various states and localities around the country (Center for Mental Health in Schools 2005d).

TOWARD A COMPREHENSIVE SYSTEM
OF LEARNING SUPPORTS

Problems experienced by students generally are complex in terms of cause and needed intervention. Therefore, in designing learning supports, school and community leaders must work together to develop a high functioning, comprehensive, and multifaceted system.

How comprehensive and multifaceted? As illustrated in figure 4.2, the desired interventions can be conceived along a continuum ranging from a broad-based emphasis on promoting healthy development and preventing problems (both of which include a focus on wellness or competence enhancement) through approaches for responding to problems early-after-onset and extending on to narrowly focused treatments for severe or chronic problems. Not only does the continuum span the concepts of primary, secondary, and tertiary prevention, but it can

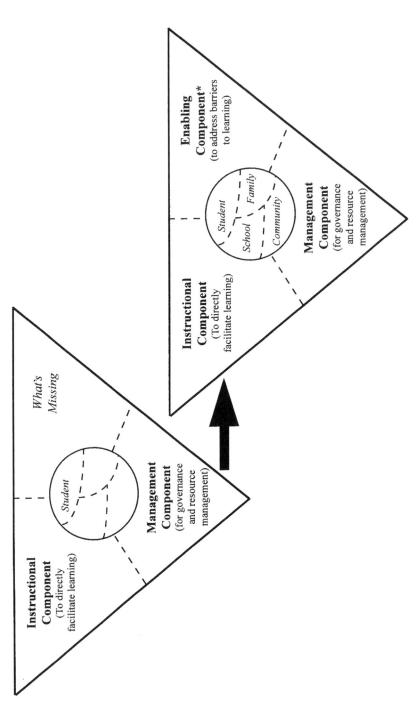

Figure 4.1. Moving from a two- to a three-component model for school improvement

FROM

TO

Direct Facilitation of Development & Learning **Developmental/ Instructional Component**

Governance and Resource Management **Management Component**

Besides offering a small amount of school-owned student "support" services, schools outreach to the community to add a few school-based/linked services.

Direct Facilitation of Development & Learning **Developmental/ Instructional Component**

Governance and Resource Management **Management Component**

Addressing Barriers to Learning **Enabling Component***

Figure 4.1. **(continued)**

School Resources
(facilities, stakeholders,
program, services)

Examples
• General health education
• Drug and alcohol education
• Enrichment programs
• Support for transitions
• Conflict resolution
• Home involvement

  • Drug counseling
  • Pregnancy prevention
  • Violence prevention
  • Dropout prevention
  • Suicide prevention
  • Learning/behavior
    accommodations and
    response to intervention
  • Work programs

    • Special education for
      learning disabilities,
      emotional disturbance,
      and other health impairments

Systems for Promoting
Healthy Development &
Preventing Problems
primary prevention – includes
universal interventions
(low-end need/low-cost
per individual programs)

Systems of Early Intervention
early-after-onset – includes
selective & indicated interventions
(moderate need, moderate
cost per individual)

Systems of Care
treatment/indicated
interventions for severe and
chronic problems

(High-end need/high cost
per individual programs)

Community Resources
(facilities, stakeholders,
programs services)

Examples
• Public health & safety
  programs
• Prenatal care
• Immunizations
• Pre-school programs
• Recreation & enrichment
• Child abuse education

• Early identification to treat
  health problems
• Monitoring health problems
• Short-term counseling
• Foster placement/group homes
• Family support
• Shelter, food, clothing
• Job programs

• Emergency/crisis treatment
• Family preservation
• Long-term therapy
• Probation/incarceration
• Disabilities programs
• Hospitalization
• Drug treatment

Systemic collaboration* is essential to establish interprogram connections on a daily basis and over time to ensure seamless intervention within each system and among _systems of prevention, systems of early intervention_, and _systems of care._

*Such collaboration involves horizontal and vertical restructuring of programs and services
a) within jurisdictions, school districts, and community agencies (e.g., among departments, divisions, units, schools, clusters of schools)
b) between jurisdictions, school and community agencies, public and private sectors; among schools; among community agencies

Figure 4.2.

also incorporate a holistic and developmental emphasis that envelops individuals, families, and the contexts in which they live, work, and play. The continuum also provides a framework for adhering to the principle of using the least restrictive and unintrusive forms of intervention required to appropriately respond to problems and accommodate diversity.

Moreover, given the likelihood that many problems are not discrete, the continuum can be designed to address root causes, thereby minimizing tendencies to develop separate programs for each observed problem. In turn, this enables better coordination and integration of resources which can increase impact and cost effectiveness. Ultimately, as indicated in figure 4.2, the continuum can evolve into a totally integrated system by enhancing the way the subsystems of intervention at each level are connected. Such connections may involve horizontal and vertical restructuring of programs and services (a) within jurisdictions, school districts, and community agencies and (b) between jurisdictions, school and community agencies, public and private sectors, among clusters of schools, and among a wide range of community resources.

As graphically illustrated by the tapering of the three levels of intervention in figure 4.2, development of a fully integrated system is meant to reduce the number of individuals who require selected and indicated supports. That is, the aim in developing such a comprehensive approach is to prevent the majority of problems, deal with another significant segment as soon after problem onset as is feasible, and end up with relatively few needing specialized assistance and other intensive and costly interventions.

OPERATIONALIZING THE CONTINUUM FOR SCHOOL-IMPROVEMENT PLANNING: REFRAMING HOW SCHOOLS ADDRESS BARRIERS TO LEARNING

An additional framework helps to operationalize the concept of an enabling or learning supports component (see figure 4.1) in ways that coalesce and enhance programs to ensure all students have an equal opportunity to succeed at school. A crucial matter is defining what the entire school must do to enable all students to learn and all teachers to teach effectively. Schoolwide approaches to address barriers to learning are especially important in which large numbers of students are affected and at any school that is not yet paying adequate attention to considerations related to equity and diversity. Leaving no child behind requires addressing the problems of the many who are not benefiting from instructional reforms.

Various pioneering efforts have operationalized such an enabling component into six programmatic arenas. We refer to these six arenas as the component's curriculum or content (Adelman 1996b; Adelman and Taylor 1998). This curriculum encompasses programs to (1) enhance classroom-based efforts to enable learning; (2) respond to and prevent crises; (3) support transitions; (4) increase home involvement in schooling; (5) outreach to develop greater community involvement and support; and (6) provide prescribed student and family assistance (see Exhibit 1 at the end of this chapter).

Combining the six content arenas with the continuum of interventions illustrated in figure 4.2 provides a full intervention picture to guide school-improvement planning in developing a system of learning supports. The resulting matrix is also shown in figure 4.2. This matrix creates a unifying umbrella framework to aid in rethinking the daily work of all staff who provide learning supports. It also facilitates mapping and analyzing the current scope and content of how a school, a group of schools (e.g., a feeder pattern), and a school district address barriers to learning and teaching.

GETTING FROM HERE TO THERE REQUIRES ANOTHER TYPE OF CONCERN ABOUT SYSTEMIC CHANGE

Those who set out to improve schools and schooling across a district are confronted with two enormous tasks. The first is to develop prototypes; the second involves large-scale replication. One without the other is insufficient. Yet considerably more attention is paid to developing and validating prototypes than to delineating and testing systemic change processes required for sustainability, replication, and scale-up (Elmore 2004; Fullan 2005; Hargreaves and Fink 2000). For example, most innovations are developed as pilots, demonstrations, or special projects at one or a few schools in a district. These prototypes are assigned special budget allocations for a period usually ranging from three to five years. Often the stated intent is not only to sustain but eventually to diffuse the prototype throughout the district. But the reality is that most prototypes disappear after the special period of funding ends. This has led some researchers to describe the failure to sustain and take prototypes to scale as "projectitis" and to an increased focus on dealing with the problem (Adelman and Taylor 2003).

School improvement obviously needs to begin with a clear framework and map for what changes are to be made. It should be equally evident that a framework and map is needed for how to get from here to there. And in both cases, the work requires strong leadership and adequate resources to build capacity for systemic change and looks to available research for guidance (Sarason 1996; Taylor, Nelson, and Adelman 1999; Vander Ark, 2002).

Elsewhere, we have discussed in some detail a basic framework highlighting how major elements involved in designing school improvements are logically connected to considerations about designing systemic change (Center for Mental Health in Schools 2005e). Figure 4.3 outlines the framework. As can be seen in figure 4.3, the same elements can be used to frame key design concerns related to school improvement and systemic change, and each is intimately linked to the other. The elements are conceived as encompassing

- The vision, aims, and underlying rationale for what follows,
- The resources needed to do the work,
- The general functions, major tasks, activities, and phases that must be pursued,
- The infrastructure and strategies needed to carry out the functions, tasks, and activities, and
- The positive and negative results that emerge.

Strategic planning for school improvement should account for each of the elements outlined in figure 4.3, first with respect to prototypes for ensuring that all the students have an equal opportunity to succeed in school and then with respect to how schools will accomplish essential changes. At the district level, the need is for a strategic plan that clarifies how the district will facilitate replication and scale-up of prototype practices.

Key considerations with respect to both (a) desired school improvements and (b) "getting from here to there" (e.g., systemic changes):

> What is the vision, long-term aims, and underlying rationale?
> What are the existing resources that might be (re)deployed and woven together to make good progress toward the vision?
> What general functions, major tasks, activities, and phases need to be implemented?
> What infrastructure and strategies are needed to carry out the functions, tasks, and activities?
> What short-term indicators will be used as process benchmarks, what intermediate outcomes will indicate progress toward long-range aims, and how will negative outcomes be identified?

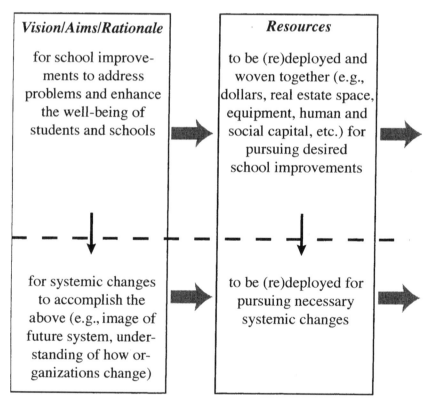

Figure 4.3. Linking logic models for designing school improvement and systemic change

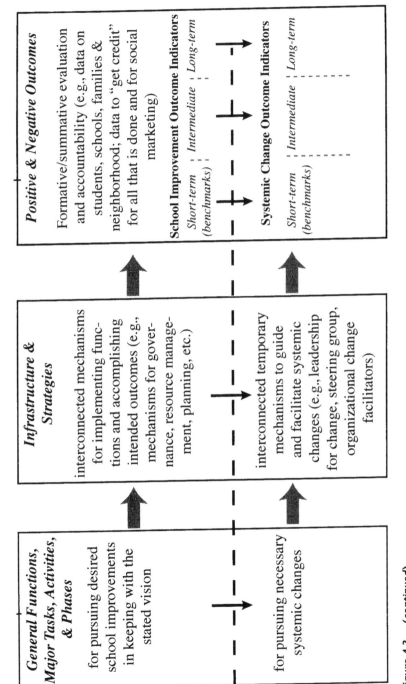

Positive & Negative Outcomes

Formative/summative evaluation and accountability (e.g., data on students, schools, families & neighborhood; data to "get credit" for all that is done and for social marketing)

School Improvement Outcome Indicators

Short-term (benchmarks) : *Intermediate* : *Long-term*

Systemic Change Outcome Indicators

Short-term (benchmarks) : *Intermediate* : *Long-term*

Infrastructure & Strategies

interconnected mechanisms for implementing functions and accomplishing intended outcomes (e.g., mechanisms for governance, resource management, planning, etc.)

interconnected temporary mechanisms to guide and facilitate systemic changes (e.g., leadership for change, steering group, organizational change facilitators)

General Functions, Major Tasks, Activities, & Phases

for pursuing desired school improvements in keeping with the stated vision

for pursuing necessary systemic changes

Figure 4.3. *(continued)*

SUMMARY

Prevailing school reform processes and capacity building (including pre-service and in-service staff development) have not dealt effectively with the marginalization of learning supports. Thus, it is not surprising that so many schools continue to struggle with enhancing student progress and closing the achievement gap. The simple psychometric reality is that in schools where students encounter major barriers to learning, test score averages are unlikely to increase much until learning support programs are rethought and redesigned.

Every school-improvement plan must meet the challenge by ensuring it focuses on development of a comprehensive system of learning supports for addressing barriers to learning and teaching. Development of such a system requires shifts in prevailing policy and new frameworks for practice. In addition, for significant prototype development and systemic change to occur, policy and program commitments must be demonstrated through effective allocation and (re)deployment of resources to facilitate organizational and operational changes. That is, finances, personnel, time, space, equipment, and other essential resources must be made available, organized, and used in ways that adequately operationalize policy and promising practices. This includes ensuring sufficient resources to develop an effective structural foundation for prototype development, systemic changes, sustainability, and ongoing capacity building. To do less is to undermine substantive systemic change and perpetuate an unsatisfactory status quo.

REFERENCES

Adelman, H. S. 1995. Education reform: Broadening the focus. *Psychological Science* 6: 61–62.

———. 1996a. *Restructuring education support services: Toward the concept of an enabling component.* Kent, OH: American School Health Association.

———. 1996b. Restructuring education support services and integrating community resources: Beyond the full service school model. *School Psychology Review* 25: 431–45.

Adelman, H. S., and L. Taylor. 1994. *On understanding intervention in psychology and education.* Westport CT: Praeger.

————. 1997. Addressing barriers to learning: Beyond school-linked services and full service schools. *American Journal of Orthopsychiatry* 67: 408–21.

————. 1998. Reframing mental health in schools and expanding school reform. *Educational Psychologist* 33: 135–52.

————. 1999. Addressing barriers to student learning: Systemic changes at all levels. *Intro to thematic section for Reading and Writing Quarterly* 15: 251–54.

————. 2003. On sustainability of project innovations as systemic change. *Journal of Educational and Psychological Consultation* 14: 1–26.

————. 2006. *The school leader's guide to student learning supports: New directions for addressing barriers to learning.* Thousand Oaks, CA: Corwin Press.

Allen, D. W. 1993. *Schools for a new century: A conservative approach to radical school reform.* New York: Praeger.

Carnegie Council on Adolescent Development's Task Force on Education of Young Adolescents. 1989. *Turning points: Preparing American youth for the 21st century.* Washington, DC: Author.

Center for Mental Health in Schools. 1996. *Policies and practices for addressing barriers to learning: Current status and new directions.* Retrieved from http://smhp.psych.ucla.edu/pdfdocs/newdirections/policiesfull.pdf, January 17, 2006.

————. 1997. *Addressing barriers to student learning: Closing gaps in school/community policy and practice.* Retrieved from http://smhp.psych.ucla.edu/pdfdocs/barriers/closinggaps.pdf, January 17, 2006.

————. 2005a. *School improvement planning: What's missing?* Retrieved from http://smhp.psych.ucla.edu/whatsmissing.htm, January 17, 2006.

————. 2005b. *Addressing what's missing in school improvement planning: Expanding standards and accountability to encompass an enabling or learning supports component.* Retrieved from http://smhp.psych.ucla.edu/pdfdocs/enabling/standards.pdf, January 17, 2006.

————. 2005c. *Another initiative? Where does it fit? A unifying framework and an integrated infrastructure for schools to address barriers to learning and promote healthy development.* Retrieved from http://smhp.psych.ucla.edu/pdfdocs/infrastructure/anotherinitiative-exec.pdf, January 17, 2006.

————. 2005d. *Where's it happening? New directions for student support.* Retrieved from http://smhp.psych.ucla.edu/pdfdocs/wheresithappening/overview.pdf, January 17, 2006.

————. 2005e. *Systemic change for school improvement: Designing, implementing, and sustaining prototypes and going to scale.* Retrieved from http://smhp.psych.ucla.edu/pdfdocs/systemic/systemicreport.pdf, January 17, 2006.

Dryfoos, J. G. 1994. *Full-service schools.* San Francisco: Jossey-Bass.

Elmore, R. F. 2004. *School reform from the inside out: Policy, practice, and performance.* Cambridge, MA: Harvard Educational Publishing Group.

Fullan, Michael. 2005. *Leadership and sustainability: System thinkers in action.* Thousand Oaks, CA: Corwin.

Gardner, S. L. 2005. *Cities, counties, kids, and families: The essential role of local government.* Lanham, MD: University Press of America.

Hargreaves, A., and D. Fink. 2000. The three dimensions of reform. *Educational Leadership* 57: 30–34.

Sarason, S. 1996. *Revisiting "The culture of schools and the problem of change."* New York: Teachers College Press.

Taylor, L., P. Nelson, and H. S. Adelman. 1999. Scaling-up reforms across a school district. *Reading and Writing Quarterly* 15: 303–26.

Vander Ark, T. 2002. Toward success at scale. *Phi Delta Kappan 84*: 322–26.

Exhibit I   Content Areas for a Component to Address Barriers to Learning

(1) Classroom-based approaches encompass

- Opening the classroom door to bring available supports in (e.g., peer tutors, volunteers, aids trained to work with students-in-need; resource teachers and student support staff work in the classroom as part of the teaching team).
- Redesigning classroom practices to enhance teacher capability to prevent and handle problems and reduce need for out of class referrals (e.g., personalized instruction; special assistance as necessary; developing small group and independent learning options; reducing negative interactions and overreliance on social control; expanding the range of curricular and instructional options and choices; systematic use of prereferral interventions).
- Enhancing and personalizing professional development (e.g., creating a learning community for teachers; ensuring opportunities to learn through coteaching, team teaching, and mentoring; teaching intrinsic motivation concepts and their application to schooling).
- Curricular enrichment and adjunct programs (e.g., varied enrichment activities that are not tied to reinforcement schedules; visiting scholars from the community).
- Classroom and schoolwide approaches used to create and maintain a caring and supportive climate.
- Emphasis at all times is on enhancing students cognition and affect related to competence, self-determination, and relatedness to others at school and reducing threats to such cognition and affect.

(2) Crisis assistance and revention encompasses

- Ensuring immediate assistance in emergencies so students can resume learning.
- Providing follow-up care as necessary (e.g., brief and longer-term monitoring).

- Forming a school-focused crisis team to formulate a response plan and take leadership for developing prevention programs.
- Mobilizing staff, students, and families to anticipate response plans and recovery efforts.
- Creating a caring and safe learning environment (e.g., developing systems to promote healthy development and prevent problems; bullying and harassment abatement programs).
- Working with neighborhood schools and community to integrate planning for response and prevention.
- Capacity building to enhance crisis response and prevention (e.g., staff and stakeholder development, enhancing a caring and safe learning environment).

(3) Support for transitions encompasses

- Welcoming and social support programs for newcomers (e.g., welcoming signs, materials, and initial receptions; peer buddy programs for students, families, staff, volunteers).
- Daily transition programs for (e.g., before school, breaks, lunch, after school).
- Articulation programs (e.g., grade to grade—new classrooms, new teachers; elementary to middle school; middle to high school; in and out of special education programs).
- Summer or intersession programs (e.g., catch-up, recreation, and enrichment programs).
- School-to-career/higher education (e.g., counseling, pathway, and mentor programs; broad involvement of stakeholders in planning for transitions; students, staff, home, police, faith groups, recreation, business, higher education).
- Broad involvement of stakeholders in planning for transitions (e.g., students, staff, home, police, faith groups, recreation, business, higher education).
- Capacity building to enhance transition programs and activities.

(4) Home involvement in schooling encompasses

- Addressing specific support and learning needs of family (e.g., support services for those in the home to assist in addressing

basic survival needs and obligations to the children; adult education classes to enhance literacy, job skills, English-as-a-second
language, citizenship preparation).

- Improving mechanisms for communication and connecting
  school and home (e.g., opportunities at school for family networking and mutual support, learning, recreation, enrichment,
  and for family members to receive special assistance and to volunteer to help; phone calls or e-mail from teacher and other
  staff with good news; frequent and balanced conferences—stu-
  dent-led when feasible; outreach to attract hard-to-reach families—including student dropouts).

- Involving homes in student decision making (e.g., families
  prepared for involvement in program planning and problem
  solving).

- Enhancing home support for learning and development (e.g.,
  family literacy; family homework projects; family field trips)

- Recruiting families to strengthen school and community (e.g.,
  volunteers to welcome and support new families and help in various capacities; families prepared for involvement in school governance).

- Capacity building to enhance home involvement.

(5) Community outreach for involvement and support encompasses

- Planning and implementing outreach to recruit a wide range of
  community resources (e.g., public and private agencies; colleges
  and universities; local residents; artists and cultural institutions,
  businesses and professional organizations; service, volunteer, and
  faith-based organizations; community policy and decision makers).

- Systems to recruit, screen, prepare, and maintain community resource involvement (e.g., mechanisms to orient and welcome,
  enhance the volunteer pool, maintain current involvements, enhance a sense of community).

- Reaching out to students and families who do not' come to
  school regularly—including truants and dropouts.

- Connecting school and community efforts to promote child and
  youth development and a sense of community.

- Capacity building to enhance community involvement and support (e.g., policies and mechanisms to enhance and sustain school-community involvement, staff/stakeholder development on the value of community involvement, "social marketing").

(6) Student and family assistance encompasses

- Providing extra support as soon as a need is recognized and doing so in the least disruptive ways (e.g., prereferral interventions in classrooms; problem-solving conferences with parents; open access to school, district, and community support programs).
- Timely referral interventions for students and families with problems based on response to extra support (e.g., identification/screening processes, assessment, referrals, and follow-up—school based, school linked).
- Enhancing access to direct interventions for health, mental health, and economic assistance (e.g., school-based, school-linked, and community-based programs and services).
- Care monitoring, management, information sharing, and follow-up assessment to coordinate individual interventions and check whether referrals and services are adequate and effective.
- Mechanisms for *resource* coordination and integration to avoid duplication, fill gaps, garner economies of scale, and enhance effectiveness (e.g., braiding resources from school-based and linked interveners, feeder pattern/family of schools, community-based programs; linking with community providers to fill gaps).
- Enhancing stakeholder awareness of programs and services.
- Capacity building to enhance systems, programs, and services for student and family assistance.

5

THE CRUCIBLE OF REFORM: THE SEARCH FOR SYSTEMIC LEADERSHIP

Thomas L. Alsbury

In response to the increased pressure for continuous improvement of student achievement, school leaders have been more active than ever promoting reforms of various types. However, strategic planning, increased accountability focus, and various school restructuring efforts still seem to result in sporadic and unsustainable student-achievement gains in most districts. Suggestions for combating unsustainable change efforts have ranged from improving the quality of the reform program itself, redistributing leadership to teachers, focusing on the school's culture, using data to enforce accountability, improving staff development, and a focus on instructional practice. Although all of these suggestions for improving the effectiveness of school reform have merit, this chapter will use past research findings and findings from an empirical study, the Crockett study, to focus on the problems leaders encounter, what is needed for systemic change to occur, and recommendations for future reform leaders.

It was the purpose of the Crockett study to conduct a four-year systems analysis of one district's initially successful reform efforts at the middle and high schools from 2001 to 2005. The study assumes the fecundity of, and is designed around, organizational reform variables recommended by Coburn (2003) and Leithwood, Aitken, and Jantzen

(2001) as necessary for program introduction, implementation, and sustainability. The chapter concludes that although systemic leadership and support is crucial to sustainable change, the quality of leadership is more crucial than who leads.

REASONS WHY SCHOOL REFORMS FAIL

Researchers have suggested that school reform may falter for a variety of reasons, including a lack of attention to systemic district support in the areas of leadership, staff development, finance, and cultural development (Coburn 2003; Leithwood, Aitken, and Jantzi 2001; Mintzberg 1993). Mintzberg noted that many school reform programs are initiated with poor or no systems analysis and planning. Leithwood, Aitken, and Jantzi focused on the importance of cultural development as opposed to a heavy-handed accountability focus noting that, "the consequences of tightening the accountability 'screws' often are a narrowing and trivializing of the school curriculum and the creation of work cultures that reduce rather than increase professional commitments" (2). Additionally, these researchers indicated that the local learning required for successful restructuring efforts is aided by feedback concerning change obstacles.

Although researchers provide a wide variety of recommendations for reform success, a theme emerges from their studies centered on the importance of a systemic approach to reform development and implementation. A long-term monitoring of broad systemic variables during, and subsequent to, a reform program revision, seems necessary if sustained change to the school and its culture, resulting in student-achievement gains, is to remain a viable goal (Deal and Peterson 1999; Fullan 2001). A continuous systemic evaluation during a reform effort not only provides valuable feedback loops to the change leaders in the organization, but may also inculcate within the organization a habit of systematic data collection, reflection, and use.

THEORETICAL PERSPECTIVES

Interest in how sustainable school reform is linked to effective leadership is not new and has been studied by a number of researchers. Fullan (2001) suggested that leaders within a district will increase long-term effectiveness if they focus on moral purpose, understand the change process, develop relationships, foster knowledge building, and strive for coherence. Deal and Peterson (1999) speak to the need for transforming school cultures and Sergiovanni (1992) focused on moral or servant leadership to realize sustained reform. Although researchers have traditionally assumed that principals at the building level would provide the leadership for reform, the issue of who leads school reform has also looked in new directions.

Researchers have begun to debate whether teacher leaders, rather than principals, are most effective in leading school reform, raising the question, "Does it matter where leadership comes from" (Harris 2004)? Adding to the debate about what is needed for effective and sustainable reform is the notion that a systems orientation, focused on crucial processes and conditions within a school district, is key (Lethwood et al. 2001). This may suggest that who leads school reform is not as important as what system changes are initiated within the school. Finally, researchers have recommended a closer analysis of systemic program components to identify those factors that may better support sustainable reform (Coburn 2003). In this chapter, all three systemic issues, who should lead reform, the importance of focusing on systemic attributes, and how successful reform can be sustained, are addressed.

WHO CAN OR SHOULD LEAD REFORM?

The recent drive for school reform and accountability has renewed the focus on the importance of effective school leadership. The centrality of school leadership, and focused on the principal in particular, is well established in research literature (Blase and Blase 1998; Gil 2001; Leithwood and Duke 1999). Leithwood and Riehl (2003) indicate that although reform efforts are most successful when principals work with teacher leaders, the principal needs to remain in the formal leadership position.

However, recently the conversation in schools and among researchers has shifted to the significance of "what happens in the classroom," bringing the relative importance of administrative leadership style or organizational structure under question. School-improvement research seems to consistently point toward the long-term benefits of teacher collaboration and the promotion of cultural rather than structural change and the increase in teacher ingenuity and innovation (Harris 2002). Although research evidence shows that effective leaders powerfully influence school effectiveness and even student achievement (Wallace 2002), there are relatively few studies that have established any direct causal links between leadership and improved student performance (Hallinger and Heck 1996).

Silns and Mulford (2002) similarly suggest that student improvement is most evident when leadership is widely distributed throughout the school community. Glickman, Gordon, and Ross-Gordon (2001) note "varied sources of leadership, including distributed leadership" in a list of characteristics of an improved school as crucial to successful school reform (49). Additional research on teacher leadership reinforces the shift from a focus on principal or central office leadership, to that of the teacher (Muijs and Harris 2003). Harris (2004) stated, "Even though the conventional wisdom of leadership as role or position tends to persist, there is a groundswell toward alternative interpretations of leadership"(4).

However, researchers have also suggested that distributed or teacher leadership models are mostly theoretical, lack empirical data in terms of student achievement (Bennett, Harvey, Wise, and Woods 2003), and describe a purely analytical tool that simply relays effective principal leadership activities (Spillane, Halverson, and Diamond 2001; Gronn 2000). Thus, principal leadership behaviors are often still the determining factors in what may appear to be teacher-led reform processes because effective building leaders initiate, implement, and maintain systems that use distributive leadership approaches.

Leadership in Context

Harris (2004) noted a variety of leadership approaches used during successful school reform efforts including top-down forms that he and other researchers found effective in the early stages of school reform, particularly in schools experiencing difficulty according to Gray (2001). These findings seem to mirror the previous claims of contingency theorists who suggested that when school personnel are unwilling and unable to reform, directive leadership may be the most effective (Blake and Mouton 1985;

Hersey and Blanchard 1977). Conversely, most researchers, although recognizing the importance of contextual effects on leadership and reform, support specific approaches for all leaders that are exclusively postmodernistic in style. Marks and Printy (2003) indicated that the most effective leadership style, called "integrated leadership," consisted of a combination of transformational and instructional leadership characteristics.

An overview of current research also reveals a focus on the development of leadership capacity within a school district and less on the individual skills of particular leaders or on who initiates shared contexts for collaborative leadership (Harris and Lambert 2003). Thus, it may be argued that leadership may be most appropriate and effective when coming from a variety of individuals or groups of administrators, teachers, staff, and even school board members, depending on the unique contextual organizational circumstances within each school system. This might lead to the suggestion that the importance of focused leadership from the principal of the school and the necessity of bottom-up versus top-down initiation of reform is a bit of a red herring. In other words, the who of leadership may be less important than the what.

FOCUSING ON SYSTEMIC ATTRIBUTES

Although the question of who leads school reform efforts may be important, research suggests that even more crucial are the processes and conditions of the organizational system (Leithwood, et al. 2001). Leithwood and others suggest that first-order changes like student goals, curriculum and instruction development, and services directed toward the teacher to accomplish those goals, have not produced sustainable improvements in schools; "First-order changes are almost never successfully institutionalized in the absence of complimentary second-order changes" (19). Second-order changes include changes in the organization of the district, in policy, in resource allocation, and in structure or culture. The authors further state that only as we focus on districtwide, holistic systemic change will student-achievement reforms be sustainable.

Leithwood and others (2001) developed a set of critical processes and conditions (as shown in the appendix to this chapter) that focused on crucial aspects of second-order change within a district. The authors incorporated seven categories derived from organizational design theory (Banner and Gagne 1995) and from research on effective schools and districts. These aspects of school organizations included mission and goals, school and district culture, management and leadership, structure and organization, decision making, policies and procedures, and community relations. The Crockett study, discussed later in this chapter, used these categories to evaluate the systemic variables crucial to a district engaging in a reform effort.

The concept of organizational learning by Leithwood and others (2001) accepts the fact that schools and districts will need to make changes and incorporate innovative programs, such as those that move from teacher-centered to student-centered, or use inquiry approaches to learning, specifically like the science writing heuristic (SWH) program used in the Crockett study. However, organizational learning focuses primary attention on the organizational structures and processes that support people engaged in program implementation. To date, school reform changes have lacked sustainability because of their exclusive emphasis on change in instructional methodology and classroom practice while ignoring the organizational structures and culture that provide the support systems crucial to their survival (Sarason 1990). Although Fiske (1992) suggested that schools put too much faith in process over results, even researchers who focus on clear measurable goals and the analysis of performance data confirm that process measures are interdependent, citing that sustainable change needs to remain focused on both process and product (Schmoker 1999).

Unfortunately, the consideration of district organizational systems and processes, also called *systems thinking* by Senge (1990), is still rare. Monitoring a school's organizational system over an extended period to inform the implementation of a reform effort would allow school leaders to monitor and adapt the organizational components needed for sustained reform; a goal that has remained elusive in most school reform efforts.

SUSTAINING SUCCESSFUL REFORM

Although researchers have confirmed the necessity to implement and monitor organizational systems changes in concert with program innovations, they have reported that most educational reform efforts lack sustained change in multilevel systems. Coburn (2003) indicated that localized successes in school reform often fail to sustain the changes as a result of multiple and shifting organizational priorities. Coburn noted that reform efforts will likely fail when exported to outside schools and districts, from school to school within a district, and even between teachers within a school, unless implementers of school-improvement programs consider a principle she characterized as reform "scale" (3).

Scale speaks not so much to who is leading but what aspects of reform culture exist in a system and the ability to sustain the change once it has begun. Coburn (2003) pointed to the fact that many successful reform efforts tend to result in significant and immediate student-achievement gain, but often these results diminish or disappear after a few years even though the reform program appears, on the surface, to still be in place.

WHAT IS SCALE?

Scale is comprised of three main components: depth, spread, and shift. All components of scale are necessary if reformers hope to maintain the initial student-achievement gains over time, with normal external forces, such as social and political changes, and administrative turnover at work. Coburn (2003) noted that depth involves a change in "teacher beliefs" (4) or in their underlying assumptions of how students learn. It also involves a change in the "norms of social interaction" (5) between the teacher and the student in the classroom. Finally, "deep change" requires a change in the "underlying pedagogical principles" (5) and in the "enacted curriculum" (Cohen and Ball 1999).

Coburn (2003) pointed to the lack of studies that measure whether changes, once implemented, are actually able to sustain over time. She noted that most studies do not continue to gather data at a school for multiple (four to six) years and not after the funding and the "hoopla" of the new program has ceased. However, Coburn and Meyer (1998) and McLaughlin and Mitra (2001) have indicated that the greater the depth of change the more likely reform will be sustained even in the face of reduced resources and an increase of competing new programs and initiatives.

Coburn (2003) suggested that the idea of spread was not only restricted to the exporting of program methods to other schools, but also in finding a way to export the issues of value, culture, and pedagogical principles embodied in depth mentioned previously. The district itself can affect spread by developing a common set of values and principles within all of the school staff and leadership. This shifts leadership of reform to the district level and provides a greater task than simply providing resources to buildings. Coburn calls this "spread within" (7).

Coburn (2003) finished with the idea of shift, described as the moment a reform effort is internalized and continued by actions of the district itself. She suggested that an outside reformer might help with this by training the district leadership in what will be needed and how to go about sustaining the change. This is different than buy-in and goes to the heart of systematic measures that work to change a district's organizational structures. The Crockett study incorporated Coburn's principles of sustainability and Leithwood's critical conditions and processes for reform in the method and analysis design and provides a rare example of a long-term study of district systemic change during the implementation of a reform effort. Findings provide a glimpse of the problem areas encountered, what was needed for systemic change to occur, and recommendations for future reformers seeking sustainable change.

THE CROCKETT STUDY

The study was conducted at the Crockett School District, a midwestern community with a population of 14,500 and a school enrollment of 2,300. This rural community is mostly comprised of middle class, blue-collar workers. The school district includes a middle school (seventh and eighth grades), a high school (ninth through twelfth grades), and five elementary schools. The SWH program was introduced in the middle and high schools in 2001 and involved all three middle school and all five high school science teachers.

Science Writing Heuristic Project

The SWH program introduced the use of writing-to-learn strategies as a crucial part of science writing. Students were stimulated to question, discuss the way they engaged in laboratory experiences, and more thoroughly verbalize and write their thought processes as they engaged with laboratory observations and experimental results. The process is inquiry based, student centered, and involves more active participation and analysis of the students' thought processes. The SWH project had been implemented in the Crockett high and middle schools during the 2001–2002 school year, introduced by the assistant superintendent and curriculum director, and all science staff were trained by the SWH university program designer and trainer. Participation in the SWH program, and the frequency of use, was voluntary, however, all chose to participate in the training and engage in some level of implementation throughout the study period.

Methods

Qualitative research methods were used in this study including interviews, observations, and document collection. Important informant interviews included all school personnel and university researchers involved in providing leadership, training, and implementation for the SWH project, including the superintendent, assistant superintendent and curriculum director, middle school principal, high school principal, high school assistant principal, all middle and high school science teachers, the project designer and trainer, and two research assistants. Researchers also observed and collected data via audio recording and transcribing of superintendent leadership team meetings and district-level all-staff in-service events.

Analysis Methods

Transcriptions from all interviews, audiotaped observations of leadership team meetings, and documents were analyzed and coded using a checklist developed from Coburn's (2003) principles of sustainability and Leithwood and others's (2001) crucial system processes and conditions (see appendix). Although not intended as a quantitative study, the frequency of responses within each category on the checklist was noted and compared across respondents.

Student Achievement

During 2002–2005, the overall student scores on the Crockett Iowa test of basic skills (ITBS), a national standardized examination, showed significant increases for overall student scores in the middle school and more mixed results at the high school. As shown in table 5.1, significant gains on the science portion of the ITBS occurred within two years of the SWH program implementation, with little change in the same student cohort scores in math and language arts, and no similar large fluctuation in test score data in previous years. More dramatic were the improvements in ITBS science scores for special education students and students of low socioeconomic status at the middle school. Despite overall test score gains among eighth graders, eleventh grade results did not show the same dramatic or sustained increases, except among special education and high poverty students in 2003–2004. Unfortunately, these increases reversed after only one year raising a question concerning why eighth grade and eleventh grade scores differed and why the reform at the high school could not be sustained. Answers to these questions emerged from the systems analysis conducted.

Table 5.1.

Year, grade	Proficient or above, all students (%)*	Proficient or above, low socioeconomic status students (%)*	Special education students (%)*
2001–2002, Eighth†	67.9	48.8	18
2002–2003, Eighth	**80.4**	**63.6**	**43.9**
2003–2004, Eighth	**77.5**	**60**	29
2004–2005, Eighth	**81.4**	**75.4**	**56.6**
2001–2002, Eleventh†	73.1	48.3	33.3
2002–2003, Eleventh	70.2	47.1	23.8
2003–2004, Eleventh	**83.3**	**86**	**87.6**
2004–2005, Eleventh	81.5	49	18.8

*Bold scores reflect significant Iowa test of basic skills gains
†SWH program introduced

Qualitative Results

Predetermined themes from grounded theory (Coburn 2003; Leithwood et al. 2001), as represented in appendix A to this chapter, make up a convenient structure with which to code and report data findings. Table 5.2 provides a frequency of response indication for each of the Leithwood et al. (2001) conditions and Coburn's (2003) principles disaggregated by respondent role and data type.

Entries were calculated by taking the number of respondents in a common role group (for example, eight teachers) and multiplied by the total number of descriptors to calculate the number of coded "tallies" possible. In other words, if a science teacher confirmed the presence of one of the descriptors at any time during their extensive interview it was tallied. The tally occurred whether a respondent merely mentioned the descriptor or spoke extensively about a principle or condition. Additionally, responses did not have to use specific language found in the descriptor checklist but common language was translated and placed in a descriptor category as appropriate. Although this procedure is not intended to indicate quantitative significance, it provided a numerical measure of how much a respondent confirmed the presence of the Leithwood conditions and Coburn principles within the Crockett school system as specifically applied to the SWH program.

As shown in table 5.2, only 27.5 percent of the sustainable reform conditions and principles were mentioned by respondents, observed, or found in documentation. This indicates that sustainable reform principles and conditions were not generally present in the Crockett school system to the extent necessary to sustain the SWH program over the long term. Despite the initial successes in the program as indicated by significant ITBS student test gains, Leithwood's and Coburn's theories

Table 5.2

Respondents annually	Leithwood (2001) conditions	Coburn (2003) principles
Teachers (8)	76 of 600 (13%)	36 of 128 (28%)
Administrators (4)	224 of 300 (75%)	27 of 64 (42%)
Researchers (3)	73 of 225 (32%)	17 of 48 (35%)
Documents (7)	99 of 525 (19%)	17 of 112 (15%)
All participants (15)	373 of 1125 (33%)	80 of 240 (33%)
All data points (23)	472 of 1650 (29%)	97 of 352 (27.5%)

would predict a measured and short-lived improvement; a result confirmed at the high school but not the middle school level. The Crockett study provides an opportunity to assess what problem areas were encountered during the reform effort, what was needed for systemic change to occur, and what others could learn from their experience.

Problem Areas Encountered

Over the course of the implementation of the SWH project, the study of the Crockett school district leadership system provided an opportunity to determine what problems were encountered that thwarted the reform effort and what activities supported the success of the SWH project. Problems that created difficulty in the Crockett reform effort included district teacher and administrative turnover, a lack of leadership from the building principals, the lack of systemic planning and coordination, differential use of the reform program external mandates, and a lack of systemic sustaining elements, like scaling.

DISTRICT STAFF AND LEADER INSTABILITY

During the introduction and implementation phases (2001–2003) of the SWH program at Crockett, science teaching staff had remained unchanged. However, in 2003, there was significant science teacher turnover in the high school. It can be argued that this was a contributing factor in the quick decline of eleventh grade science scores and the observed drop in implementation frequency and quality among these teachers. This is likely to have been caused by two factors.

First, staff turnover meant that only some of the current high school teachers were present at the time the initial decision was made to begin the reform program. As confirmed by interview data this led to a diminished buy-in and support from the science staff in the high school. Second, science staff initially trained by the university designer and trainer indicated that the training had motivated them to reconsider their general belief about teaching; a phenomenon Coburn (2003) indicated was crucial for sustained change and an indicator of depth. Interview data from the new high school science staff, in 2003–2004, indicated a decrease in teacher buy-in, a diminished understanding of the SWH content, and a decline in implementation frequency and quality.

In addition to teacher turnover at Crockett, there were also a few key leadership changes during 2004. Although the current assistant superintendent for curriculum and instruction, who introduced the program and continued coordinating its implementation, remained constant, the middle school principal and the school superintendent changed. Surprisingly, systems analysis data did not indicate this change as a major factor to the success of the reform. This is primarily because neither the superintendent nor the principles at the building level had been involved in the SWH project and delegated full leadership for the reform effort to the assistant superintendent and curriculum director.

Finally, the university researcher, who functioned as the project designer and trainer left the SWH project in 2004. Interview data from science teachers indicated that the university professor was a vital figure in motivating staff to change their pedagogical views and properly implement the SWH program, particularly at the high school level. In this particular instance, it appears that the leadership of the university trainer and collaborator had a significant impact on the success of the sustainability of the reform at the high school.

Overall, there was relative stability among the key stakeholders, trainers, leaders, and staff within the district during the inception and implementation phases of the project in 2001–2003. With the superintendent and principal turnover deemed as inconsequential, it appears that change in the university trainer and collaborator and the teaching staff was mostly responsible for the failure to sustain the reform effort at the high school.

LACK OF LEADERSHIP AT THE BUILDING LEVEL

Table 5.2 indicates that science teachers reported the presence of only 15 percent of the necessary reform conditions and principles, whereas administrators identified the presence of 69 percent of these within the system. Another verification of a potential disconnect between administrators and teachers was the frequency in which respondents not only did not mention key reform principles and conditions, but also reported in the negative that these were not present in the Crockett district. Administrators reported in this study that 1.4 percent of the reform principles and conditions were definitely absent from the Crockett system, whereas teachers reported negatively almost six times as much (6.6 percent). Documentation also indicated a disconnect between leaders and staff, with documentation citing the presence or promotion of only 18 percent of the reform principles and conditions.

Interview data from Crockett principals indicated they were not actively involved in initiating activities or systemically promoting the SWH reform effort. Principals did, however, frequently discuss the importance of, and their belief in the principles and conditions for effective reform. Similarly, the staff reported the absence of key reform conditions and principles, and some assigned little importance to the need for leadership to come from the principal at the building level as long as they were receiving support from the university trainer and the assistant superintendent and curriculum director. However, several of the high school science teachers expressed a need for additional support from their principal noting:

> This could suggest that building-level leadership might be more critical at different grade levels or within different teacher contexts. For example, it could be argued that, at Crockett, the teacher team at the middle school were stable and had developed a strong working relationship. Conversely, the high school science staff were more isolated from each other, experienced more turnover, and possessed a wide variance of beliefs about student learning; a context requiring more principal leadership to sustain a reform effort such as the SWH program. (Alsbury 2004)

Documentation and interview data, from the Crockett district, revealed a lack of systems that would support collaborative planning, coordination, and communication between the central office, principals at the building level, and the science teachers. For example, no leadership or curricular teams exists at the building level that introduces, implements, or assesses reform efforts like SWH program. The curriculum director introduced the SWH program to science teachers. Teachers indicted general support from, but a lack of knowledge and involvement of, principals in the SWH program, and principal interviews supported that contention. One teacher noted, "I think it would take some encourage-ment from the supervision above to say hey, this [the SWH program] is something we need to continue. You know just as well as I do, that I'll just go back to my old way because change is tough, and not everybody wants change" (eleventh grade science teacher; Alsbury 2004).

Although school leaders in Crockett have an understanding of some of the reform conditions and principles deemed important by Leith-wood and others (2001) and Coburn (2003), there are others that seem conspicuously absent. For example, one of Leithwood's management conditions—regular monitoring and supervision of staff using data col-lection measured against school goals and staff development and ac-countability—was not mentioned by school leaders in Crockett. Re-spondents spoke only to this descriptor, inasmuch as they noted the presence of a staff development program in Crockett.

DIFFERENTIAL USE OF THE REFORM

Data findings confirmed that not all science teachers were at the same level of proficiency with the SWH program, the program was used with varying success and frequency among teachers, and not all teachers fully embraced the use of the program in their classroom. These variations in buy-in and use of the SWH program were expressed by the following science teachers who said:

> They bought us new toys and inquiry materials . . . but in the end I don't have time. . . . So the support I think is there in theory, but with the time commitments that we have that's dumped on us as teachers right now, the support's there but we can't get to it (eighth grade science teacher).
>
> I don't have a very good taste in my mouth about it. I think it's good, but I don't think I was ready. I don't know if I was ready to do it or if I wasn't supported well or if I didn't know how to do things right" (eleventh grade science teacher).
>
> They (the district) almost do too much. I mean it's kind of overwhelming to us as teachers. There's always something coming down the pike, and we're getting bombarded with a lot of different things, and it's really hard to keep track of everything and keep it straight. We feel like we don't really

complete anything before we jump on the bandwagon for something else."
(eighth grade science teacher; above quotes in Alsbury 2004)

Even among teachers who supported and found classroom successes
through frequent use of the SWH program, quotes like these evidence
a lack of systemic buy-in caused perhaps by, among other things, a lack
of a bottom-up, values-driven mission recommended by many researchers and evident in schools with effective reform efforts (Fullan
2001; Leithwood et al. 2001).

In interviews, researchers and administrators stated that they intended
SWH to change instructional pedagogy to create a more positive and successful science classroom experience leading to significant student improvements. The presence of a shared, positive mission and culture or a
sense of teacher empowerment seems to be absent among some of the
SWH teacher participants as a result of an organizational structure that
directed reform efforts from the central office to teachers, bypassing
building principals. Although this approach did not seem to negatively
impact Crockett middle school science teachers, it was particularly problematic among the less-cohesive Crockett high school science teachers.

External Mandates

Respondents in the study spoke frequently of top-down directives
from outside the Crockett school district as well; namely No Child Left
Behind (NCLB). Although the presence of accountability measures like
NCLB need not have the ultimate influence on the mission or motivation behind reform efforts like SWH, this appears to be the case. Crockett science staff seemed to indicate that they had a reform effort for the
sake of raising ITBS scores to satisfy NCLB, but neither connected to,
nor emanating from, a shared mission based on educational values or
moral purpose. This is evidence by interview data that tallied, from 100
percent of the respondents, confirmation of the presence of a long-
range goal at Crockett but specifically defined that goal as raising student test scores. One teacher said, "That's what NCLB has done, we
have to improve scores in order to be a successful school. That's what
we're being graded on, so that's where the push is. I don't know if that's
right" (eleventh grade science teacher; Alsbury 2004).

LACK OF SUSTAINING SYSTEMS

Mechanisms that might institutionalize reform program like incorporation of the reform conditions and principles into teacher evaluation documents, line items in the permanent budget for SWH, permanent/yearly staff development programs for SWH, or written hiring policies seeking teacher skills and predispositions congruent to SWH were not present in Crockett.

This sustainability principle was noted by Coburn (2003) as the institutionalization of reform through program processes, such as teacher evaluation and supervision criteria, and practices that systematically reinforce shared curricula or instructional methods. No such systematic assessment of the SWH program existed within the supervision or evaluation forms or processes of the Crockett school district. One teacher commented, "He's [the principal] just trying to encourage us . . . this is something we're trying, let's just give it a whirl to see what's happening. Never anything like, you're going to have to do this" (eleventh grade science teacher; Alsbury 2004).

Although this teacher's comments were meant as a compliment to the administrator in appreciation for allowing total academic freedom and an unobtrusive leadership approach, it speaks to the lack of program goals embedded into a supervision or evaluation system; one of the conditions for school with effective and sustainable reform efforts.

LACK OF SYSTEMIC PLANNING AND COORDINATION

Organizational systems of several kinds were present in the Crockett school district, including committees of grade-level teachers within buildings called *horizontal teams*, and subject-specific curriculum committees, composed of teacher representatives across grade levels called *vertical committees*. However, the vertical science/health curriculum committee consisted of all three middle school science teachers, but only two of the five high school science teachers. Also, neither the middle nor high school principals were on this committee.

Interview data confirmed that teachers and principals not on the committee were less supportive and knowledgeable about the SWH program.

It might also be noted that despite the composition of the vertical science curriculum committee, interview responses indicated that teachers overwhelmingly viewed the SWH program as coming from the central office and reported the curriculum director as their contact for everything concerning SWH program including requests for resources and training.

It may be argued that systematic hierarchical arrangements that bypass support resources at the building level, like budgets, schedules, and program priorities, tend to fragment goals or allow accidental roadblocks that serve to slow down or destroy reform efforts (Fullan 2001). At Crockett, the diminished participation by key science teachers in the curriculum system may have contributed to the lack of sustainability at the high school level.

LACK OF SHARED CULTURE

Another important condition for effective school reform is the presence of a shared culture (Deal and Peterson 1999). Crockett teachers mentioned the condition descriptors for culture for reform the least of all the conditions and principles, providing almost no comments referencing the following descriptors from Leithwood and others' (2001) conditions: (a) openness to change, (b) participative decision making, (c) school/districts as systems, (d) values directed decision making, and (e) a substantial agreement among staff about the basis on which day-to-day decisions are made. Ironically, the only one of Leithwood's conditions that yielded a high frequency of response was the one noting that error and uncertainty was inevitable.

Other data indicated differences between various respondent role groups. For example, although no group spoke extensively about mission or school culture, administrators spoke most often about management conditions, whereas teachers spoke the least about this area. Teachers spoke most often about the importance of student-achievement gains in terms of policy and procedures. All respondents spoke least often about structure and organization and community partnerships. Ironically, researchers spoke most often about leadership components. Overall, the findings seem to indicate that people within the Crockett system follow fairly traditional roles; central office focuses on policy, principals focus on management, teachers focus on raising test scores, researchers talk about leadership and few talk about mission, systems, collaboration, or community.

HOW TO SUPPORT SYSTEMIC CHANGE REFORM

Although it is instructive to explore the reform conditions and processes that may appear to be absent in the Crockett district, it is also important to recognize the contradictory evidence of fluctuating ITBS scores, especially among low socioeconomic status and special education students. Table 5.1 shows that despite what might have been lacking in the Crockett reform effort, test scores generally did increase and sustained, especially at the middle school. This begs the questions as to how to make systemic reform continue after the initial pilot years. Findings from the Crockett study and other research provides several suggestions including (a) the development of pedagogical shift and depth, (b) institutionalizing reform, (c) staff stability, (d) systemic planning and coordination, (e) consistent use of reform, and (f) a shared culture. Research also suggests that context matters. Thus, although providing the principles of sustainability is crucial to reform success, who provides them may not be as important as once thought.

Systemic Reform Requires Pedagogical Shift and Depth

Coburn (2003) suggested that districts that lack depth and shift will not have sustainable reform. In the Crockett district interviews, these sustainability principles were rarely noted by administrators, even by those who frequently mentioned Leithwood and others's reform conditions (75 percent). The one Coburn principle that was addressed the most frequently was that the university designer and trainer had helped them internalize the SWH program and change their internal beliefs and pedagogy about student learning. Teachers said,

> It's changed the way I teach to a large degree. I no longer engage in days of lecturing and note-taking by students. I have a lot more student engagement and student involvement. (eighth grade science teacher)

The biggest change for me is having the students be responsible for their own learning. Before, I just told the kids we're going to get on the bus, and you're going to follow along, and if you start to struggle, just hang on . . . I'll back it up, and we'll hop back on and away we go. With the inquiry approach, I'm no longer the bus driver. They are now driving their own bus, and I'm in the back facilitating and trying to keep things moving along. (eighth grade science teacher; Alsbury 2004)

Systemic Reform Requires Institutionalization

The Crockett findings indicate that the university designer and trainer was able to motivate and shift the staffs thinking about teaching pedagogy and may have significantly contributed to the immediate success of the SWH program in 2001–2003. In addition to the university trainer, the assistant superintendent and curriculum director provided the emotional drive, the resources, and the priority focus that continues to sustain the SWH project in Crockett. In the unique context of the Crockett school district, the sustainability of the SWH reform effort appears to be embodied in champions for the program; the university designer and trainer, the assistant superintendent, and a few teachers.

However, few of Coburn's other principles of sustainability that would lead to the institutionalization of the SWH program seem to exist. Coburn (2003) contended that without multiple and varied institutionalizing principles in place, the district may be hard pressed to successfully shift and spread the responsibility for training, creation of buy-in, or motivation for the SWH program in the future. Unfortunately, starting in 2004, the university designer and trainer, a key source of reform sustainability as mentioned previously, was no longer directing the project, and several administrative and teacher changes also occurred in Crockett within the previous two years.

When asked to identify how the program will be sustained, some administrators pointed to informal, teacher-to-teacher reinforcement and training, and offered little assurance of continued, systematic district support of the program. Coburn (2003) suggested that school districts interested in systemic change need to institutionalize the reform through what she calls shift. Shift activities can include: (a) ensuring that the leaders at all levels of the district and the teachers understand the pedagogy and nature of the reform; (b) creating a method for ongoing staff development; (c) continued funding of the reform; (d) finding ways to hold the district formally responsible for continued spread of the reform, perhaps weaved through policy, hiring practice, budgeting, scheduling of time, and procedures within buildings; and (e) reform-centered ideas and methods of school or in-district decision making that involves the staff and key leaders involved in the reform.

Systemic Reform Requires Staff Stability and Consistent Instructional Application

Data from this and other studies on educational reform suggests that teacher stability may be crucial to sustained reform efforts. In this study, it was evident that student test scores started to drop in the high school only after science teacher turnover led to a diminished level of science department buy-in to the SWH project. In addition, new staff had not been trained in the program nor had they been inspired to change their teaching pedagogy like those teachers originally trained by the university trainer and designer.

Other data collected in the study indicated that teachers with the best student results were observed using the SWH program often while maintaining the integrity of the inquiry approach. Staff who used the program infrequently or who did not deliver it properly reported less support of the program and posted poorer student test results.

In Crockett middle school, where staff were stable and participated in the selection of the project, the training, and the implementation, both quality and quantity of delivery remained high. Also, teacher buy-in and enthusiasm remained high as did their student-achievement gains, as seen in table 5.1. These findings support the notion that teaching staff who are not involved in the initial decision to adopt a reform program need to be taken through a similar decision-making process and instructional training to use the program. In other words, new staff must be taken through the same process as the original staff.

It is also necessary to continue to observe the teachers as they implement a program to determine frequency of use and quality of delivery and provide feedback. Although university collaborators provided this service during 2001–2003, the Crockett district needed to institutionalize this procedure through principal or peer observation and support. In this study, as this support waned, staff delivery quality declined, some staff discontinued frequent use of the SWH program, and many reported a feeling that the program was no longer a priority for the district. In the absence of a clear directive to continue the reform program, some staff opted to focus on other, newer demands.

Systemic Reform Requires Planning and Coordination

Evidence from this study suggests that a collaborative approach to goal setting and decision making needs advancing in Crockett to better develop teacher buy-in and knowledge of vision and mission and other reform principles and conditions mentioned infrequently or absent from the respondent transcriptions. Low evidence of Coburn's principles for sustainability and Leithwood and others's conditions for effective reform and the ensuing change in the middle school principal and superintendent may potentially exasperate the already apparent lack of coherence in teacher's internal beliefs and pedagogy or depth, and the lack of staff internalizing the program or shift as it applies to the SWH program. As a result, the initial success of the program may be short lived.

It seems clear from the findings that Crockett teachers are not aware of or are not confirming the shared establishment, understanding, or support of a district mission that drives reform efforts. This might suggest that Crockett administrators do not fully understand the importance of systems thinking, organizational learning, or collaboration present in effective schools and noted by Leithwood and others (2001). However, in the study interviews, Crockett administrators in fact did indicate an understanding of these conditions. They said:

> if you want something sustained, it's got to be with your teachers. It can't be built within the administration because the administration leaves. So to have this sustained, the teachers have to be trained, they have to support it, and the have to implement it and get it as part of their teaching practices (middle school principal).
> [About sustainability:] I think just consistent implementation of activities that are based on that theory and then also for the teachers to see suc-

cess as a result of that, and I think for kids to get more used to and accustomed to those approaches to learning. (district curriculum director; Alsbury 2004)

WHO SHOULD LEAD?

Leithwood and others (2001) describe organizational learning as crucial to sustained school improvement. Organizational learning promotes a collaborative culture, shared decision making, goal consensus, and time for professional collaboration. Within this and other leadership theory, the principal is assumed to be irreplaceable in providing direction, facilitation, and leadership in successful reform efforts. Fullan (2001) points to the need for creating and sharing knowledge and providing coherence. In fact, some researchers consider the use of teacher leaders as a more crucial factor in sustainable school improvement (Lambert 2003) than district administrators.

However, Peterson (2000) contended that increased school board and central office involvement, in some cases, has led to a decline in student achievement, whereas other studies indicate that school boards and programs they support have a positive effect on school renewal with the goal of improved student achievement (Cotter 2001; Parelius 1982; Russell 1997; Scott 1991; Underwood, Fortune, and Cleary 1985). We are left with the idea that while all staff and leaders must be involved in successful school reform, there is little agreement or indication of who plays the most important or crucial role.

The findings of this study seemed to support the argument that a traditional, hierarchical and even top-down leadership approach initially can result in a dramatic overall improvement in student achievement, even among marginalized student groups. In the Crockett study, a university researcher and an assistant superintendent provided primary leadership to a team of science teachers of what currently appears to be a successful reform particularly at the middle school level.

This and other research seems to indicate that there are a variety of contextual variables that need to be considered when developing a system for effective change. This attention to context presents a challenge to current beliefs about the necessity of principal facilitation in systematic transformation, organizational learning, and cultural change for sustained student-achievement gains and points to the legitimacy of centralized, traditional leadership approaches in certain organizational contexts.

REFERENCES

Alsbury, T. L. (2004, November). Leadership, scaling and succession in school reform efforts in an accountability age. Paper presented at the annual convention of the University Council for Educational Administration, Kansas City, MO.

Banner, D. K., and T. E. Gagne. 1995. *Designing effective organizations: Traditional and transformational views.* Thousand Oaks, CA: Sage.

Bennett, N., J. A. Harvey, C. Wise, and P. A. Woods. 2003. *Distributed leadership: A desk study.* Retrieved from www.ncls.org.uk/literature, October 20, 2004.

Blake, R. R., and J. S. Mouton. 1985. *The managerial grid.* Houston, TX: Gulf.

Blase, J., and J. Blase. 1998. *Handbook of instructional leadership: How really good principals promote teaching and learning.* Thousand Oaks, CA: Corwin.

Coburn, C. E. 2003. Rethinking scale: Moving beyond numbers to deep and lasting change. *Educational Researcher* 32 (6): 3–12.

Coburn, C. E., and E. R. Meyer. 1998. *Shaping context to support and sustain reform.* Paper presented at the American Educational Research Association Conference, San Diego.

Cohen, D. K., and D. L. Ball. 1999. *Instruction, capacity, and improvement.* Philadelphia: Consortium for Policy Research in Education.

Cotter, M. E. 2001. Strategic leadership for student achievement: An exploratory analysis of school board-superintendent governance and development practices. *Dissertation Abstracts International* 62 (6): 1993, UMINo. 3017528.

Deal, T. E., and K. D. Peterson. 1999. *Shaping school culture: The heart of leadership.* San Francisco: Jossey-Bass.

Fiske, E. B. 1992. *Smart schools, smart kids: Why do some schools work?* New York: Touchstone.

Fullan, Michael G. 2001. *Leading in a culture of change.* San Francisco: Jossey-Bass.

Gil, L. S. 2001. *Principal peer evaluation: Promoting success from within.* Thousand Oaks, CA: Corwin.

Glickman, C., S. Gordon, and J. Ross-Gordon. 2001. *Supervision and instructional leadership: A developmental approach.* Boston, MA: Allyn and Bacon.

Gray, J. 2001. Using the past to plan the future: Making sense of almost four decades of research. *School Effectiveness and School Improvement* 12 (2): 259–63.

Gronn, P. 2000. Distributed properties; A new architecture for leadership. *Educational Management and Administration* 28(3) 317–338.

Hallinger, P., and R. Heck. 1996. Reassessing the principal's role in school effectiveness: A critical review of empirical research 1980–1995. *Educational Administration Quarterly* 32 (1): 5–44.

Harris, A. 2002. *School improvement: What's in it for schools?* London: Falmer Press.

———. 2004. *Distributed leadership and school improvement: Leading or misleading?* Paper presented at the Annual Meeting of the American Educational Research Association, San Diego.

Harris, A., and L. Lambert. 2003. *Building leadership capacity for school improvement.* Buckingham: Open University Press.

Hersey, P., and K. Blanchard. 1977. *Management of organizational behavior: Utilizing human resources.* Englewood Cliffs, NJ: Prentice-Hall.

Lambert, L. 2003. *Leadership capacity for lasting school improvement.* Alexandria, VA: ASCD.

Leithwood, K. A., and D. L. Duke. 1999. A century's quest to understand school leadership. In *Handbook of research on educational administration*, 2nd ed., ed. J. Murphy and K. Seashore Louis, 45–72. San Francisco: Jossey-Bass.

Leithwood, K. A., R. Aitken, and D. Jantzi. 2001. *Making schools smarter: A system for monitoring school and district progress*, 2nd ed. Thousand Oaks, CA: Corwin Press.

Leithwood, K. A., and C. Riehl. 2003. *What we need to know about successful school leadership.* Philadelphia: Laboratory for Student Success, Temple University.

Marks, H. M., and S. M. Printy. 2003. Principal leadership and school performance: An integration of transformational and instructional leadership. *Educational Administration Quarterly* 39 (3): 370–97.

McLaughlin, M. W., and D. Mitra. 2001. Theory-based change and change-based theory: Going deeper and going broader. *Journal of Educational Change* 2 (4): 301–23.

Mintzberg, H. 1993. *The rise and fall of strategic planning.* New York: Free Press.

Muijs, D., and A. Harris. 2003. *Teacher leadership: A review of research.* Retrieved from www.ncIs.org.uk/literature, October 20, 2004.

Parelius, R. J. 1982. *The school board as an agency of legitimation and change.* Paper presented at the Annual Meeting of the American Educational Research

Association, New York, NY. ERIC Document Reproduction Service No. ED 217556.

Peterson, S. A. 2000. Board of education involvement in school decisions and student achievement. *Public Administration Quarterly* 24 (1): 46–68.

Russell, M. 1997. A study of the relationship between school board leadership behavior and advancement of instructional quality. *Dissertation Abstracts International* 57 (8): 3349, UMI No. 9700667.

Sarason, S. 1990. *The predictable failure of educational reform.* San Francisco: Jossey-Bass.

Schmoker, M. 1999. *Results: the key to continuous school improvement*, 2nd ed. Alexandria, VA: Association for Supervision and Curriculum Development.

Scott, H. J. 1991. *Leadership imperatives for school board members in the reform and renewal of public schools.* Paper presented at the Annual Meeting of the National School Boards Association, San Francisco. ERIC Document Reproduction Service No. ED 336857.

Senge, P. M. 1990. *The fifth discipline: The art and practice of learning organization.* London: Doubleday.

Sergiovanni, T. 1992. *Moral leadership.* San Francisco: Jossey-Bass.

Silns, H. C., and W. Mulford. 2002. Leadership and school results. In *Second international handbook of educational leadership and administration*, eds. K. Leithwood and P. Hallinger. Norwell, MA: Kluwer Academic: 561–612.

Spillane, J., R. Halverson, and J. Diamond. 2001. *Toward a theory of leadership practice: A distributed perspective.* Chicago: Northwestern University, Institute for Policy Research.

Underwood, K. E., J. C. Fortune, and F. J. Cleary. 1985. Heads up: Here's how school boards are energizing public education. *American School Board Journal* 172 (1): 25–28.

Wallace, M. 2002. Modeling distributed leadership and management effectiveness: Primary school senior management teams in England and Wales. *School Effectiveness and School Improvement* 13 (2): 163–86.

APPENDIX A

SYSTEM AND PROCESS EVALUATION OF THE BOONE SCIENCE HEURISTIC WRITING PROJECT

Interview Protocol Response Checklist

Note: The following represent areas that the respondent may discuss, which are connected to the main research purposes and supported by multiple researchers as exemplars for effective school reform. The response checklist was modified from the student and district surveys found in Leithwood, Aitken, and Jantzi (2001, 133–77) and Coburn (2003).

COBURN'S PRINCIPLES OF SUSTAINABILITY

Depth

____ There is a change in the teachers' internal beliefs or a change in pedagogy.

____ The reform has been internalized by key staff leaders.

Spread

____ The researcher has trained and prompted the organization to take-on, internalize, and institutionalize the project values and program essentials.

____ The district has established policy or procedures to institutionalize.

____ The school has established policy or procedures to institutionalize.

____ Processes are designed for ease of spread among teachers.

____ Processes are designed for ease of spread among schools in the district.

____ Processes are designed for ease of spread among other districts.

Shift

___ The researcher trained the administration and staff to internalize the program.

___ The researcher trained the administration and staff to institutionalize the program.

___ Leaders at all levels understand the underlying pedagogy of the project.

___ Resource capacity is built in to ensure ongoing staff development surrounding the project.

___ Ongoing funding is established for the project.

___ Hiring policy and procedures support the continuation of the project.

___ Budget policy and procedures support the continuation of the project.

___ Reform methods of decision making is institutionalize through policy, mission, or procedures.

LEITHWOOD'S CRITICAL SYSTEMS PROCESSES AND CONDITIONS

Mission, Goals, and Organizational Culture

___ Clarity: goals and mission are clear and can be readily understood.

___ Meaningfulness: Goals and mission are considered valuable and worth striving for (commitment).

___ Awareness: District and school staff are aware of goals and mission (consensus).

___ Usefulness: Goals and mission influence decisions at district, school, and classroom levels.

___ Currency: Goals and mission are reviewed and revised periodically.

___ Congruence: Goals and missions of the school are congruent with one another.

___ Value based: Goals and missions are expressions of a set of fundamental values.

___ Immediate focus: Instrumental in fostering productive change.

___ Long-range focus: Oriented to defensible outcomes for students.

School Culture Norms

___ Mutual respect among staff.

___ Openness to change and risk taking.

___ Use of different perspectives for problem solving.

___ High expectations.

Beliefs

___ In the dignity and worth of all individuals.

___ Implementing change involves considerable "local" problem solving.

___ One learns from failure; good ideas may be found in many different places.

___ Student centered.

Values

___ Participation in decision making by all legitimate stakeholders.

___ Accountable to students or clients.

___ Knowledge, personal mastery.

___ Values-directed decision making.

Assumptions

___ All decisions ultimately must be justified in terms of student welfare.

___ Schools or districts are "systems": changing one part has implications for other parts.

___ Error and uncertainty is inevitable; learning is never ending.

___ Schools are to be positive, safe, and orderly.

Strength of Culture

_____ There is substantial agreement among staff about the basis on which day-to-day decisions are made.

_____ Staff demonstrate a wide variety of approaches to learning and have divergent perspectives that they share together.

_____ Proposals for change are given serious consideration by staff.

Forms of Culture

_____ Encouragement is provided for individual and team problem solving.

Management

_____ Operational planning: Each team regularly develops, reviews, and refines a plan for its operation.

_____ Information for planning: The views of those served are collected and considered.

_____ Organizing: Roles and responsibilities are defined by teams and structures are developed to assist staff in carrying out their tasks.

_____ Staffing: Staffing practices help ensure high levels of capacity for contributing to the teams' operational plans.

_____ Supervision and evaluating: Performance of staff is monitored in a manner appropriate, regular, data supported, and measured against the district or school goals and operational plans.

_____ Staff development and accountability are the functions of supervision and evaluation.

_____ Coordinating: Operational plans are coordinated across all teams and focused on the district's strategic plans.

_____ Communication and reporting: Information about the operational plan and its inception and implementation procedures are widely disseminated across and within teams.

_____ Budgeting: Financial and human resources are allocated according to priorities identified in the teams' operational plans and the districts' strategic plans.

School and District Leadership

___ Provides vision or inspiration.
___ Models behavior.
___ Provides individualized support.
___ Provides intellectual stimulation.
___ Fosters commitment to group goals.
___ Encourages high performance expectations.
___ Visibly acknowledges good work.
___ Strongly encourages individual improvement.

Instructional Services

___ Instruction is carefully planned collaboratively horizontally and vertically.
___ Instructional goals are appropriate and clear.
___ Instructional content is challenging.
___ Instructional strategies are suited to instructional objectives and students' needs.
___ Instructional strategies reflect defensible principles of learning.
___ Instructional time is used effectively.

Structure and Organization

___ Engages in continuous efforts to find the most productive locus for decision making.
___ Organizational structures facilitate day-to-day work of staff.
___ Organizational structures facilitate organizational learning and long-term problem-solving capacity.
___ Collateral or parallel groups are established to foster developments of alternative points of view; these may be ad hoc groups.
___ Heterogeneous student grouping is used.
___ Collects optimum amounts and types of information.
___ Information is used to assist in decision-making processes that range from highly participative to autonomous, depending on the issue.

___ Decisions regarding the stream of problems associated with school-improvement initiatives are distributed among many teachers and administrators.

___ School staff recognizes their limitations and are open to assistance from external sources.

___ Student assessment practices in the classroom yield valid and reliable information.

___ Student assessment information collected in the classroom is used to improve instruction.

Policy and Procedures

___ Maintains a balance between district, school, and staff autonomy.

___ Support the accomplishment of the district and school goals.

___ Personnel devote special attention and most of their time to areas key to accomplishing student-achievement goals like staff development, evaluation, curriculum and instruction, and school improvement.

___ Student policies emphasize student achievement.

___ Student policies minimize disruptive behaviors.

___ Student policies provide for students with special needs.

___ Student policies foster students' sense of affiliation with the school.

District Community Partnership

___ District at "peace" with larger community, generally a passive acceptance.

___ Communicates mission in many formal and informal ways.

___ School develops community partnerships.

___ School has a productive relationship with the postsecondary sector.

___ School has incorporated parents into the programs.

___ School helps produce educational culture at home.

6

LEADERSHIP AND THE SELF-ORGANIZING SCHOOL

David F. Bower

Complexity theory offers new concepts, such as self-organization and emergence, that may assist schools to find more holistic ways to sustain reform and improvement. This chapter summarizes a qualitative phenomenological study that examined the experiences of the staff of one middle school to better understand the phenomena of self-organization and its role in sustaining school improvement. Self-organization and renewal sustain reform and improvement indirectly and are also related to emergence. Leadership supports and sustains the dynamics of self-organization, renewal, and improvement in individual and collective ways. This study suggests that processes of self-organization can help schools to sustain reform and improvement by internalizing purpose and focus.

INTRODUCTION: DROPS OF WATER ON A HOT SKILLET

This chapter offers a conceptual framework for sustaining change. It will suggest how ownership of reform initiatives can emerge from within a school and how leadership can support this process. Examining a school through the lens of complexity theory or self-organization theory is a relatively new way to view the phenomenon of sustained improvement and reform. Much of what we want and need in our schools—and probably in other organizations as well—will not be gained by mandates. Renewal, sustained change, growth, and creativity emerge from within. We cannot create these qualities by fiat or by devising lists of goals and objectives. We can, however, help to create the conditions that allow for these qualities to emerge and to grow naturally.

Patience over Time Yields Results

A colleague once described fads and trends in public education that come and go by saying, "They're like drops of water on a hot skillet— lots of hiss and fizzle but no substance. They're gone in a second." This insight is readily understood by many veteran teachers who see reforms come and go. But why is this phenomenon so common?

Amid the demands for better schools we find a jumble of reform strategies that have found their way into schools in the form of programs, policies, and laws. Some of the demands are contradictory and lead to confusion within schools (Lambert and McCombs 1998, 491). Fullan (1994) noted a similar problem with top-down leadership: "Topdown strategies are problematic because complex change processes cannot be controlled from the top" (190). Ironically, many imposed reform plans actually reinforce the system that reformers want to change. Demands for educational change and reform often ignore the history of public education and the structures that support schools. Without such a critical knowledge base, reform efforts may actually perpetuate or create other problems in the target system (Tye 2000).

Tye (2000) referred to this phenomenon as the "deep structure" of schooling (3). Society generally agrees that schools should look and function much as they have for the last several decades. Schools look and function in similar ways—a nine-month calendar, six periods in a day, classrooms full of student desks, grade levels organized by age, and teachers who deliver instruction. Inhibiting forces that perpetuate this phenomenon include: social context, structures of schools themselves, financial constraints, parent and community beliefs, and the teaching profession itself (3). Tye concluded, "[r]eforms of any kind won't 'stick' unless they are compatible with the existing deep structure of the society or with the direction in which the deep structure may be shifting. If true, this may help to explain much of the failure of both liberal and conservative education reforms in the United States since the end of World War II" (4).

The heritage of public school systems derived from a machine-age model has left us with organizations that are cumbersome, fragmented, and isolated. Laszlo (1996) noted that we have inherited a fragmented view of the world that is represented in specialties that do not connect; the result is isolation. Without connections, we have no coherence. Holism is a place to look for solutions to the problems we have inherited. Quantum theory and the science of chaos remind us that we are unified. Many of our problems stem from continuing to use mechanistic views to examine parts of problems rather than the whole or the context. We challenge schools to do more and do better without looking at the many factors that affect how children learn. We mandate change to systems and unknowingly perpetuate those same systems. We must move beyond thinking of our world and ourselves as disconnected fragments if we are to ever achieve lasting and thoughtful change.

COMPLEX ADAPTIVE SYSTEMS

Marion (1999) provided a useful definition to begin an exploration of chaos and complexity. He suggests, "A complex system is one whose component parts interact with sufficient intricacy that they cannot be predicted by standard linear equations; so many variables are at work in the system that its overall behavior can only be understood as an emergent consequence of the holistic sum of all the myriad behaviors embedded within" (27–28).

Chaos and complexity theory lead to some ways to think about managing an organization. Morgan (1997) offered a challenge to rethink beliefs about organizations, learn to manage contexts, learn to use small changes to create big effects, live with transformation as a daily event, and be open to new metaphors. We can rethink organizations as we learn to live with order that emerges from disorder and as we discern patterns that emerge naturally. Top-down management practices give way to flexible and adaptive methods of organization. We can learn that the role of leaders is to "shape and create the 'contexts' in which appropriate forms of self-organization can occur" and that "transformational change ultimately involves the creation of 'new contexts' that can break the hold of dominant attractor patterns in favor of new ones" (Morgan 1997, 267).

One way to understand complexity is to view the relationship between complicated and complex systems (Davis, Sumara, and Luce-Kapler 2000). Complicated systems may be understood by examining their parts. They are "predictable sums" of those parts (55). Complex systems, however, may not be understood by examining parts; they exceed their parts and may only be understood in relation to the parts. Complex systems are "self-organizing, self-maintaining, dynamic, and adaptive" (55) and unpredictable. They exist between order and chaos. Complex adaptive systems change because of a flow of information into them. If the system can incorporate the information, it adapts.

Pascale (1999) described four tests to see if an entity is a complex adaptive system. A complex adaptive system: 1) is comprised of many agents acting in parallel; 2) continually shuffles these building blocks and generates multiple levels of organization; 3) subject to second law of thermodynamics (entropy)—that is, winding down unless replenished with energy; and 4) exhibits capacity for pattern recognition to anticipate the future (85).

Lewin (1999) summarized rules by which complex adaptive systems operate: "The source of emergence is the interaction among agents who mutually affect each other. . . . Small changes can lead to large effects. . . . Emergence is certain, but there is no certainty as to what it will be. . . . Greater diversity of agents in a system leads to richer emergent patterns" (202–203). A complex adaptive system finds its capacity "not in the individual parts but in the function of the whole" (Wah 1998, 27). Isolating the parts results in the loss of context of the whole. An example of this parts isolation in education change efforts is implementing a team concept in a school without examining changes needed in scheduling, planning time, and teaching strategies.

Ellinor and Gerard (1998) noted a connection between holonomy and self-organization[1]:

> Quantum mechanics likens the organization to a hologram wherein all parts contain the whole and the whole is made up of unique parts. If we apply this holographic image to human systems, it becomes important that

each worker, no matter at what level in the organization, have mental images of how the whole organization operates and knows what is important to it on a timely basis. Information becomes vital, communication between and among all the parts is essential. What one knows must be available to all so that the essential life of the organization is maintained. . . . Self-organizing systems theory likens the organization to a self-referencing system, which maintains itself around an evolving core identity. Adaptation to changing conditions is the norm. If we apply this image to organizations, we see that top-down direction needs to be supplemented with information moving to all parts of the organization through rapid networks of communication. Each part of the organization needs to be able to reference what all other parts are doing. In this way, the whole organization can adjust to changing internal and external conditions fluidly. (43)

SELF-ORGANIZATION

Self-organization can be explained by technical definitions or by simple analogies. Sherman and Schultz (1998) described self-organization as:

the spontaneous emergence of non-equilibrium structural organization due to collective interactions between a large number of objects . . . Scientists have found that when the control factor is removed and the complexity is allowed to emerge, self-organization takes place. Within the sciences of complexity, this notion is coming to be recognized as a biological fact that is radically changing how we understand the way systems work. (85–86)

Wheatley (2001) described self-organization as an inside-out process:

The way that change happens in life is not from the top down, it is not from somebody writing out a strategic plan, developing the architecture, and then being the boss and delivering it. Life does not use bosses. Life uses a process called self-organization, which one way to think about this is that life organizes from the inside out; it organizes from lots of local actions that when they become connected to one another, great changes are possible. (5)

Self-organization comes from the ability to respond to the moment, to organize to meet the challenge, and to respond to the task at hand. Self-organized systems are flexible, adaptive, and fluid. They use information as fuel for responses and encourage the dispersal of information throughout the system to aid thought and reflection (Wheatley 1992). Capra (1982) delineated two complementary processes in self-organized systems. These are self-maintenance (the processes of self-renewal, healing, and adaptation) and self-transformation (the processes of learning, development, and evolution). This delineation helps to explain the difference between stability and equilibrium. Capra notes that, "self-organizing systems have a high degree of stability . . . the stability of self-organizing systems is utterly dynamic and must not be confused with equilibrium. It consists in maintaining the same overall structure in spite of ongoing changes and replacements of its components" (270–71). Equilibrium presents its own challenges, as does the edge of chaos.

Self-organization develops through interactions. Interactions in schools occur on many levels—between adults, between students, between adults and students, between learners and their work. Interactions must be guided by the values and vision of the organization, especially as these are expressed in dialogue, discussion, problem solving, inquiry, and reflection. Linear ways of leading do not always serve a more networked or webbed practice. For example, a leadership style that uses a hierarchical system like the "inverted tree" used in some organizations tends to shut down communication. Communication tends to flow only through established "branches" rather than throughout the entire system.

THE RESEARCH STUDY

My 2003 research study examined the dynamics of self-organization in one school using these questions:

1. What characterizes self-organization and renewal within a school?
2. How do self-organization and renewal sustain reform and improvement?
3. How does leadership support and sustain the dynamics of self-organization, renewal, and improvement?

This qualitative phenomenological study examined the experiences of the staff at Roosevelt Middle School in Albuquerque, New Mexico, to

Figure 6.1.   Conceptual framework characterizing self-organization

better understand the phenomena of self-organization. Figure 6.1 summarizes the study conceptually. The core of the organization, characterized by principles, philosophy, and values, influences processes like feedback, communication, dialogue, sense making, and relationships. These processes in turn support what emerges from the organization—ownership, renewal, creativity, a safe and trusting environment, engagement, and self-organization.

Focus

Principles, philosophy, and vision are overlapping concepts that several teachers cited as important to the focus they give to their work.

Principles and philosophy help to provide the core around which a system may organize. In this way they have the power of "strange attractors" in a system that is self-organizing. Cutright (2001) said:

> What, then, allows chaotic systems to develop any sense of pattern, to stay within boundaries? It is the existence of attractors. Attractors are those elements in a system that have drawing or organizational power. The presence of multiple attractors, while establishing boundaries on a system, results in unstable, complex patterns, with the attractors acting upon one another, and demonstrating greater sensitivity to influx. It is the presence of attractors that also gives chaotic systems the quality of self-organization, the ability to recreate order and pattern, at least temporarily, despite continuous compensation for internal and external shocks to the system, or turbulence. (5–6)

Self-organizing around a clear philosophy or principles provides a way to give focus without limits. McMaster (1996) noted that "a relatively small set of principles, or attractors, will be sufficient to create the elements by which a system self-organizes" (48). He also says that, "a rich variety of expressions is possible from a simple set of rules or 'attractors' when energy is directed or expressed through them. In the case of corporations, the 'attractors' can be thought of as values, or operating principles" (63).

Internalized focus means that teachers have found ways to balance their personal beliefs about teaching with the priorities and focus adopted by the school. This seems to be where the collective focus of a school shapes and directs individual work. One teacher described his role in this level of work in this way:

> Something else that helped was going through our vision and mission statements. We haven't done that for a few years, but what helped was that we internalized it by saying, 'what's my part in that' and we came up with a mission and vision for the entire school. But we all took a part and said, 'How am I contributing to this?' (Tom) (Bower 2003, 172)

Process

Self-organization and renewal sustain reform and improvement in a school through relationships, communication, sense making, and dialogue and conversation.

Relationships   Teaching teams support relationships and have been in place at Roosevelt for over a decade. They emerged naturally at first in the early 1990s and then became the norm of the school as grade-level teachers organized themselves into teams. In 1999 a health and wellness team was formed that consisted of counselors, social worker, nurse, special education chair, an administrator, and family counselor. Relationships and teams provide context and a sense of "fit" for teachers. When teachers speak of relationships or teaming, they are talking about connecting with others and finding support for their work. A comment by one teacher shows the importance of being a member of a teaching team:

> Working on a team—well, I would not want to be working by myself. Just me all alone [chuckle]. Because there's just not that support, and there's lots of different kinds of support. Parent support—we all go into a conference and we have the same concerns. I think it helps the students to have community, and there's just so many things we take for granted with teams. I've always taught on a team and I wouldn't want to teach without one. (Jennifer) (Bower 2003, 179)

Interaction, especially as supported by teams, contributes to the processes that characterize self-organization and renewal. Teams pull people into the school culture, as one respondent noted. Teams provide connections to others and to principles. Support is also important, especially the support from peers. Teams provide interaction that sparks creativity during the exchange of ideas. Several teachers noted that it is hard to be creative in isolation. Relationships also help to push teaching into a more public arena; teachers can not hide, and as a result, are more likely to adapt their practices to meet standards and goals that they have internalized through a team relationship.

Communication   Communication is an essential process that supports relationships and teams. Communication also provides information that helps people to know the place and role within the school. Feedback is a component of communication, but it is mentioned specifically in interviews, and so the term is stated here more explicitly. Feedback is an essential element of systems. Biological systems rely on feedback to regulate autonomous functions like respiration, temperature, and reflex actions. Many feedback loops are hooked together to allow for regular adjustment.

Communication is an essential process that supports relationships and teams. Communication also provides information that helps people to know the place and role within the school. Feedback is an important element in effective communication.

Sense Making   If open systems depend less on structures and more on processes, something must assist individuals to self-organize their role, function, and purpose. If there is less emphasis on structures and more emphasis on processes, sense making becomes essential (Weick 1995, 70).

Collective sense making refers to how people work together through interaction and communication. The categories of "individual" and "collective" sense making are somewhat artificial because there is an interaction between individual and collective processes. However, it is useful to examine the data in these categories to understand the different aspects. Collective sense making means working in a group that provides the means to understand individual work in a larger context. When people can make collective sense of their work, they are not working in isolation. They have ways to know how they are doing and how to make adjustments as needed.

Individual and collective sense making provide a way to internalize the purpose of the school and to determine how an individual responds to that purpose. The individual and collective levels are the microlevels and macrolevels of an organization. Sense making was most often described through interaction between individual (micro) and the collective (macro) levels. This interaction is holonomy, the interplay between individual/team/school levels of the organization. What is clear is that relationships support sense making. The collective level of work also helps individuals find their place and their sense of fit within the larger organization.

Dialogue and Conversation   Dialogue and conversation are key processes to support sense making and the flow of information. Dialogue can restore a sense of wholeness that is often missing in fragmented organizations. Wheatley (2001) wrote:

> having conversation is as ancient as our species. As soon as we had fire, we sat around the fire and we began to tell stories to one another of our day, or our challenges, of our adventures. We believe that conversation is the natural, normal way that human beings think together, and in the midst of this

crazy culture, in the midst of this speedup, in this time when we do not have time to just sit and reflect, we are not only losing good thinking, we are losing this ancient process by which we connect and develop new ideas. (3)

Dialogue has an ancient and seemingly universal history: "dialogue has no traceable beginning. It has journeyed broadly throughout the course of human history and has had many contributory sources" (Ellinor and Gerard 1998, 3). These sources include the early Greeks, preliterate Europe, indigenous peoples, and various spiritual traditions. African American and American Indian cultures have practiced dialogue and remind us of "that which we have forgotten to remember." In American Indian culture, the process requires talking and talking until the talking starts. Dialogue is also central to systems thinking (Chawla and Renesch 1995, 155).

Dialogue can be useful to bridge the microelements and the macroelements in organizations that I mentioned previously. In this way, dialogue relates to holonomy. Bohm (1996) contrasted individual and collective thought, noting that much of our thought comes from a collective background; most of our assumptions come from our collective experience in the world. "The collective thought is more powerful than the individual thought" (14). "Everyone who works as part of an organization or team today needs to feel how what they do is making a difference to the whole. In our rush for results, this is too often overlooked. Dialogue, when it is practiced routinely, can continuously keep our individual and collective juices flowing and the energy level high" (Ellinor and Gerard 1998, 16). A result of dialogue is that "[a]s people begin to see more of the whole of what is being accomplished together, they each see where he/she can add more value" (18).

Finally, dialogue supports the communication skills needed for self-organization. "Self-organization can be in many forms . . . there is emphasis on open communication, active listening, a recognition of the learning opportunities, and the capacity for the individual to be self-motivated and self-regulated. This is what Stacey calls 'communities of practice'" (Gunter 1995, 16). The interaction of elements at the process level is well summarized by this teacher's comment:

I read what's happening on the national and district level and all of that's important to me, but actually how I make sense of my work is much farther down the scale with my team of teachers and with individual teachers here at Roosevelt. I piece that together with the district and the national things that are happening and I don't ignore everything that the district is saying, but I think most of my direction comes from right here at Roosevelt with teachers that I work with. One thing that really helps me is when we have time to discuss things as a group. Because we may get dissention on one side and other opinions and I think finally evolving into a final decision as a school or a team. (Lefty) (Bower 2003, 206)

For me, what renews me is the working relationship, with my team, or with a co-partner. Because you're talking about it—you're not just doing it and planning everything—you share it and you get fresh new ideas, new viewpoints, and it makes you go back and look critically at what you've done and it gets better and it works out better for the students. I understand why teachers get burned out in other schools. I don't get it so much here because there's that sense of being a team and we work together. We're constantly bouncing ideas off of each other. (Barry) (Bower 2003, 189)

Emergence

Like flowers in a garden, emergent qualities arrive on their own schedule. What we want for our schools and for ourselves emerge from within the organization. They do not result from directives or from lengthy lists of goals and objectives. Emergence gets to the heart of self-organization. What characterizes self-organization within a school is what emerges from within. This concept seems logical in a school like Roosevelt Middle School. However, it seems counter to many current theories of school reform that thrust initiatives into a school from the outside, such as high-stakes testing or packaged curriculum plans. Emergence is a key concept in complexity theory and self-organization. It has implications for understanding new approaches to organizational theory and leadership.

McMaster (1996) offered an operational definition of emergence as, "a phenomenon that occurs out of the interplay of forces, information or energy being channeled through a system composed of a few basic principles (or 'attractors') and beyond a threshold point of containment. This interplay results in an identifiable phenomenon of rich variety and expression" (14).

Johnson (2001) described the complexity of natural systems that draw on intelligence at the bottom, rather than the top, of an organization:

They [systems] get their smarts from below. In a more technical language, they are complex adaptive systems that display emergent behavior. In these systems, agents residing on one scale start producing behavior that lies one scale above them: ants create colonies; urbanites create neighborhoods; simple pattern-recognition software learns how to recommend new books. The movement from low-level rules to higher-level sophistication is what we call emergence. (18)

These concepts have important implications for leaders. Leaders who understand the dynamics of emergence will be alert to emerging ideas or initiatives. Identifying these ideas or initiatives is the first step in bringing them into focus within the organization.

An emergent system is an aspect of holonomy—the larger wholes produced by parts. Marion (1999) states that "[t]he emergent system is truly greater than its parts. The whole has a grasp of a 'larger picture' that is unavailable to the parts . . . it violates the second law of thermodynamics by growing and becoming stronger rather than dissipating (entropy); and it can maintain its integrity in the face of perturbation" (29). Emergence as described by Marion helps to explain how an organization sustains itself and taps into the power of renewal. Rather than declining or weakening, an emergent organization finds strength to survive.

Safe and Trusting Environment

Closely related to freedom is a safe and supportive environment. Working in an environment that makes it safe to take risks and to be creative seems to allow individual strengths and abilities of staff members to emerge. A safe and supportive environment is one that encourages and values risk taking, creativity, and personal choice.

Renewal

One result of feedback is self-renewal or what scientists call "autopoiesis." Wheatley (1992) cites a concise definition of *autopoiesis* (from the Greek for self-production) as "the characteristic of living systems to continuously renew themselves and to regulate this process in such a way that the integrity of their structure is maintained" (18). Chilean scientists Humberto Maturana and Francisco Varela challenge the idea that organizations are open to changes in the external environment and that these changes force organizations to respond and adapt. Maturana and Varela argue that "all living systems are organizationally closed, autonomous systems of interaction that make reference only to themselves (quoted in Morgan 1997, 253). They use the term *autopoiesis* to describe the processes of self-renewal, self-creation, and self-production in a closed system. Living systems must maintain an identity and responding to changes becomes secondary to this maintenance. Interactions with the environment are self-referential with the result that "a system's interaction with its 'environment' is really a reflection of its own organization. It interacts with its environment in a way that facilitates its own self-production; its environment is really a part of itself" (Morgan 1997, 254).

Ownership

If people support what they create, then creativity and ownership are linked. Ownership allows teachers to say, "This is my work" or "This is our work." Ownership shifts the responsibility for implementation or problem solving from an external source to an internal source. If people support what they create, they also support what they own.

LEADERSHIP IN A COMPLEX WORLD

The challenges of a complex world suggest a need for a new approach to leadership. One way that the context is changing is through an emerging emphasis on systems and viewing systems as wholes. Beavis (1995) uses the term *quantum weirdness* as he makes reference to systems as wholes and to the belief that the relationship between parts is what matters, that "understanding leadership for example, is not a matter of how the organizational chart reads—who reports to whom, what is the hierarchy—or what are the traits of an effective leader. The new map shows that leadership must be seen in terms of relationships—who are the followers? Who is being empowered by the leader?" (27–28). Fritjof Capra, in *The Hidden Connections* (2002), refers to the emergence of novelty in his chapter on life and leadership in organizations. He claims,

"The phenomenon of emergence takes place at critical points of instability that arise from fluctuations in the environment, amplified by feedback loops. Emergence results in the creation of novelty that is often qualitatively different from the phenomena out of which it emerged" (116–17).

The concept of emergence offers some important implications to help leaders understand the dynamics of organizations. McMaster (1996) suggests that leaders seeking transformation will benefit by linking theories to emergent phenomena. "For a transformation to occur, a theory consistent with the emergent interactive self-organizing nature of human organization is required" (69). Santosus (1998) argues that "managers should allow creativity and efficiency to emerge naturally within organizations rather than imposing their own solutions on their employees" (1). An implication here is that leadership is less about imposition than drawing forth. Senge (1999) agrees, noting that "one key to achieving this [balance between local leadership and executive leadership] lies in understanding the interplay between 'design and emergence.' Executives should design the governance mechanisms to support the day-to-day organizational practices on the local level" (365).

Another implication for change leaders is to address the conditions that support emergence rather than trying to impose an answer or solution. "Think of strategy as an emergent phenomenon; we too often work on the strategy rather than on the conditions that support the emergence" (Lewin 1999, 202). Lewin is suggesting that we can only replicate the conditions that support innovation or reform, not the innovation or reform itself.

The challenge that the concept of emergence presents to us is that we can not make it happen by direct efforts. We get to emergence by more indirect efforts. Tetenbaum (1998, 26) says that chaos is self-organizing and emergent; we cannot "force" what emerges. MacIntosh and MacLean (1999) explain that when we consider complexity theory, Newtonian laws may apply, but not in all cases. Nonlinear relationships add to the complexity and to the feedback loops. Random developments can move a system to places never imagined. A system may become chaotic; in this case, small events (like the butterfly concept) combined with nonlinear feedback may cause something new to emerge (300–01). What emerges may or may not be what was intended.

Emergence may be preceded by difficult times. If we have the wisdom to recognize and appreciate this uncertainty we can be patient while the emergent process takes place. As a former theater teacher, I appreciate the connection that Capra makes between artistic and emergent processes. For example, Capra (2002) says that the "experience of tension and crisis before the emergence of novelty is well known to artists, who often find the process of creation overwhelming and yet persevere in it with discipline and passion" (118). Further on he explains:

> Artists and other creative people know how to embrace this uncertainty and loss of control . . .the sudden emergence of novelty is easily experienced as a magical moment. . . . In human organizations, emergent solutions are created within the context of a particular organizational culture, and generally cannot be transferred to another organization with a different culture (119).

Lambert and McCombs (1998) cite a need for principals to see the relationship between learning and change (496). This is similar to Burns' (1977) reference to the "teaching role of leadership" (425). Tasks of the principal include reducing isolation, increasing capacity, providing a caring environment, and promoting quality. "These functions are fulfilled by modeling, coaching, attending to detail, observing ceremonies, rituals, and traditions, and telling stories that identify heroes and heroines[2] who support the school's mission" (Lambert and McCombs 1998, 496). Characteristics of a culture that sees change as learning include the ability to include the opinions of everyone and thus avoid damaging conflicts, finding hope and excitement in the change process, and fostering change forces from with the organization by using inquiry and reflection (497).

McMaster (1996) says that leadership is a "naturally arising phenomenon that occurs in a complex dance" (71). He also describes leadership as interaction. McMaster suggests that lack of a management theory, especially in bureaucratic systems, creates problems. "As a result of this thinking, management considers systems as controls on people, communication as directional (certain kinds 'upwards' and certain kinds 'downward'), authority as hierarchical, and reward systems as a means for motivation" (6). McMaster also describes a more holistic approach to leadership. "Authentic leadership is present when there is a connection to the whole, coupled with a willingness to be responsible for one's part in it. . . . [Leaders] will trust the results of dialogue. . . . Their touchstones will be theory, dialogue and feedback from outside the system" (76).

Leadership in complex organizations requires a shift in our perceptions of its locus. A shift in thinking is needed to move leadership from the "hero leader" to the collective. Organizations might respond in one of two ways: find a hero leader or develop leadership throughout the organization (Chawla and Renesch 1995, 35). When an organization shifts the burden of leadership to the "hero," the result is an increase in that organization's powerlessness because it does not tap into its own greater potential. Nor does the organization develop collective intelligence. McMaster (1996) suggests that leadership is more about intelligence than the role of an individual. "What is leadership in the context of a complex intelligent system? . . . A system with its own intelligence is not missing leadership in the ordinary sense—so providing it may prove detrimental" (68).

Leadership in complex organizations calls for transformation. "By defining leadership as 'to show the way by going first,' we bring together personal and organizational transformation" (McMaster 1996, 73). Leaders must be willing to transform themselves. McMaster describes an aspect of this transformation beginning "with the assumption that transformation is an emergent phenomenon. That is, there is no such thing as transformation by decree, by decision, or even by any planned linear process. Rather, transformation occurs or emerges from a rich interplay of many factors and forces. . . . Transformation can be viewed as a non-linear result" (73).

McMaster (1996) links transformational leadership to the self-organizing concept of inside out:

> The idea of 'top down' or 'bottom up' loses its meaning in the phenomenon of transformation. To the extent that transformation requires leadership (which is to a very large extent) it is a function of 'inside out.' That is, what is thought, felt, imagined and desired within ourselves must be expressed into the social world of the corporation through our speaking and actions. (75)

Thus transformational leadership is about drawing out from within, both on individual and collective levels.

INDIVIDUAL LEADERSHIP: PRINCIPAL

Teachers identified a need to be buffered from a variety of initiatives and demands for their time. The principal is perceived as being a primary "buffer" or filter. Teachers find reassurance in knowing that someone like a principal who sees the "big picture" can help to determine what work needs to be done and what work can be set aside. Being buffered means that they are supported through engagement in meaningful work rather than meaningless compliance.

SHARED LEADERSHIP IN COMPLEX ORGANIZATIONS

James McGregor Burns, writing on transformational leadership "posits that people begin with the need for survival and security, and once those needs are met, concern themselves with 'higher' needs like affection, belonging, the common good, or serving others" (Heifetz 1994, 21). If leaders provide basic needs to the individual level of organizations, then other elements should emerge from the collective organization. These elements may include creativity. "Complexity theorists argue that managers should allow creativity and efficiency to emerge naturally within their organizations rather than imposing their own solutions on their employees" (Santosus 1998, 1). This type of leadership requires a shift in focus. Heifetz (1994), for example, states: "Imagine the differences in behavior when people operate with the idea that 'leadership means influencing the community to follow the leader's vision' versus 'leadership means influencing the community to face its problems.' In the first instance, influence is the mark of leadership. . . . In the second, progress on problems is the measure of leadership" (14).

In any organization, including schools, these shifts can be difficult. "Such a shift in the locus of control, a blurring of the roles of leader and follower, makes many schoolpeople uncomfortable" (Neuman and Simmons 2000, 10). Although these shifts allow for adaptive processes, they also may expose problems, as Heifetz (1994) points out:

> Adaptive work consists of the learning required to address conflicts in the
> values people hold, or to diminish the gap between the values people

stand for and the reality they face. Adaptive work requires a change in values, beliefs, or behavior. The exposure and orchestration of conflict—internal contradictions—within individuals and constituencies provide the leverage for mobilizing people to learn new ways. (22)

Further on Heifetz indicates that leaders must acknowledge that members of organization may still long for the hero leader who will save the day:

> [o]ur expectations of authority figures become counterproductive when our organizations and communities face an adaptive challenge—when the application of known methods and procedures will not suffice. We continue to expect our authorities to restore equilibrium with dispatch. If they do not act quickly to reduce our feelings of urgency, we bring them down. Sometimes, we kill them. (125)

Leaders must be prepared to address these problems as they emerge. The advantage, though, is a move toward distributed leadership. Neuman and Simmons (2000), for example, urge that

> school leadership needs to be redistributed in ways that share responsibilities across the school community and that value collaborative decision making. 'Distributed leadership' calls on everyone associated with schools—principals, teachers, school staff members, district personnel, community members, and students—to take responsibility for student achievement and to assume leadership roles in areas in which they are competent and skilled. 'Leadership' is no longer seen as a function of age, position, or job title. Indeed, it is a characteristic less of an individual than of a community and is a responsibility assumed with the consent of the community. (10)

Shared leadership allows for more participation and engagement in the work of the school. It means that teachers do not have to give up their autonomy or independence to the control of another. It means that the input and ideas of all are valued. Whyte (2001) notes that leaders do much the same thing, that "[t]he core act of leadership must be the act of making conversations real. The conversations of captaincy and leadership are the conversations that forge real relationships between the inside of a human being and their outer world, or between an organization and the world it serves" (61).

One role of leadership is to move the organization to the edge of chaos where creativity is found. Leaders must be comfortable with resisting stability that may be appealing but in reality will lead to equilibrium that will paralyze the organization. A leadership challenge—perhaps related to the art of leadership—is knowing when to give focus and push and when to step back and allow things to emerge. As an example, grade-level teams have identified an isolation that comes from not meeting together. As of yet they have not found their own purpose and reason to meet jointly. Should I, as leader, provide the purpose and reason, or should I wait patiently and allow it to emerge? Perhaps the solution is to do a little of both.

Leadership removes barriers in organizations to sustain renewal and transformation. Self-organization helps us see some ways to do this by allowing natural processes to work. When we know what is natural and understand the dynamics, we can be more effective leaders. A comment from the school librarian illustrates how she views these dynamics:

> After our conversation this morning, I realized that what we often describe in terms of a leader is management, and that is what is difficult for outsiders to understand. Everyone expects the leader to make the household decisions; what time is breakfast, who takes out the garbage, etc. It is an essential, consuming job need to keep 600 people functioning. But when leadership transcends management we have that elusive breakthrough. Leaders keep the lighthouse working. The light is highly visible from long distances and in storms, but is protected from the elements. The vision must be built upon a sound foundation, i.e.: student needs, all voices need to be heard, valued, and constant maintenance of the structure itself, which occasionally means replacement of parts, re-grouting, incorporating new discoveries when appropriate and keeping an ebb and flow of people aware of the importance of the lighthouse. Each maintenance worker for the lighthouse is responsible for various parts and functions autonomously it seems, making his or her own decision, but in reality their autonomy is simply a different component in maintaining the light. No one is really autonomous, because to be so would mean a breakdown in the continuum. When it does happen it creates a ripple in the force that everyone feels, but may not know the cause, but the result is a feeling of uneasiness until the equilibrium is re-established. And that equilibrium may be different than before. (Glenda) (Bower 2003, 238)

IMPLICATIONS FOR PRACTICE

A self-organized school requires that "organizing structures" like vision, purpose, and focus, be internalized within the members of the school. The implication here is that attention to individual and collective process, like sense making, is crucial. The structures that exist, like teams and other groups, are more fluid and more linked to process. This is a key element of adaptability. Induction of new members is crucial. If people make sense of an organization at the microlevel, then new members of the organization make sense of where the organization is in terms of value, vision, or focus through their relationships with others. This process of sense making reinforces the new culture and supports self-organization.

Self-organization is a key to overcoming the problems of a loosely coupled system. When people are collectively engaged in the work of a school, have internalized the vision and purpose, and hold each other accountable, it matters what they do in their classrooms. When teaching and learning become public, the loosely coupled system becomes more tightly coupled. Leadership in self-organizing schools must move from individual to collective. Leaders must understand both the theory and practice of this work. This points to the need for new theories and examples. We need to learn from schools where the dynamics of self-organization are in place.

The current climate of school improvement is characterized by a push for quick results. Schools must improve now if not yesterday; change must be immediate; and there is little time for dialogue or reflection. Conflicting and contradictory mandates complicate this climate. Schools are expected to personalize and standardize at the same time. Schools must teach higher level thinking skills and also have high test scores for basic skills. Mandates for reform are external and usually are about compliance rather than promoting internal ownership and change.

The word *education* comes from Latin roots *ex* meaning out and *ducere* meaning lead. If education truly is about leading out, then education is about what emerges from within. This is the power of self-organization and emergence, and the power of leadership to sustain and support this dynamic. Perhaps what we have made so complicated is really simple.

REFERENCES

Beavis, A. K. 1995. *Towards a social theory of school administrative practice in a complex, chaotic world.* Paper presented at meeting of the American Educational Research Association, San Francisco. ERIC document no. 391243.

Bohm, D. 1996. *On dialogue.* New York: Routledge.

Bower, D. F. 2003. *Leadership and the self-organizing school.* Albuquerque: University of New Mexico.

Burns, J.M. (1977). Leadership. New York: Harper and Row.

Capra, F. 1982. *The turning point: Science, society, and the rising culture.* New York: Bantam Books.

———. 2002. *The hidden connections: A science for sustainable living.* New York: Anchor Books.

Chawla, S., and J. Renesch, eds. 1995. *Learning organizations: Developing cultures for tomorrow's workplace.* Portland, OR: Productivity Press.

Cutright, M., ed. 2001. *Chaos theory and higher education: Leadership, planning, and theory.* New York: Peter Lang.

Davis, B., D. Sumara, and R. Luce-Kapler. 2000. *Engaging minds: Learning and teaching in a complex world.* Mahwah, NJ: Lawrence Erlbaum Associates, Inc.

Ellinor, L., and G. Gerard. 1998. *Dialogue: Rediscover the transforming power of conversation.* New York: John Wiley and Sons, Inc.

Fullan, Michael. 1994. Coordinating top-down and bottom-up strategies for educational reform. In *The governance of curriculum,* ed. R. Elmore and S. H. Fuhrman. Alexandria, VA: Association for Supervision and Curriculum Development: 186 – 202.

Gunter, H. 1995. Jurassic management: Chaos and management development in educational institutions. *Journal of Educational Administration* 33 (4): 5–20.

Heifetz, R. A. 1994. *Leadership without easy answers.* Cambridge, MA: Belknap Press of Harvard University Press.

Johnson, S. 2001. *Emergence: The connected lives of ants, brains, cities, and software.* New York: Simon and Schuster.

Koestler, A. 1967. *The ghost in the machine.* New York: MacMillan Co.

Lambert, N. M., and B. L. McCombs. 1998. *How students learn: Reforming schools through learner-centered education.* Washington, DC: American Psychological Association.

Laszlo, E. 1996. *The systems view of the world: A holistic vision for our time.* Creskill, NJ: Hampton Press, Inc.

Lewin, R. 1999. *Complexity: Life at the edge of chaos.* Chicago: University of Chicago Press.

MacIntosh, R., and D. MacLean. 1999. Conditioned emergence: A dissipative structures approach to transformation. *Strategic Management Journal* 20: 297–316.

McMaster, M. D. 1996. *The intelligence advantage: Organizing for complexity.* Boston: Butterworth-Heinemann.

Marion, R. 1999. *The edge of organization.* Thousand Oaks, CA: Sage Publications.

Morgan, G. 1997. *Images of organizations.* Thousand Oaks, CA: Sage Publications.

Neuman, M., and W. Simmons. 2000. Leadership for student learning. *Phi Delta Kappan* 82 (1): 9–12.

Pascale, R. T. 1999. Surfing the edge of chaos. *Sloan Management Review* 40 (3): 83–94.

Sherman, H., and R. Schultz. 1998. *Open boundaries.* New York: Perseus Books.

Santosus, M. 1998. Simple, yet complex. *CIO Enterprise Magazine.* Retrieved www.cio.archive/enterprise/041598_qanda_content.html. Accessed 2002.

Senge, P. 1999. *The dance of change: The challenges to sustaining momentum in learning organizations.* New York: Doubleday/Currency.

Tetenbaum, T. J. 1998. Shifting paradigms: From Newton to chaos. *Organizational Dynamics* 26 (4): 21–32.

Tye, B. 2000. *Hard truths: Uncovering the deep structure of schooling.* New York: Teachers College Press.

Wah, L. 1998. Welcome to the edge. *Management Review* 87 (10): 24–30.

Weick, K. E. 1995. *Sensemaking in organizations.* Thousand Oaks, CA: Sage Publications.

Wheatley, M. J. 1992. *Leadership and the new science.* San Francisco: Berrett-Koehler Publishers, Inc.

Wheatley, M. J. 2001. *Hope from the four directions.* Retrieved from www.fromthefourdirections.org/articles/ Accessed 2002.

Whyte, D. 2001. *Crossing the unknown sea: Work as a pilgrimage of identify.* New York: Riverhead Books.

NOTES

1. Holonomy helps us to grasp the whole. Koestler (1967) coins the word *holon* from the Greek *holos* for whole and the suffix *on* which suggests a *part*, as when used in words like proton or neutron.

2. Stories help to make the work of the organization understandable in a narrative form. Validating the work of the heroes and heroines validates the function of leadership throughout the organization.

STRANGE ATTRACTORS
IN SCHOOL LEADERSHIP

Sarah Smitherman Pratt and Angelle Stringer

Strange attractor is a peculiar term. In complexity theory, attractors are defined as "states to which the system eventually settles, depending on the properties of the system" (Lewin 1992, 20), where these states are not fixed but are generally considered within certain bounds. Strange attractors are a description of one such set of attractions, or states, to which a system can cycle. Mathematicians in chaos theory examine these cycles and display them in various patterns (Alligood, Sauer, and Yorke 1996). Perhaps the most well-known graph of strange attractors is Lorenz's Butterfly, displayed as two sets of points around which lines form open circles, resembling butterfly wings. The lines are connected and move between the two points, yet they never remain fixed around one or the other point, and the lines do not oscillate precisely from one to the other. Rather the pattern shows "basins of attraction," or boundaries around a point, in which these boundaries are fluid, open, and constantly in flux (Lorenz 1993).

We employ the metaphor of strange attractors in leadership as a way to describe a different set of interactions in a school system that is complex, not hierarchical. Connecting to a systems theory approach of interpreting patterns, we seek to expound on how relationships in schools are interconnected, dynamic, and influence the vitality of the school as a system. This interpretation is similar to Robert Phillips's (2006) research and his pursuit to find different ways of making meaning out of his interactions as a leader in his school district. Though he resides in Australia and we live in North America, we agree that a systems theory perspective can offer a different interpretation for what it might mean to be a leader in a school. We examine our interpretation by first exploring what a systems theory approach means. Then we move to examples in which school leadership might be (re)considered from this perspective. We conclude by reflecting on what it means to be a leader as a strange attractor.

SYSTEMS THEORY

In systems theory, the study of relationships within and among systems is a key focus. Nonlinear relationships are a crucial aspect in the study of dynamical systems. Our world is not linear, and our experiences in the world are examples of such nonsequential moments and memories. As a way to examine patterns of dynamical interrelationships, nonlinear, dynamical systems are explored in depth through chaos theory (mathematics) and complexity theory (science). Though these two theories are often used interchangeably, they actually have different histories and foci (see Smitherman 2005). Researchers in the two areas, however, mutually inform each other's research interests, and developments in one area influence the other. This is an example of a nonlinear relationship. Researchers in systems theory do not look at cause-and-effect relations, as in a linear manner; instead, systems theorists focus on reciprocating, mutually informing, interrelated interactions.

Summarily, complexity theory is a form of scientific research that looks for patterns of self-organization. Many applications, such as in the area of insect populations, traffic patterns, and economic systems, emerge out of complexity theory (Johnson 2001; Taylor 2001). *Complexity* is a term used to describe a system in which the system—parts and whole—transforms and changes as interactions occur. In these interactions, occurring in open, dynamical systems, newness emerges. An open system, according to Prigogine and Stengers (1984), is defined as a system that exchanges energy, matter, or information with its environment (xv). Living systems are open systems because boundaries are shifting, changing, and renegotiating as the system continues to redefine itself. Open systems differ from closed systems, which are mechanical, predictable, and controllable, because open systems do not remain fixed. Boundaries in a closed system are structures, such as walls of concrete, whereas boundaries in open systems are like membranes that are constantly in flux. Living systems are often considered complex because for a system to live, changes, adaptations, and transformations must occur, otherwise, death occurs. So when we refer to dynamical systems in this article, we mean open systems as well.

Chaos theory is a branch of mathematics that explores how chaos (unpredictable patterns) can emerge out of a predetermined set of functions. Involved in this exploration is the method of iteration. A value is put into a function, and the resulting value of the function is then put back into the function again, and again, and again. What emerge are different sets of numbers, some with predictable patterns, whereas others do not have those predictable patterns. Recursive relationships are the key. Chaos mathematics is a study of nonlinear relationships, a folding back on itself, yet with the expectation that something different can emerge. Patterns of unpredictability offer a surprise in an otherwise fixed situation.

Together, complexity theory and chaos theory provide a different language for investigating patterns in science and mathematics that can influence our worldview. Terms such as *recursion, interconnectedness, webs of relations, emergence,* and *transformations* carry significance that may not before been understood or accepted as a valid way of knowing. These theories explore systems, rather than individuals, and parts and wholes together because parts and wholes are only momentary labels that are created to deal with a particular idea. A system is never in isolation, and the context becomes part of the system. This idea, that systems are momentary creations for our own ways of imagining the world, becomes important in viewing our relationships, our identities.

Along with research in nonlinear dynamical systems, a postmodern perspective can greatly influence the way we perceive the world. The term *postmodern* is often employed to distinguish how something is not merely a modernist view. For differences between modern and postmodern frames, refer to Doll (1993). A postmodern frame is one that embraces multiple perspectives, uses difference, eschews rigidity, and thrives on questioning. The ways in which we interact, form, and (re)create relationships are not predictable; life itself is unpredictable. Open, inviting, engaging conversations enliven our world, our existence, and in turn (re)vitalize who we are becoming. By embracing and inviting difference, we ask questions to which we do not know the answer. We "allow" others to influence—though that does not mean that we necessarily agree—what we think, how we think, and who we are.

Postmodern ways of thinking include considerations for benefits and limitations of ideas. Rather than thinking in a modernist frame, in dichotomies of either this or that, postmodern ways of thinking include consideration of how a system is both thriving and dying, simultaneously—a both/and rather than an either/or logic—and how that system might change if there are different interactions that occur. We seek a postmodern perspective of nonlinear, dynamical systems to shift the conversation of school leadership away from control and hierarchies toward an engagement in responsibilities and webs of relationships that allow for transformations. Complexity theory is one way to investigate webs of relations, patterns of connections, and interplay of ideas without eliminating or starting over. Chaos theory is an additional means of examining the complex set of relations at the boundaries of order and chaos.

A SMALL CHANGE CAN MAKE A BIG DIFFERENCE

One such interpretation of an idea in chaos theory is a popular phrase, "The Butterfly Effect." This term comes from the work of a meteorologist, Lorenz (1963), who discovered two truly groundbreaking ideas: 1) small changes can make big differences; and 2) systems are sensitive to initial conditions. With the first idea, Lorenz (1993) asks the question: "Does the flap of a butterfly's wings in Brazil set off a tornado in Texas" (14). A nonlinear interpretation allows for the possibility that small differences can stimulate major shifts in the system. In a complex system, relationships are not in one-to-one, cause-effect situations. Relationships that are situated within a system are interconnected, mutually informing and influencing how certain aspects within a system change. These relationships cannot be predetermined or controlled. In terms of a system of interactions, relationships are only momentary suspicions for what we interpret as occurring at that moment, then the moment passes us by. We can only hope that as we play a part in the system, we can possibly contribute in a positive way to the system as it changes and transforms. Small decisions we make can influence, inspire, and generate major shifts, transitions, and new patterns of relationships. These changes generate a positive or a negative change, depending on our decisions. For example, if an administrator chooses to spend at least one day in each classroom over the course of a semester, maybe even substitute for an hour for the teacher, that person would acquire a different perspective of students, teachers, the classroom dynamics, and even a different way of viewing the school. Interacting in a different space, though just a small change, could create a significant difference in perspective. This small change creates the opportunity to inspire and influence some significant changes in the dynamics of the school relationships.

Lorenz's (1963) second idea, which relates to the first, is that systems are sensitive to how they start. One example that Lorenz (1993) uses as a way to describe how systems are sensitively dependent on their starting points is by describing a path a skier might travel on a slope with moguls. In his mathematical model, Lorenz demonstrates how slight variations at the beginning of the descent by either a skier or a board can lead to large variations in trajectories and outcomes by the bottom of the run. In other words, although the slope and gravity ensured descent down the slope, similar starting points by multiple skiers or boards would not conclude in the same trajectories or completions. This illustration depicts what Lorenz believes is an "essential property of chaotic behavior, . . . [for] nearby states will eventually diverge no matter how small the initial differences may be" (32). Divergence, or difference, becomes a distinguishing trademark of a system that exhibits. Similarly, in a classroom, repeating the same activity a second time will never achieve precisely the same results as the first. The situation and the context are never the same, and even if the same people are involved, they are not the same people because life is dynamic, people are altered by their experiences, and a different perspective (even if slight) is brought to bear on the situation. Predictability becomes impossible, uncertainty creeps in, and control escapes us. Instead of thinking in terms of repetition, which we now know to be impossible, let us consider recursion. Repetition involves a recurrence of the same event with the intent of achieving the same result, whereas recursion is the recurrence of the same event and expecting something different.

Taking these two ideas together, that small changes can make big differences, and initial conditions set apart different opportunities for decisions, we now explore a scenario in which one of us (Angelle) was faced with a dilemma. Parental involvement was quite limited, which we both believe is not enough to encourage student success in school. According to Jung-Sook Lee and Natasha Bowen (2006), parents can have significant influences on their children's academic achievements, though the manner in which they have a positive impact may not be found in traditional forms. Lee and Bowen state that the most significant form of involvement is not *how* the parents are involved in the school, but if they are involved in *any* way at school (212). The authors conclude from their research that:

> addressing the achievement gap through parental involvement strategies need not involve radical changes in the culture of the school or of parents from nondominant cultural groups. Instead, it may involve recognizing the common values of parents and schools and modifying ways in which opportunities and resources for parent involvement at school and at home are made available to all parents. (215)

Radical changes are not necessary, but changes in our perceptions of others might be. We offer one story.

One of us (Angelle) experienced a poignant moment in which she learned that a small change can make a big difference. While teaching a group of rural, high risk middle school students, I found it quite paradoxical that the parents were supportive when called them on the phone, responded promptly to written correspondence, but would not, under any circumstances, attend any form of parenting meeting. Athletic events were fine but to attend a conference to discuss the child's academics or behavioral challenges did not seem to be high on the priority list. This was disturbing because I knew the parents cared for their children's successes. I could not understand the underlying obstacles.

Luckily, I happened to encounter two quite verbose parents in a local store. Taking the opportunity to update them on their children's successes, I also took the opportunity to inquire about their hesitancy to attend the schoolwide parent conference events and their resistance to come to school to meet with me when they were both extremely supportive and friendly on the phone. After an uncomfortable pause, one of the mothers explained. She said that as a child, she did not like school—she was not good at it and it was not a pleasant memory. She had no desire to go to school and relive those bad memories. The other mother said she hated being forced to meet with the teacher or the principal, either of whom was sitting behind the desk whereas she was relegated to either the student desk or some smaller chair in an oppressive office. Another comment was made concerning attire. One mother said that she did not have any business suits or fancy jackets to wear to attend school meetings, whereas one could wear T-shirts and jeans to football and basketball games.

I was humbled. I had never thought about how some of the parents felt when they came to the school. I always had such great personal experiences in school and am now a lifelong learner and educator. The idea that school could be a scary place for these adults never occurred to me. Through more discussion, we decided I would host a parent get-together. Student work was posted, and I was able to share a great deal of information about our class with them. It was warm and friendly. Taking into consideration this new information, I redesigned the nature of my parent meetings. I turned the teachers' lounge into a coffee-house-style setting and provided refreshments. I wore business casual clothing. I asked the two mothers to help me contact other parents. The participants at the first meeting came in cautiously but soon relaxed, and we all came together as caregivers of our students. In meetings that followed, more parents attended, and the involvement in the students' overall academic lives dramatically increased. It was not about who knew algebra or how to diagram sentences; it was about honoring the gift of education and encouraging students to embrace the opportunities available.

Not only did I learn how to better engage the parents in a friendly, comfortable, yet professional manner, but I also learned a great deal about how to further stimulate interest and foster care for my students. Because I was open to meeting the parents where they were, they began to trust me with anecdotes of their families' lives. These "windows" into their worlds greatly enhanced my ability to bring new and personal topics into the classroom (of course, without revealing any information about their home lives). In truth, I think I grew the most. I still maintain relationships with some of the students and parents.

This scenario is just one example for how our perceptions are limited by our experiences and education. We need opportunities to be shown how we are limited, and we should respond with an open heart and an open mind. In this story, I could have been dismissive to the parents and ignored what became for me a moment in my teaching that changed my entire perspective toward her students, the school community, and how to seek out meeting others where they are. This one small change, listening to the needs and struggles of others, created a drastic change not only in my classroom but also in the entire school community. As educators, our limited experiences and interpretations can lend themselves to incorrect conclusions. By listening to these parents, all were able to work toward the significant goal of parents and teachers conversing about the successes and challenges that face students. This one small event shifted the community of parents toward becoming their own agent and participant in the education process. The parents became co-leaders. They invited other parents, and they became advocates for what I was doing in my classroom. These parents became a source of strength for how the community perceived the school. The one small change, creating a meeting where the parents would be comfortable, made a significant difference in many people's lives for years to come.

We believe that this transformation can be made possible in many circumstances, whether through some major interventions or small changes. Just like the small changes for the location and atmosphere of the parent conferences, minor tweaking of the process can put forth potentially incredible shifts in relationships in the system. In an open, dynamical systems perspective, and through a postmodern lens, we consider how little decisions can have significant, long-term influences in how the system changes. Though we cannot predict how these decisions might transform, reflecting back on situations can allow us to recognize how we have changed, and how changes occurred. In complex, open systems, there is life. There will be change. This change, however, is not a controlled, directive form of intervention in which changes will occur. Instead, what we suggest is that we hope by listening and struggling together, we make decisions that could lead to important changes in a positive way. In life, we cannot control the choices and decisions of others.

From a systems perspective, we are but one part of what constitutes our system. As leaders in this system, our role is to listen, foster opportunities for all of us to change, and continually pursue how all of us can contribute to the success of our community.

TRANSFORMATIONS ARE INEVITABLE

Structures of change can be complex. Our modernist tendencies affect the categorization of knowledge, subjects, people, and ourselves, and this categorization appears as a tiered, top-down, hierarchical structure. Doll (2002; 2005a) attributes this, in part, to Peter Ramus (1515–1572) and his method for breaking down subject areas into discrete pieces. This structuring, or ramification, can be easily found today in administration mappings and standards in subject areas. In Doll's (2005b) presentation to division B of the American Education Researchers Association (AERA), he shows how Ramus's map of reducing "more complicated" topics into "more simplified, manageable" pieces when turned on its side reveals a hierarchical structure that is similar to many administration mappings. The principal is at the head, then the assistant principals, then lead teachers, and finally classroom teachers. In this model, though, is the principal truly the "head" of the table, the one in charge, in isolation from the rest of the group? Does the principal only interact with the assistant principals? If one reads a flow chart of administrative responsibilities as a top-down model, this assumption could be made. This mentality, that if we continuously break something down, we will eventually be able to work with the pieces, influences our ways of perceiving the world.

Basics-as-breakdown is a notion prevalent in teaching, an idea which Jardine, Clifford and Friesen (2003) vehemently oppose. Their notions of teaching and learning embrace hermeneutical engagements in conversations around ideas, emergent within the community of learners. They imagine school as different, and they share their ways of being in the world:

> Schools can be treated as dealing, not with the dispensation of finished, dead, and deadly dull information that students must simply consume, but rather with troublesome, questionable, unfinished, debatable, living in-

heritances and with the age-old difficulty of how to enthrall the young with the task of taking up the already ongoing conversations of which their lives are already a part (xiii–xiv).

Their struggles and desires to enthrall their students and to invite them to participate in the "already ongoing conversations" lend a different approach to leadership in schools.

Jardine (1992/2004) takes an ecological perspective to education in which he describes flow in terms of shared moments of experience. In his later work with Clifford and Friesen (2003), they describe this flow as sharing the world together. Let us, instead, imagine flow—relationships in schools—in a different way. Flow is a life force, a part of nature. Different examples exist. A tree has a particular flow to it. It flows from the initial seed to the inner planting of its roots and outward growth of a trunk and branches. Although predictable in general terms how it might change and grow, exactly how it does grow is unpredictable. Wind, rain, temperature, location with respect to other plant life, animals, and geography all contribute to its flow of change.

We wish to caution the reader that although change is everywhere and ongoing, even under the cover of stagnation, life exists. Under the surface of a still pond, activity occurs. These systems may not be the healthiest design for the environment, but growth still occurs. Because there is no constant flow of water, the ecosystem is imbalanced. Left unattended, certain plants and life forms dominate. Just because we wish for transformations and changes to occur does not mean we will always be able to generate healthy, balanced systems of relationships. We are not glorifying that we know what is best and that school leaders must follow our models if they want to be successful. Instead, we would like to encourage conversations in which all are listening, participating, and respecting the views of others. Just like the stagnant pond, the undercurrent of a seamlessly lifeless school begins to dominate the momentum—or lack thereof—of the school. Complacency breeds toxic apathy, disharmony, low morale, and a basic overall discontent that will eventually pollute and poison the system. It is the responsibility of the leadership team to facilitate a positive system—not by force or conflict, but through collaboration—rolling, tumbling, struggling, breathing—but moving forward—holding fast to some elements while exorcising other parts—gasping for new or renewed purposes. Imbalanced systems need interventions to stimulate change and nurture a more healthy set of relations. As we described previously, it might only take a small change to ignite a big difference.

Life includes cycles of change, of growth, and of death. These cycles exhibit patterns of relationships. In biological terms, Bateson (2002) describes two kinds of changes that can occur in living beings. The first is somatic change, which means that a body adapts to its current environment. Travel from lower to higher altitudes and the blood in the body will change to accommodate the less dense air. The second type of change is genetic change. As a being exists in a particular ecological system, over time this influences genetic transformations that will be passed on for generations. These changes can be subtle or prominent, but either way, future generations (and thereby ecological systems) are never the same as previous.

Relating this to leadership, consider how we interact with another in the midst of a conversation. We can pay attention to body language, intonation, personalities, and adjust accordingly. This involves listening, not just hearing. We will be challenged, affirmed, rattled, encouraged, stumped, confused, and so on, which will have some kind of impact on our psyche, perhaps even unnoticeable until some time passes. We walk away from this exchange, changed, transformed, and subsequent interactions will be influenced by this. Although someone might not be (or believe that he or she is) changing the person with whom he or she is conversing, that person can invite difference and consider how he or she is changed and what he or she can learn from the experience (Jardine 2006). This could be termed a dance of interactions in which the participants mutually influence each other and adjust as interactions occur.

In group dynamics, there are different systems at play. In a school system, no one is in isolation. All interact with others in some way. Together, the principal, assistant principals, office staff, teachers, support staff, and students all form a system we call a school. Parents, communities, school boards, and governments, just to name a few, are also part, yet not part, of the system. The system of a school has different roles. The principal will have an influence in the morale of the school, but the principal is not the only one. Leadership becomes collaboration, not delegation. Everyone works together, whether toward success or failure. Jardine, Friesen, and Clifford (2006) liken this to an ecological interpretation of our world in which we are all working together, in our own unique ways, to think the world together. In a systems interpretation of interactions, we recognize that each of us is interdependent on other aspects, other contributors, other "parts" of the whole. We are never in isolation. The leaders involved in the school, from the principal to the support staff to the teachers to the students, all together will influence the "student's chances of academic success" (Marzano, Walters, and McNulty 2005, 3). More importantly, all can work to influence change and success in each other. Just as in the example of Angelle's interactions with the parents mentioned previously, her teaching and ways of perceiving others was radically changed by her interactions with those parents.

LEADERS AS STRANGE ATTRACTORS

A leader in complex, dynamical interactions acts as a facilitator by asking questions to which the answer is not yet known and inviting different perspectives, all the while promoting ownership for everyone who has influence in affecting change. This is not to say that anarchy will rule or that relativism should run rampant. Ideologies and objectives are important. To view these as rigid, set, or predetermined, however, is to limit the growth and vitality of a system. Boundaries are important, but these bounds should be more fluid in their structure, in a biological sense. Fluidity of structures allows for a flow, a shift and change as aspects, traits, and characteristics of the system grow and change.

We are encouraging a different way of perceiving those involved in the school. Our suggestion for a different perspective does not mean that we will move from one hierarchy to another—namely from a top-down model to a bottom-up approach—we wish to advocate a collaborative, interactive, web-like structure of interrelationships. Schlechty (2001) states that, "one of the fundamental tasks of those in authority is to understand the concepts of shared leadership and participatory management and to empower others to lead" (177). In this complex model, an important task is for leaders to recognize the strengths and limitations of the participants and work toward highlighting areas in which individuals excel and supporting each other in areas of struggle. Schlechty likens this approach to that of a jazz band "where leadership is passed around among the players depending on the what the music demands as the moment and who feels most moved by the spirit to express that music" (178). Jazz is not about precision or about prescriptive models of control but about allowing for a freedom of flow and expression.

Please note that "musicians," to extend the metaphor, are not only the administrators or teachers, but also include all members of the school staff. Teachers' aides, cafeteria workers, custodians, parent volunteers, bus drivers, and many other staff are all essential to the melody and harmony of the school. Their input and observations come from different perspectives yet help to balance out the care of the students. Empowering these paraprofessionals to contribute to the growth of the school is essential to the morale of the school. For example, to fully understand the magnitude of the cafeteria worker's input, spend a week standing by the lunch line entrance. Listen to the student conversation. Many times the students do not feel the cafeteria staff is listening. Their interests, their concerns, and their fears are discussed in the line. A kind word, a nurturing smile, or direct action may be needed, but in any case the students know they are cared for and safe at that school. A leader who maintains a systems perspective should include all involved in the school as integral to the educational process.

Flexibility, or the "ability and willingness to adapt leadership style to the needs of the current situation" (Marzano, et al. 2005, 106), must be a strong characteristic for any strong administrator. Heifetz and Laurie (2001), and Heifetz and Linsky (2002) refer to flexible administrators as those who are able to take the "balcony view:" "Get off the dance floor and onto the balcony. Leadership is improvisational. It cannot be scripted. On one hand, to be effective a leader must respond in the moment to what is happening. On the other hand, the leader must be able to step back out of the moment and assess what is happening from a wider perspective" (Heifetz and Linsky 2002, 4). Their intent in this phrase is to encourage and to push leaders to be people who reflect in action. They follow this metaphor with important questions to ask, to reflect while in the moment, in the midst of the action: "What is really going on here? Who are the key parties to the problem? What are the stakes they bring to this issue? How will progress require us all to reevaluate our stakes and change some of our ways?" (Heifetz and Linsky

2002, 5). We agree that these questions should be asked while we are in the midst of action, to consider in the moment what might be occurring, and be willing to grow, change, and adapt as needed.

IN ALL FAIRNESS FOR NEW TEACHERS

Conversations as a means of investigating can lead to complex, dynamic relationships. Preconceived notions of change are deterministic. A nonlinear, complex view of relationships allows for living, changing systems that do not deny we are all always changing who we are, why we choose to do as we do, and how that influences the system in which we are involved.

Stagnant ponds are not dead but are an example of an extremely unbalanced ecosystem. The term *balance*, however, should not imply equal distribution. For example, in shared responsibilities, all teachers are not and should not be considered the same. In our years of experience in working as teachers and now as supervisors of teachers, we see a pattern in schools that we find unfortunate. New teachers are often required to begin their first year of teaching with extra duties, such as sponsoring a club or coaching a team, and they often become overwhelmed, putting energy into the extracurricular activities rather than their primary objective of instructional planning and implementation. To be fair—not equitable or pawning off of new responsibilities—consider that "first year teachers have one basic goal I mind—survival" (Mandel 2006, 67). New teachers should be allowed the freedom, the time, and the space in which they can reflect on their teaching practices. Consider these new teachers from a systems perspective. They should have support, mentors, collaborative opportunities, and conversations about their teaching; they should not be burdened with working additional hours and exerting extra efforts to activities beyond the scope of teaching in the first year. Johnson and Kardos (2002) have found:

> What new teachers want in their induction is experienced colleagues who will take their daily dilemmas seriously, watch them teach and provide feedback, help them develop instructional strategies, model skilled teaching, and share insights about students' work and lives. What new teachers need is sustained, school-based professional development—guided by expert

colleagues, responsive to their teaching, and continually through their early years in the classroom. (13)

As they grow, mature, transform, and experience teaching, opportunities for further involvement can emerge. These opportunities should be limited and maintained only to the degree that their teaching will not suffer.

Many school districts have set into place support for new teachers in the form of monthly meetings or one mentor. We believe that these meetings, although beneficial, may not be enough. Alternatively, we would like to suggest that learning teams, in which teachers in the same subject area or grade level, provide a different form of interaction that can be a meaningful time for new teachers. Learning teams gather to discuss successes and challenges, strategies, lesson plans, and professional obligations (such as record keeping, communication with parents, and district requirements). This mode of interaction provides assistance and comfort to new teachers struggling to survive the enormity of that first year. An experienced teacher facilitates this time and holds meetings biweekly to not overburden yet provide enough time and opportunities to share. The most important aspect of this interaction is the feeling of camaraderie that grows, especially with the knowledge that everyone is stressed and seeking advice in ways to grow and develop as professional educators. These learning teams create conversations in which reconsiderations of roles and modes of inquiry occur and encourage teachers to reflexively reflect on their teaching. Further, allowing for a group of people to interact—more than merely two people, namely mentor and mentee—creates opportunities for dynamic interactions. Webs of relationships and interconnectedness can lead to richer, more complex forms of conversation.

A SENSE OF COMMUNITY

Researchers have shown that parents and community volunteers can increase children's academic success through involvement with schools and communities (Lopez, Scribner, and Mahitivanichcha 2001; Lee and Bowen 2006). Parental involvement improves student and staff morale, attitudes, and achievement across all subject areas. Thus, by having schools invite parents to get involved, the risk of academic failure and the rate of students dropping out before graduation can severely decrease. Discipline problems decrease, and children's attitudes about school and its value increase actively cultivating an environment that promotes learning (Elam, Lowell, and Gallup 1994).

By what measure is success determined? One function of a school is to provide a well-rounded cohesive education for students who will be, in the near future, the responsible parties for our own communities. Too often, schools become the little kingdoms of the adults instead of a space in which children are allowed to be children (Jardine 2006). Celebrating the successes within the school is of vital importance to the life of the school's future. When the administrator, head of the department, parent, or teacher takes the time to compliment another whether in public or private, the gesture serves to fuel continued success. Many vehicles are available for "bragging"—school newspapers, in school television, school assemblies, bulletin boards, parent newsletters, morning announcements, and press releases to the local media. Let the entire school community know of the wonderful things happening within the halls of academia. The old saying "Nothing succeeds like success!" holds true. It gathers a momentum that will drive the school to greater heights.

Couched in success, administrators can continue to lead through positive opportunities. We would like to conclude our ideas and suggestions for leadership by problematizing what we perceive as certain concerns in school leadership and offer instead different forms of leadership that can facilitate and nurture a system that is open, dynamic, and alive. First, leading in a school system does not mean dissemination of directives that are to flow down in a hierarchical manner. Neither is leading allowing everyone to act in their own way without consequences or intervening and trying to do the job for others. A top-down approach does not allow for weblike interactions, and a bottom-up approach does not either. Both models are forms of hierarchical, linear interactions. Fleener (2002) called this modernist interpretation of leadership an "oppressive framework of value-hierarchical thinking [that] values dualisms and a logic of domination" (47). Fleener opposed this "logic of domination" and wished to discard "the lenses of modernism and [find] suitable replacement lenses, [and this] may make all the difference in the world—as long as we realize that even our new lenses filter our way of seeing and living. We must endlessly recreate heart" (195). It is in this recursive pattern of recreation that we continue to find different ways of conversing, experiencing and interpreting our complex, dynamical interpretations of our world. In the back and forth, ebb and flow, movement between strange attractors, where no one is in control but rather in relation, in this space we can seek moments to recreate heart.

Similarly, what we would like to convey is a different notion of leadership, not controlled by a modernist, hierarchical interpretation, but also a postmodern and a complex systems perspective. By considering how a school is a system in which there are strange attractors and in which all involved in the system are transformed in the daily interactions at school, we believe a leader should consider how the following might be carried out in the system that is the school:

- Minister to the needs of those whom they have been entrusted.
- Facilitate growth and positive change through a generous spirit.
- Honor the privilege that has been bestowed to work with others.
- Take responsibility for the focus and condition of the school.

Although this list is by no means exhaustive for what it means to be a complex leader, we believe by seeking how to become a leader that is not dominated by hierarchies or prone to allow free-for-alls. In the space between, we believe there is a place in which those involved in the school can nurture the complexities and nuances that occur as we all interact together. As strange attractors, let us be involved without control, allow ourselves to be transformed as we transform others, and nurture each other in a living, open, dynamical system in which we are situated.

REFERENCES

Alligood, K., T. Sauer, and J. Yorke. 1996. *Chaos: An introduction to dynamical systems.* New York: Springer.

Bateson, G. 2002. *Mind and nature: A necessary unity,* 5th ed. Cresskill, NJ: Hampton Press.

Doll, W. 1993. *A post-modern perspective on curriculum.* New York: Teachers College.

———. 2002. Ghosts and the curriculum. In *Curriculum visions*, ed. W. Doll and N. Gough, eds., 23–70. New York: Peter Lang.

———. 2005a. The culture of method. In *Chaos, complexity, curriculum and culture: A conversation*, ed. W. Doll, J. Fleener, J. St. Julien, and D. Trueit, 19–76. New York: Peter Lang.

———. 2005b. *Teaching good*. Paper presented at the annual meeting of the American Educational Research Association, Montréal.

Elam, S., C. Lowell, and A. Gallup. 1994. The 26th Annual Phi Delta Kappa/Gallup poll of the public's attitudes toward the public schools. *Phi Delta Kappan* 76 (1): 41–56.

Fleener, M. J. 2002. *Curriculum dynamics: Recreating heart*. New York: Peter Lang.

Heifetz, R. A., and Laurie, D. L. 2001. The work of leadership. *Harvard Business Review* 79 (11): 131–40.

Heifetz, R. A., and Linsky, M. 2002. *Leadership without easy answers*. Cambridge, MA: Belknap Press of Harvard University Press.

Jardine, D. 2004/1992. A bell ringing in the empty sky. In *Contemporary curriculum discourses*, ed. W. Pinar, 262–77. Scottsdale, AZ: Gorsuch Scarisbricks.

Jardine, D. 2006. *Piaget and education primer*. New York: Peter Lang.

Jardine, D., P. Clifford, and S. Friesen. 2003. *Back to the basics of teaching and learning: Thinking the world together*. Mahwah, NJ: Lawrence Erlbaum.

———. 2006. *Curriculum in abundance*. Mahwah, NJ: Lawrence Erlbaum Associates.

Johnson, S. M., and S. M. Kardos. 2002. Keeping new teachers in mind. *Educational Leadership* 59 (6): 12–16.

Johnson, S. 2001. *Emergence: The connected lives of ants, brains, cities, and software*. New York: Simon & Schuster.

Lee, J., and N. Bowen. 2006. Parent involvement, cultural capital, and the achievement gap among elementary school children. *American Educational Research Journal* 43 (2): 193–218.

Lewin, R. 1992. *Complexity: Life at the edge of chaos*. Chicago: University of Chicago Press.

Lopez, G., J. Scribner, and K. Mahitivanichcha. 2001. Redefining parental involvement: Lessons from high-performing migrant-impacted schools. *American Educational Research Journal* 38 (2): 253–88.

Lorenz, E. 1963. Deterministic nonperiodic flow. *Journal of Atmospheric Science* 20: 130?41.

———. 1993. *The essence of chaos*. Seattle, WA: The University of Washington Press.

Mandel, S. 2006. What new teachers really need. *Educational Leadership* 63 (6): 66–69.

Marzano, R. J., T. Waters, and B. A. McNulty. 2005. *School leadership that works: From research to results.* Alexandria, VA: Association for Supervision and Curriculum Development.

Phillips, R. 2006. *Pink flamingos and educational orthodoxy: A conversation on complex systems, chaos and leadership in schools and school districts.* Presentation given to the Louisiana State University College of Education, Baton Rouge.

Prigogine, I., and I. Stengers. 1984. *Order out of chaos: Man's new dialogue with nature.* New York: Bantam Books.

Schlechty, P. C. 2001. *Shaking up the school house: How to support and sustain educational innovation.* San Francisco: Jossey-Bass.

Smitherman, S. 2005. Creating wholes and holes in curriculum. In *Chaos, complexity, curriculum and culture: A Conversation,* ed., W. Doll, M. J. Fleener, J. St. Julien, and D. Trueit, 153–80. New York: Peter Lang.

Taylor, M. 2001. *The moment of complexity: Emerging network culture.* Chicago: University of Chicago Press.

8

SHARED ACCOUNTABILITY: AN ORGANIC APPROACH

Carlos A. Torre and Charlene Voyce

> Despite its long history, accountability in education means different things to different people. There is little consensus about how to apply the concept intelligently and creatively in schools. (Frymier 1996)

As far back as ancient Greece, there is evidence of concern with establishing lines of responsibility or accountability for children's learning: "Fathers themselves, ought every few days to test their children and not rest their hopes on the disposition of a hired teacher: for even those persons will devote more attention to the children if they know they must from time to time render an account" (Plutarch, quoted in Wynne 1972, 30). In Victorian England, the British Parliament established a plan through which teachers were paid on a "payment by results" basis according to their students' achievement. Yet, as Frymier attests, educators fail to agree on what it means to be accountable and countless attempts at educational accountability[1] have been equally unsystematic, hit or miss, or misguided.

Over the last century, trends toward accountability in education have been based mostly on models better suited to describe and regulate the functioning of machines or other inanimate systems than that of vigorous teaching and learning practices. Our system of education (and just about every other sector of society) has been influenced strongly by

Isaac Newton's[2] body of beliefs about how the world works and is organized. "Newtonianism," now identified as "classical science," holds that: 1) all "systems" (including people and human systems) are orderly, regular, uniform, and can be understood and regulated or controlled if we reduce their complexity ("reductionism") by isolating and subdividing their basic components into ever smaller parts; 2) systems function in a linear, step-by-step manner. Their actions and reactions are proportional, such that small exertions are used for small problems and large ones for large problems. Each cause has one effect and each effect results from one cause ("mechanics" or "mechanical"); and, 3) systems seek stability and equilibrium, and so theoretically should be as predictable as clockwork ("determinism"). For these reasons, we refer to educational paradigms that adhere to Newtonian ideas as *mechanistic*.

In contrast to Newton's clockwork perspective, teaching and learning call for the coordination of large, diverse groups of people in situations in which lines of authority are not always clear, individual roles are stretched by multiple responsibilities, and ordinary actions produce seemingly unpredictable consequences. Because these kinds of processes are representative and characteristic of the behavior of living organisms, we refer to them as *organic* or natural.

A new scientific paradigm, nonlinear dynamical systems theory (or nonlinear dynamics, for short—also known as chaos and complexity theory), presents a more organic perspective of how the world works and is organized than that obtainable through classical science. Because nonlinear dynamics focuses on such everyday issues as diversity, unpredictability, instability, disequilibrium, and qualities that emerge out of the interaction among things ("the whole being greater than the sum of its parts"), it constitutes an intuitively understandable picture of how order, change, and transformations take place. This new paradigm offers some vigorous and compelling insights that can help galvanize the nature of educational accountability through a better understanding of such concepts as communication; interaction; collaboration; reconciliation; how people and things self-organize; appreciating and drawing on peoples' resistance to change; and distributed control via relational rather than bureaucratic models. As a theoretical perspective, nonlinear dynamics does vastly more justice to educational processes than does the classical predisposition to reduce all systems and their activities and interactions to the sum of their parts. Thus, drawing on one research example, we propose its application as a more organic conceptual framework conducive to creating effective, efficient processes of educational accountability.

This chapter describes how education leaders can perceive and develop effective accountability processes that take into account education's inherent complexities and its accompanying assortment of interrelated family, social, and community matters. Specifically, we provide:

- A discussion of how a great many insights fundamental to nonlinear dynamics have been applied intuitively (as "common sense") in New Haven, Connecticut's two-year process to create an effective practice of accountability. With appropriate adaptations, this experience can have national and international applicability.
- A historical review of educational accountability (trends and foci) in the United States.
- A summary of how the sciences have influenced education and of how nonlinear dynamics can help generate a new perception of education and educational accountability.
- Recommendations for designing effective educational accountability processes.

ACCOUNTABILITY IN U.S. EDUCATION: A HISTORICAL REVIEW

During the first two decades of the twentieth century, school districts in most major urban areas of the United States were characterized by "efficiency bureaus" staffed by educational "efficiency experts," who toiled, seemingly around the clock, devising scoring formulae to quantify teacher performance and by this means, prescribe "scientific" remedies for the ills of education (Callahan 1962). This system of educational accountability can be traced to Frederick Taylor's claim at the start of the twentieth century that schools would function efficiently if "scientific management" principles were used to structure their programs as well as the activities of teachers and administrators.

During the 1930s, 1940s, and most of the 1950s, calls for educational accountability faded considerably in the United States. Then, in 1957,

the successful Soviet launch of Sputnik touched off spontaneous per-
functory measures for school reform. The results were large-scale efforts in school output evaluation (Project TALENT)[3] through standardized tests; increased emphasis on sciences, reading, writing, and math;
revamping curricula including the development of "new math" and in-
quiry-based learning; and the lowering of the age of initial enrollment in
school. Despite the influence of the inclusive human development approaches inspired by the Civil Rights Movement (e.g., the Elementary
and Secondary Education Act [ESEA]) of 1965, designed to make re-
medial support in math and reading available to underprivileged students; the establishment of Head Start in 1964, designed to address the
cognitive, social, and health needs of underprivileged preschool children to prepare them better to succeed in first grade and beyond; and
the passing of legislation related to the education of children with special needs, this period symbolizes the beginning of federally mandated
accountability for government-funded programs and techniques.[4]

Hansen (1993) provided the following assessment of the purposes
and eventual results of these procedures:

> The principles underlying these techniques were very similar to those that
> had been applied without effect in the first quarter of the century. Their
> thrust was to improve efficiency and cost effectiveness, while focusing pri-
> marily on input and process variables. . . . Accountability in the 1970s
> seemed to focus on getting 'more bang for the buck'. (14–15)

The tools of that period[5] were intended to enhance the efficiency of
schools, not the quality of education as indicated by student outcomes.
"Control," not necessarily "improvement," seems to be the dominant
operative concept in most efforts toward educational accountability.

When the U.S. Department of Education's report, *A Nation at Risk:
The Imperatives for Educational Reform*, was published, again, initial
reactions concentrated unreservedly on accountability through test
scores (National Commission on Excellence in Education 1983). Their
students' scores on standardized tests determined the success or failure
of teachers and schools. Bonuses and other rewards were conferred for
increased scores; penalties were applied for declines in test scores. Test
scores were compared among teachers, classrooms, schools, and dis-

tricts, and the federal government compared scores of U.S. children to their counterparts in other countries. Over time, U.S. education has become increasingly dependent on these single measures to gauge student development and decide on future educational strategy as evidenced by the enormous influence on educational accountability, which the National Assessment of Educational Progress has made since the first countrywide testing took place in 1970.

A Nation at Risk was highly critical of public schools, linking the decline of the United States' ability to compete economically in the world to an alleged deterioration in the quality of its system of public education. In part, it stated that: "A rising tide of mediocrity . . . threatens our very future as a nation and a people. We have, in effect, been committing an act of unthinking, unilateral disarmament" (U. S. Department of Education 1983, paragraph 1, p. 1).

This follows on the thinking of economist Milton Friedman (1955) who conceived of schools as being important parts of a nation's economic system. He maintained that schools are like factories. Children are the products fashioned by schools. To produce a better product, the same forces that regulate free enterprise must control schools: "choice" and "competition." Frymier (1996) countered, however, that schools are not factories, and that children are no more products of schools than patients are products of hospitals or prisoners products of jails. He denounces strongly this analogy of schools as factories and children as products and admonishes those who agree with it because of the great disservice done to students and the profession of education.

Friedman's (1955) perspective, and that of the proponents of most efforts toward educational accountability discussed here, relies on mechanistic models that follow Newton's theories. In the following sections, we critique this point and propose the application of nonlinear dynamics as a more organic conceptual framework for education leaders in designing effective systems of educational accountability.

THE INFLUENCE OF THE SCIENCES ON EDUCATION

Classical science holds that every event in the universe is determined by initial conditions (step-by-step, proportional cause and effect) that can theoretically be uncovered and understood perfectly. Nothing is unintended because neither coincidence nor chance plays a role in how all the pieces of the universe assemble and work together. Everything (people included) is reducible to the sum of its parts. By isolating and subdividing anything repeatedly, we can reduce or eliminate its complexity—revealing its orderly, regular, uniform, stable, and balanced nature—as a way to understand and regulate. Consequently, every thing and event should be as predictable and controllable as clockwork: With enough information, one can foretell everything about the future and reconstruct everything about the past (Pierre-Simon, Marquis de Laplace 1796).

The unprecedented success of industry during the Industrial Revolution resulted in the eager, universal application of this factory model to everything from other innate systems (railroads), to social systems (governments[6] and community agencies), and even individual living organisms (that is, workers through efficiency experts and the production of poultry, beef, shrimp and other living commodities in controlled environments). In this manner, Newtonianism came to permeate most if not every sphere of society, including education. Wrought by the economic, cultural, and political forces of the time, the Newtonian model became a lens through which all else was viewed.

The vast majority of efforts at educational accountability over the last 100 years have been mechanistic in nature. As discussed previously, such efforts have been characterized by the explicit, "full-strength" application of Frederick Taylor's (1967) "scientific management" principles, with their attendant efficiency bureaus and efficiency experts, large-scale school-output evaluations, and extensive use of engineering principles and procedures along with practices from the defense and business sectors.

The tendency to address issues of educational accountability through standardized testing, comparison, and competition is rooted deeply in education. At its core is a firm allegiance to centralized control, in which power and authority are vested in a "controller" of the total system's behavior, someone or something or small group at the top of a pyramidal structure who makes decisions for others to carry out. Langton (1989) recounted that, throughout the extensive history of clockwork automata, most earnest efforts consist of a "manager" program (e.g., a revolving cylinder with dowels tripping switches successively) that determines the behavior of the entire model. How the system danced was dictated by this regulating mechanical or electronic device.

In education, this controller is an overriding administration, or administrator, at the neighborhood school, local district, and state levels. When mechanistic models are applied at any of these levels, rigid bureaucracies and constraining hierarchical structures usually arise. Such bureaucracies greatly limit the kinds and frequency of communication and interactions that are possible. Noncontroller constituents of such bureaucracies usually feel alienated and superfluous to the mission of the organization. When questioned about senseless or detrimental policies or decisions, their corresponding attitude is usually, "I don't make the rules, I just enforce them." Diffusion of new ideas, such as educational accountability, in such rigid environments is futile or, at best, uncreative.

Friedman's (1955) regarding of schools as factories and children as their products is a commonly made analogy. It provides added evidence that the application of mechanistic Newtonian concepts to the process and structure of education is indeed quite prevalent. Applying industrial, economic, engineering, or other such mechanistic principles to education, allows for a line of reasoning that reduces an extremely complex process to its superficial appearances. For example, proponents of vouchers contend that competition will improve education because if competition is allowed with private and religious institutions, public schools will have to outperform the competition or "go out of business." Parental choice in education, consequently, becomes the force that sets the wheels of reform into motion.

The obvious flaw with this argument is that public schools are, and need to be, nonprofit organizations. As a taxpayer, consider whether or not it is your intention to require the local board of education to yield profits year after year (Frymier 1996). Most people would probably agree that their primary mission to educate all children, dictates that service, not profits be the main commitment or responsibility of the public schools. Further, if we follow Friedman's (1955) line of reasoning, that students are products of the schools, to a consistent conclusion it backfires because the "excellence" of a "product" does not depend solely on the quality of the process to which it is subjected. Excellence depends heavily on the quality of the "raw material" to be processed. Logically, then, some students should be rejected as being subpar. To do otherwise would reflect poorly on the school's quality control. Consequently, the assumption behind vouchers, that public schools will be driven to improvement by a profit motive, is not only invalid, it is inappropriate and irresponsible.

The mechanistic perspective remains a dominant paradigm in education. Notwithstanding, the seriousness of the issues that we face currently in education (and thereby the need for effective educational accountability) and the transformational nature of the economic, political, and social changes taking place in our society oblige us to admit and deal squarely with the enormous limitations of mechanistic models applied to education or to any other human activity.

AN ORGANIC PARADIGM OF SCHOOL REFORM AND ACCOUNTABILITY: TOWARD A NEW PERCEPTION OF EDUCATION

To understand better how an organic paradigm can provide a more realistic representation of educational processes, we must take a closer look at some of the basic differences between mechanical (nonliving) and organic (living) systems that render conventional (Newtonian) analysis highly ineffective when applied to living systems.

Organic versus Mechanical Systems

Both mechanical and organic systems can self-organize.[7] Self-organization is the tendency of systems, in situations of great turmoil, to apparently and spontaneously, bring themselves into existence or rearrange themselves into new forms or patterns, that is, to produce order (the emerging of tornados, mobs, or special interest groups are good examples). We say "apparently" because the "self" part of this term gives the inaccurate impression that these systems create themselves in isolation from and in opposition to their environment. In fact, self-organization is brought into existence by interaction with the environment, through the processes of ecological interconnectedness and coevolution that result from disequilibrium among the system's constituent elements or members. Disequilibrium, then, generates interactions among these same constituent elements. If a system is in total balance or equilibrium, nothing can happen. It is static and, in a sense, dead. Disequilibrium, therefore, produces and (for a time) maintains the newly self-organized structure. This structure, in turn, dispels energy (that is, through friction) thereby reducing the initial amount of imbalance.

Unlike mechanical systems, however, organic systems (microorganisms, animals, institutions, and governments) try to take control of their environments by seeking out a sufficient amount of "thermodynamic disequilibrium," such as food, money, or power, to keep themselves alive. In nonliving systems, like clouds and hurricanes, when the level of disequilibrium has diminished sufficiently the systems cease to exist or function: Clouds evaporate and hurricanes dissipate. Thus, a basic difference between mechanical and organic systems is the ability of organic systems not only to self-organize, but also to evolve to fit their environments better; search for new, more conducive environments; or even generate environments wrought to benefit the system itself. This is why the mechanistic, one-size-fits-all attempts at accountability do not work: They are not responsive to the situation at hand. Clearly, organic systems present a degree of complexity immeasurably beyond anything possible in the realm of mechanical systems.

Prigogine and Stengers (1984) warn us that, "the more complex a system is, the more numerous are the types of fluctuations (inconsistencies in its functioning) that threaten its stability" (188). That being the case, how do organic systems as complex as the ecology or human organizations or a new process of educational accountability manage to evade perpetual chaos?

Organic systems avoid complete turmoil by doing what mechanical systems cannot: manage and influence information. All life forms and organizations possess a sort of blueprint or paradigm of themselves and how they relate to their environment (as found in chromosomes and other genetic material, mission statements, bylaws, and constitutions). By applying the information found in their blueprints, organic systems keep themselves alive and continue to evolve, discover, and create. The evidence demonstrates that the threshold of stability in organic systems is determined by how the system reacts when it experiences opposition between instability caused by fluctuations and the stabilizing effect of communication and diffusion processes.[8] In other words, how the system deals with problems (what Torre called "reconciliation," 1984; 1987; 1989; 1995a; 1995b).

Reconciliation results when the opposing forces of "activation" (to want to move in a particular direction) and "restraint" (to be held back from moving in the given direction) are integrated. In other words, a third force resolves the opposing forces of activation and restraint: reconciliation. Reconciliation goes beyond the concept of "compromise" (concessions or middle ground) to stimulate new ways of thinking and acting so that all constituents get what they need (see Appendix 1 as an example).

Educational accountability implies moving a particular school or district in a different direction or through a different method (activation). Typically, one will encounter resistance (restraint) from those set in their ways, those leery of your intentions or those wanting to think through the implications. Reconciliation of these opposites requires the interweaving of the nonlinear interactions among cognitive (intellectual), affective-perceptive (emotions), and pragmatic (action or "hands-on") mental processes in an individual or the analogous processes in an organization (i.e., fluctuations, communication, and diffusion processes). Solutions (reconciliation) emerge out of this interaction. For this reason, in complex organizations in which people interact in a variety of ways, communication and diffusion processes among a variety of individuals are likely to be efficient.[9]

In organizational development, resistance to change is portrayed or implied as negative, reactionary, or counterproductive. In fact, it is often blamed for the failure of new programs and ideas and the resistant groups and individuals are ostracized. But resistance to change (restraint) can provide creative tension in a system. Rather than dissipation of tension through compromise or imposition of beliefs, reconciliation takes into serious consideration the objections brought by the opposition, thus ensuring optimal decisions based on everyone's needs. Without resistance to change, however, there is nothing to keep us from acting too quickly on a half-baked idea. Although there are those who resist change for obstructionist or selfish reasons, most resistance is presented by people with less sinister motives. Resistance might represent reflection on the part of someone asking: "Why are we doing this?" Or, "Does this new approach avoid previous mistakes or help us do more of what we really need to do?" Alternately, some resisters may be simply awaiting social clues that the innovation is accepted, safe, or okay for them to try.

When we say that human institutions are resistant to change, we understand that this is so because many of the individuals who make up the institutions question challenges to the status quo. But lumping all of these different forms of resistance together hinders our ability to reconcile apparently opposing forces into constructive paths-forward (Torre 1995a; 1995b). By recognizing the variety of motives for resistance, we can move toward better solutions and avoid the detrimental "groupthink" (the party line) and perpetual regurgitation of ineffective ideas. An organic perspective sees resistance to change as an indispensable and potentially beneficial quality of the process of innovation (Torre 1984; 1987; 1989; 1995a; 1995b) and the process of reaching reconciliation ensures a more effective solution to the problem at hand.

The promise of this kind of organic approach to organizing the various teams required to undertake the process of educational accountability is that a system based on these principles can better address the issues that place students at risk of failing educationally or falling through the proverbial social cracks. Organic systems are not reducible to their physical components. They must also function at a coherent, representational level, a level at which momentous interactions can take place. Out of such interactions (as this section demonstrates) we get the process of emergence, in which qualities or characteristics (that do not exist in any single component) come forth in the system, effectively enabling the whole to be "greater than the sum of its parts."

AN ORGANIC PARADIGM:
TOWARD A RELATIONAL MODEL

Given what we now know about the differences between mechanical (nonliving) and organic (living) systems, our paradigm for informing an effective process of educational accountability needs to approach shared responsibility in a new way. We need a paradigm that ensures that students, parents, teachers, administrators, neighborhood, business, and faith communities, and municipal and state officials are unified around the complex demands of continually determining and assessing what our children should know, understand, and be able to do, and how we continue to involve and evolve all who need to share the responsibility for helping them fulfill this purpose. Our paradigm needs to go beyond the mere analysis and observation of individual and collective behavior and interaction. It needs to facilitate the answer to such fundamental questions as *why* and *how* these behaviors and interactions emerged in the first place, what are the appropriate conditions that allow or foster the self-organization of constituents toward beneficial action and how can we stimulate the emergence of such conditions.

We know that the ability to control information and diffusion processes highlights the enormous difference between organic and mechanical systems. Any organic paradigm designed to develop a process of educational accountability needs to provide processes designed to encourage sincere consideration of new thinking and change and means for clear, honest, and meaningful communication and interaction among all constituents. This is what we mean by a relational model. The process by which things happen and people interact is given at least equal consideration along with the "content" and direction of decisions made. This is not possible in a bureaucratic (mechanistic) model.

Conventional (classical science) analysis is only useful when applied to stable, linear, continuous, smoothly changing phenomena. Human behavior and social interaction, however, is idiosyncratic, disjointed, and often perplexing, with apparently whimsical reasoning and unpredictable changes. Thus, the more propitious approaches to modeling complex or organic systems are approaches that do away with the idea of an overall regulator (controller) of behavior and alternatively concentrate on means for the distributed control of behavior and responsibility.

Dynamism in a group or institution emerges out of the organized interactions of a large number of individuals, with no overall controller in command of the behavior of every component. Instead, each player, himself or herself, represents a behavior. Rather, than solving pieces of a puzzle and putting them together to understand the entire system, organic systems must be considered as a whole. Thus, instead of starting with a particular behavior and trying to dissect it into its component parts (top-down), one would bring together elements of a phenomenon a little at a time until the interaction among these recreate the qualities and or behaviors of the whole; that is, bottom-up (Langton 1989).

Our organic paradigm, therefore, uses a bottom-up, dispersed (distributed control) determination of behavior as its fundamental approach to the modeling of realistic organizational dynamics. Its main purpose is understanding and influencing the emergent properties and behaviors of the processes aimed at educational accountability. It is not possible to understand this process with a top-down analytical approach. We would only mimic its superficial mechanics. Such artificially mechanized schemes can seem credible because they are so common in a society established on Newtonian principles, yet teach us little about the nature of human behavior and interaction.

NONLINEAR DYNAMICS IN ACTION: NEW HAVEN'S PLAN FOR SHARED ACCOUNTABILITY

Contrary to mechanical, linear models of organization, organic nonlinear ones often emerge out of everyday interaction and functioning. By definition, organic models presume that the best fitting solution to any problem will emerge if the principal parties involved participate earnestly, openly communicate their individual or group needs, and give the process an honest chance to work. Rather than arriving at a solution through application of a model, this interactive process leads participants to an effective solution intuitively. Such was the case in the development of the New Haven shared accountability plan. In a sense, the relatively recent advent of the dynamical sciences may be evidence of how science is ultimately beginning to catch up to our better wisdom and intuitions.

As in other urban districts around the United States, New Haven's low test scores were presumed to reflect the quality of the instruction and programming taking place in its public schools. Simultaneously and contradictorily, the district was receiving data from the Connecticut Department of Education indicating that students in New Haven were learning at a faster pace than their suburban counterparts. They were finishing the race behind but were actually running faster. The problem was that New Haven students were starting the race behind students from neighboring districts.

Faced with increasing pressure to improve its schools, New Haven created a task force, chaired by renowned child psychiatrist Dr. James Comer, to develop a plan. In addition to parents, teachers, administrators, and board of education members, the task force included influential members of the business and faith communities, college and university faculty, and local community organizations. A previous group of similar representatives from the district had assembled around the question: "What is important for our children to know, understand, and be able to do?" These efforts led to the development of curriculum frameworks, subject area standards, and grade-level standards. The new accountability task force subsequently addressed the questions: "How do we demonstrate the full range of what schools do?" and, "What should we assess and how should we assess it?"

The accountability task force believed firmly that schools, were neither solely responsible for student success, nor could they accomplish student success by themselves. Academic achievement is a result of multiple influences including schools, parents, poverty, health, nutrition, and family structure. Having a sense of who else needed to be involved in this process, the task force addressed the issues of how to get others to share the responsibility and do their part to help New Haven's children learn and develop. After two years of meeting to study and discuss the accountability movement in vogue throughout the country, the task force had developed a comprehensive plan designed to meet the needs of the many constituents, to be fair to all involved, and to focus on the challenges unique to the district. The resulting plan reflects many of the principles of nonlinear organization and functioning discussed previously.

First, the entire structure of the New Haven shared accountability plan takes into account the notion that teaching and learning—and the functioning of our schools —takes place in the context of complex social interactions, both within the school and between the school and the community. Given the organic nature of school and community structures, efforts at accountability focus on the individual level—the interactions between students and teachers, between students and their parents, and among students—but also on an institutional level, with the schools and other community organizations and structures each functioning as a living entity. The idea of shared accountability, with responsibilities held collectively among all school and community constituents, recognizes the importance, in fact the necessity, of these interdependencies.

Shared accountability also recognizes the importance of multiple influences (causes) as determinants of developmental and educational outcomes and the need to distribute, rather than centralize, control of the entire process through a variety of parent, teacher, parent-teacher, school-community, and other such teams who come together regularly to fine-tune the expected outcomes, process and goals, and decide on new capabilities to be developed by students, teachers, administrators, board of education members, or the district as a whole. In this manner, the structure of the accountability plan itself was fractal in nature and provides the appropriate level of disequilibrium required to generate interactions among these same constituent elements. Most organic systems exhibit a quality we call "fractal structure." Fractals (Mandelbrot 1982) are mathematical (or real-world) objects whose organizational structure replicates itself (reiterates) repeatedly in roughly the same way at different scales or levels of magnification. Ferns, cauliflower, broccoli, trees, and many other plants are examples of fractal structure. If you cut off one of its branches, you will notice that the branch resembles the whole plant. Do the same with a branch of the branch, and note that it resembles the branch, which resembles the whole plant. You can continue this procedure, as long as physical limits allow, with similar results.

Based on these ideas, the task force identified ways in which each sector of the community (the proverbial "village") could support the academic achievement and more general development of its students. Starting with the schools, the task force outlined responsibilities at each level of the system: the central office, the educational leader at the school, the collective staff at the school, individual teachers, and students.

Once these responsibilities were specified, members identified other significant determinants of student success and extended the list of responsibilities into the surrounding community. The group called on parents, area businesses, faith-based organizations, colleges and universities, and individual citizens to do their part to ensure the healthy development of every child. For parents, this meant making sure that their children get enough to eat, get adequate rest, and come to school on a daily basis. Further, parents needed to familiarize themselves with the curriculum and ways to support, at home, what goes on in school.

For area businesses, this meant offering release time and flexible scheduling for parents to encourage them to be involved in their children's schools, supporting high quality daycare and preschool programs for children of employees, offering internships to high school students to provide real-life work experience and help students see meaning in school, or providing financial support for school activities.

Area colleges and universities were asked to support children by opening campus activities and performances to families in surrounding neighborhoods, establishing partnerships with city high schools to provide opportunities for students to take classes, participate in campus activities, and use selected facilities, and developing programs, like the New Haven Teachers' Cohort programs (two graduate degree programs specifically designed to meet the needs of the district).

Community-based organizations and faith communities were asked to provide supports such as family literacy services, after-school and weekend enrichment programs, parent education and English-language instruction for non-English speakers. Individual community members were asked to volunteer as tutors or mentors and contribute to local community-based organizations that offer services to children and families. In this way, the plan recognized that schools should be responsible for providing high-quality instruction, for encouraging and supporting students, and ensuring equitable access to all programs and that the responsibility for meeting the many other needs of students could be met through cooperation and collaboration.

Another theme that emerged through the planning process is the belief that schools do more than teach students discrete skills that can be measured by tests. The overdependence on single measures or standardized tests to gauge student development and decide on future educational strategy is an outgrowth of the application of mechanistic practices to educational accountability: If the world is seen in terms of mechanistic inputs and products, measuring success with tests makes sense. Unfortunately, standardized tests have most often been used to diminish the scope of education, settling for easily measured results that may be of dubious relevance for the target students and districts. The New Haven shared accountability plan does not eliminate the use of these tests, but rather gives them a limited role and places them in proper perspective as valid and reliable formative instruments and procedures that have the potential to help raise academic standards.

The plan recognizes that it is not the possession of these skills alone that will prepare young people for responsible and purposeful lives. Rather, it is the entirety of their development as whole living organisms. The future success of the students enrolled in our schools depends on our capacity to value and support the full range of their development.[10] In New Haven, the accountability task force considered a range of skills, behaviors, and characteristics that are important to future success. Among these are the capacity to work collaboratively with others, a strong work ethic, responsibility, flexibility, and creativity. These attributes are not easy to measure and the details of how to assess some of them remain to be worked out, but they are at least as crucial as the capacity to read scientific texts and perform algebraic functions. Thus, the members of the task force believed strongly that it was important to include them in the plan. Undoubtedly, New Haven will focus on what we measure (i.e., standardized tests). Yet, we are clear that just because something is easy to measure does not mean that it is the most important factor to assess. Honest educational accountability requires that continuous efforts be made to develop ways to assess those more organic attributes that we know, intuitively and through our collective experiences, have enormous influence on children's academic and life success.[11] Thus, the shared accountability plan includes measures of school characteristics that foster the development of these individual qualities: assessments of school climate, student and staff morale, school-home communication, the number and kind of family supports offered, and opportunities to participate in the visual and performing arts, receive instruction in a world language and participate in cultural exchange and travel abroad programs.

The New Haven shared accountability plan further illustrates the non-linear model of organization by incorporating a "diagnostic assessment" process that allows the system to recognize the uniqueness of each circumstance and be responsive to the particular needs of students, teachers and administrators. In response to complex multidimensional situations, we need to develop multiple paths to arrive at the desired destination (e.g., different approaches to reading instruction for children growing up in different cultures with different language traditions) and recognize that similar paths do not lead to the same outcome for all children (e.g., not every teaching method works with every child). Such situations argue for a more organic approach to accountability. Rather than applying a formulaic, one-size-fits-all intervention, the diagnostic assessment is conducted by a team that examines the particular situation that has resulted in low performance or slow progress. This team includes the individuals who are the "target" of the accountability intervention and will bear the responsibility for carrying out the intervention. After identifying the factors that contribute to the performance problems, the team creates a unique improvement plan, designed to address the specifics of the situation. In this way, the plan allows for participation—self-regulation—in the process of developing a solution to the identified problem(s). In other words, this assessment process fosters the self-organizing of a focused living system that can address areas of restraint, organically, and with a goal of reconciliation rather than a compromised solution that may, in the end, be no better than the practice it replaces.

Finally, the plan allows for feedback in all directions: up; down; and laterally in the system's hierarchy. For example, in addition to being assessed within it, students will be given opportunities to assess their educational experience. Parents will receive feedback regarding their support and participation in the school but will also be given opportunities to share their perceptions and assessment of the school through surveys and parent meetings. Teachers will be evaluated by their supervisors but will also be given opportunities, through surveys and focus group discussions, to express their thoughts and feelings about their experiences in the school and treatment by administrators. This strengthens the process of self-organization or self-regulation through the flow of information and the continuous dissemination and diffusion of information about the process, progress being made, modifications, and the like. Thus, managing information as a way to address the instabilities caused by inconsistencies in individual expectations vs. achieved results (fluctuations) through the stabilizing effect of communication and diffusion processes. By giving the process through which things happen and people interact at least equal consideration with the content of the curriculum and direction of school or district, this relational model allows the system to work together at many levels (and diverse ways) to formulate more effective plans to support the children it serves.

The plan's structure, which encourages multidirectional communication, also allows the district to draw benefit from peoples' resistance to change. A large number of teams and other vehicles for participation are provided so as to generate much dynamism through the organizing of many kinds of interactions among a large number of individuals, without the need for an overriding regulator in charge of directing the behavior of every group or individual. As an alternative to imposing top-down, pre-determined solutions to identified problems, the New Haven shared accountability plan distributes responsibility among constituent groups and individuals and brings them together in an attempt to create the conditions necessary to achieve our expected outcomes by taking their objections, comments, concerns, and questions into serious consideration before final decisions are made (bottom-up). Out of such interactions we expect that the process of emergence will generate solutions and forward paths unlikely to be obtained from any single constituent.

CONCLUSION

The predominant metaphor used to explain or justify accountability systems is that of quality control as it exists in the world of manufacturing. Using this metaphor, the schools are seen as institutions that process raw material (students) and produce a product (educated students). Efforts based on such perspectives do not take into account the level of complexity that exists in schools or in their educational processes. Associated practices tend to treat individuals and groups more like parts of a machine than as complex, interacting living organisms. Such models relegate problems and solutions to the simplest, often caricature, forms of themselves, thereby forcing insular responses to complex dilemmas. These responses may themselves further escalate problems. Most often, these interventions simply modify existing conditions, which return to their prior state when the intervention is discontinued.

Nevertheless, this classical science perspective has had an enormous impact on how education and educational accountability are perceived and approached in the United States. Accountability is often code language for blaming teachers for the ills and inefficiencies of our educational institutions. Politicians frequently employ harsh and inflexible language in their election campaign rhetoric that reduces the concept of accountability to the mechanics of firing teachers and administrators, restructuring schools, tightening up already burdensome rules and regulations, or other similar quick fixes. Equally as reductive is the tendency to look for "magic bullet" solutions by vaulting from one fad packaged curriculum program or teaching method to another, seeking to hit upon the "right" button or answer that responds to the complex social, economic, political, and biological challenges confronted by children throughout the world.

The individual and societal trauma generated by this approach is profound. It restrains children's ability to learn, interact in beneficial ways with peers and teachers, and be nurtured through the development of their emotions and creativity. High drop-outs rates, absenteeism, failing grades and test scores, behavior problems or violence, and other issues intended to be addressed by efforts at accountability persist and are sometime made even worse.

In contrast to mechanical models, nonlinear dynamics allow one to perceive and develop effective educational accountability processes that take into account the inherent complexities of education and the accompanying assortment of interrelated family, social, and community matters that affect everyone. An organic paradigm facilitates the recognition and anticipation of typical patterns of interaction and systemic barriers to the achievement of desired goals. A process of accountability based on an organic perspective can serve as the vehicle through which a school district transforms itself from a mechanical bureaucracy into a dynamic, flexible, and responsive process of education.

A better, more organic metaphor than that of schools as factories is one that views schools as gardens and teachers as gardeners. When a gardener—whose livelihood depends on cultivating healthy, vital flora—approaches a plant that has weathered a drought, struggled in infertile ground, fought pests and disease, and been choked by weeds, he or she must provide the plant whatever it needs. The goal is to help the plant survive and gain strength so that it may become productive. Using this metaphor, schools are responsible for nurturing the growth of students to their greatest potential.

If we extend the gardening metaphor further, we can reach solutions that the manufacturing metaphor does not allow:

- Plants—and people—are most vulnerable to environmental stresses during their earliest development. Adequate support for young children and their families, including childcare and preschool education, is crucial if we are to support our children's optimal growth.

- Neither the gardener nor the teacher is responsible for all successes and failures. External conditions influence outcomes. Just as governments provide emergency relief and support for areas experiencing drought or flooding, State and federal governments need to recognize and provide support for cities bearing the major burden of society's ills.
- It is possible—and necessary—to predict and prepare for harmful external conditions. State and federal governments have provided billions of dollars to design and build massive irrigation systems for agriculture. If these leadership bodies and the public they represent are serious about ensuring optimal educational attainment for our students, we need to be prepared to support the development of optimal conditions for student growth.

The extension of this metaphor does not remove accountability from schools, teachers, or students. Just as a good gardener must keep abreast of current research, techniques, and information, good teachers and administrators must know and implement strategies that have proven to be successful in the local climate. It is still they who must tend the garden, but they should do so in the best conditions the community is capable of providing.

REFERENCES

Callahan, R. E. 1962. *Education and the cult of efficiency.* Chicago: University of Chicago Press.

Elliott, E. J. 1989. *Accountability in the post-Charlottesville era.* Los Angeles: University of California Center for the Study of Evaluation.

Friedman, M. 1955. Role of government in education. pp. 123–144. In *Economics and the public interest*, ed. R. Solo. New Brunswick, NJ: Rutgers University Press.

Frymier, J. 1996. *Accountability in education: Still an evolving concept.* Bloomington, IN: Phi Delta Kappa, Fastback 395, ERIC # ED404758.

Hansen, J. B. 1993. Is educational reform through mandated accountability an oxymoron? *Measurement & Evaluation in Counseling & Development*, 26(1), 11–22.

Langton, C. G. 1989. *Artificial life.* Redwood City, CA: Addison-Wesley.

Laplace, P. Marquis de. 1796. *Exposition du Système du Monde* (The System of the World). Retrieved from eBooksLib.com on July 21, 2002.

Mandelbrot, B. 1982. *The fractal geometry of nature*. W. H. Freeman, San Francisco.

National Commission on Excellence in Education. 1983. *A nation at risk: The imperative for educational reform*. Washington, DC: U.S. Government Printing Office.

Prigogine, I., and Stengers, I. 1984. *Order out of chaos: Man's new dialogue with nature*. New York: Bantam Books.

Sarason, S. B. 1990. *The predictable failure of educational reform: Can we change course before it's too late?* San Francisco: Jossey-Bass.

Taylor, F. 1967. *The principles of scientific management*. New York, NY: W. W. Norton.

Torre, C. A. 1984. Problem solving and decision-making: An integration of cognitive, affective, and pragmatic operations. Paper presented at the second biennial International Conference on Thinking. Boston.

———. 1987. Thinking, culture, and education. Paper presented at the third biennial International Conference on Thinking, Manoa, Hawaii.

———. 1989. *El Proyecto Cayey: Una Investigación Sobre la Calidad del Pensamiento* [The Cayey Project: A Study on the Quality of Thinking]. Cayey: University of Puerto Rico.

———. 1995a. Chaos, creativity, and innovation: Toward a dynamical model of problem solving. In *Chaos theory in psychology and the life sciences*, ed. R. Robertson and A. Combs, 179–98. Mahwah, NJ: Lawrence Erlbaum Associates, Inc.

———. 1995b. Chaos in the triadic theory of psychological competence in the academic setting. In *Chaos theory in psychology*, ed. A. Gilgen and F. Abraham, 279–94. Westport, CT: Praeger: Greenwood Publishing Group.

Wynne, E. 1972. *The politics of American education*. Berkeley: McCutchan.

NOTES

1. The devising of ways to assess student achievement and establish lines of responsibility for their success.

2. Isaac Newton (1642–1727) was an English physicist and mathematician whose work describes three laws of motion known as Newton's laws: 1) inertia; 2) action and reaction; and 3) acceleration proportional to force. See also Newton, Isaac. 1687. *Philosophiae Naturalis Principia Mathematica* (Mathematical

Principles of Natural Philosophy): Facsimile of third edition (1726) with variant readings; Vols. 1 and 2. by I. Bernard Cohen. Harvard University Press; (January 1, 1972).

3. This project analyzed the performance of students from a large number of schools on uniform objective and traditional tests, against such variables as levels of expenditure, size of classes, qualifications of teachers, and student socioeconomic background. Not intended as an accountability effort, it, nonetheless, had a profound effect on accountability legislation that followed (Hansen 1993). See also New Haven Accountability Task Force. 2001. Greater achievement through shared accountability. A report of the Accountability Task Force. New Haven, CT: The New Haven Public Schools.

4. Federally mandated accountability procedures explicitly called for the extensive use of business principles in education through the use of concepts such as *performance contracts*; *educational outcome audits*; *cost accounting strategies*; and *outcome measures* that bind expenditures and outcomes.

5. Some of these government programs were: Program Planning and Budgeting Systems (PPBS); management by objectives (MBO); Management of Information Systems (MIS); and Program Evaluation and Review Techniques (PERT).

6. Interestingly, the checks and balances created for governing in the U.S. Constitution and Metternich's "balance of power" in Europe, were influenced by Newton and Laplace's writings.

7. The field of self-organization seeks general rules about the growth and evolution of systemic structure, the forms it might take, and methods that predict the future organization that will result from changes made to the underlying components.

8. A diffusion process is the course of action required for an innovation (i.e., accountability) to proliferate across a school, district, or society. An example is what happens as a cube of sugar dissolves in a cup of tea by spreading (diffusing), eventually, throughout the entire volume, dispersing evenly without stirring.

9. Indeed, as Sarason (1990) pointed out so clearly, attempts at school reform in the past have failed, at least in part, because they have not taken a systemic approach. According to Sarason, reform efforts that do not treat the school as an integrated system comprising numerous interacting subsystems (e.g., teaching-learning, administration, organization, socializing) are doomed to failure.

10. The New Haven public schools address many of these concerns through the six developmental pathways of the school development program and the

"Emotional Intelligence" focus of the social development program. Details of these approaches are available on request.

11. Initial efforts at accessing such organic attributes come via our social and health assessment instrument administered by Yale University. Details are available on request.

APPENDIX I

THE DAYCARE CENTER AND THE FIRE STATION

After teaching the concepts of activation, restraint, and reconciliation to a group of my students, I asked them to deliberate on a particular situation abstracted from an out-of-town newspaper:

A municipality needs to provide funds for a daycare center and a fire station at the end of its fiscal year. Both agencies have requested financial support for expanding their physical plants and for the purchase of new equipment. The municipality does not have sufficient money to fund both agencies' projects, but the entire pot of available funds is in excess of what is needed to fund either project alone. The problem is how best to meet the child-rearing and fire safety needs of the community with the available resources.

Discussions in the City Council led to the expected arguments in defense of a variety of standard "solutions" to the predicament:

1. Allocate all funds to one project, with the expected outcome that it will be able to meet its commitments and obligations, while the other is left to subside or would have to deesclate its services. As a result, either the daycare or fire fighting needs of the municipality will not be met.
2. Divide available funds between both projects according to some formula to be negotiated. Presumably, neither project will go by the wayside but, realistically, would probably be unable to fulfill its obligations entirely.

After some deliberation, the students in my course offered a third, nonstandard approach to the situation. They proposed that the city council:

3. Allocate all of the funds to the fire station so that it could expand its physical plant beyond its needs, thereby creating sufficient room to house a soundproof (also expanded) daycare

facility. The city could, then, sell the old daycare's center's physical plan, generating the additional funds necessary for purchasing the equipment needed for both the fire station and daycare center.

The students' proposal would not only solve the problem posed originally; it also solved subsidiary problems not even considered in advance. It rendered the daycare center about as safe and secure as it could possibly be (the center would now be housed in the fire station) and provided a built-in field trip for the children in the daycare center because they could easily and frequently visit the fire station. And the proposal provided relief from the boredom the fire fighter normally experienced waiting for a fire to occur—they would now have the children around to divert them during periods of inactivity.

9

EXPLORING THE SHAPE OF CHANGE: USING THE POWER OF SYSTEM DYNAMICS IN K–12 EDUCATION

Lees Stuntz, P. Jeffrey Potash, and John F. Heinbokel

In the summer of 2001, a small group of educators gathered in Essex, Massachusetts, with some of the world's finest system dynamicists to begin to address the question, "How can we utilize system dynamics to create systemic change in K–12 education?" System dynamics is a problem solving approach that uses pencil-and-paper tools and computer simulation to understand the underlying causes of change in the systems that surround us. The educators in attendance were among an elite group from across the country who, for more than a decade, had engaged in far-reaching experimental projects to adapt and apply the tools of system dynamics to K–12 education, tools used in major universities, businesses, and government agencies around the globe to address environmental, economic, and social problems.

Notwithstanding the group's impressive credentials and experience, the challenge framed by the group's convener, Massachusetts Institute of Technology (MIT) professor Jay Forrester,[1] was presented using a powerful analogy. A gathering at MIT in 1947 was organized by the Navy to contemplate the implications over the next twenty years of a new technology, called *the computer*. At the time, that technology was literally in its infancy, characterized by limited processing capacity, and house-sized machines incorporating thousands of vacuum tubes that overheated at irregular intervals. The challenge presented to the group of scientists and government officials in the "Whirlwind" gathering was to contemplate how and where this fledgling technology could be productively applied, how those applications could and would spark future innovations, and how those innovations could in turn drive new applications. In short, the challenge entailed taking what was known, and then building thoughtful and reasonable next steps, using feedback analysis, to incrementally move toward a future that could then be planned and regularly evaluated by the scientists and the military.

That same challenge was now directed on the Essex gathering for using system dynamics to create systemic change in K–12 education. Where had we been, what did we know, and how could we leverage our imaginations and systemic thinking to plot what Forrester suggested needed to be another twenty-year plan for initially humble, yet ever expanding growth?

The known could be readily summed up as follows: A collection of experiments, both government (National Science Foundation) and privately (Waters Foundation, Amber Blocks, Bemis Trust) funded, provided impressive evidence that the tools and concepts of systems-thinking and system dynamics could be effectively applied across a variety of curricular areas in addition to exploring a number of organizational topics. Equally impressive, there was proof that the tools of system dynamics could be, with differing emphasis, employed across the full range of K–12 education. Students were using system dynamics to understand how a bank balance accumulates interest, how a revolution gains momentum, how heat dissipates from a cup of boiling water, how the population of mammoths became extinct, how an epidemic of smallpox spreads, and how fish stocks around the world are being depleted by overfishing, to name just a few applications. Teachers found that using system dynamics to enhance their current curriculum made education more engaging, learner centered, collaborative, interdisciplinary and relevant for their students. They were also impressed with their students' depth of understanding of sophisticated problems and shared the belief, earlier recognized during the Educational Testing Service's (ETS) experimental STACI project in the late 1980s, that their students had "a greater capacity to understand the interrelated and complex nature of phenomena that they will encounter in their daily lives" (Mandinach and Cline 1994, 150).

These common experiences led the otherwise heterogeneous group of educators (elementary, middle, and high school teachers, hailing from all four corners of the country, and reflecting a diversity of content interests and expertise including mathematics, science, and the humanities) to quickly form a consensus around a list of key attributes associated with an education infiltrated with system dynamics, fostering student growth, educator recruitment and retention, and organizational change. Noteworthy in the process of describing student learning was the shared perception that the individual learning being fostered was characterized, not simply by a set of thinking skills, but by a complementary set of attitudes and behaviors. The product of an education infused with system dynamics, envisioned by the Essex gathering, would be individuals who were systems citizens (Lyneis et al. 2002)

For example, if students learn through classroom experience with many different systems, that all actions have consequences, often unintended, they will begin to internalize that concept. They might look at the profound effects on the ecosystem of the elimination of Aleutian Islands sea otters on one island and not another as one system and the consequences of overusing antibiotics as another. Soon they will begin to internalize these lessons and live by them. Systems citizens would think carefully about the environmental consequences of their own actions and of larger government policies and would incorporate those concerns into the actions and policies they would advocate. As students demonstrate these ways of thinking and acting, the benefits will become apparent to others from the grassroots up.

With some further support from the professional system dynamicists to make the vision operational, and some late night concept mapping by Barry Richmond,[2] we developed a "closed loop" concept map of our vision that depicted an educational learning process with several reinforcing feedback behaviors that nurtured the development of systems citizenship over time. An abstract of that concept map appears (figure 9.1), which broadly illustrates the dynamic interplays through which systems skills and attributes mutually reinforce one another.

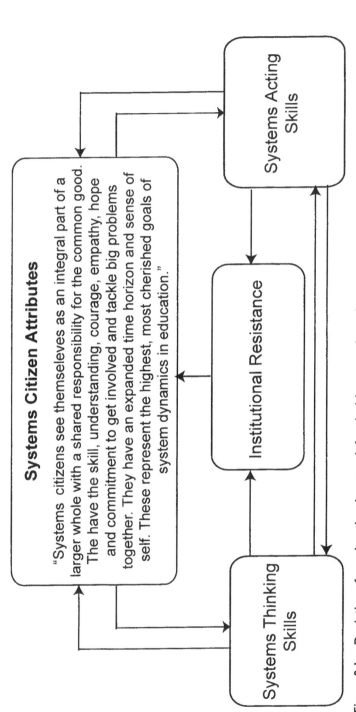

Systems Citizen Attributes

"Systems citizens see themseleves as an integral part of a larger whole with a shared responsibility for the common good. The have the skill, understanding, courage, empathy, hope and commitment to get involved and tackle big problems together. They have an expanded time horizon and sense of self. These represent the highest, most cherished goals of system dynamics in education."

Systems Acting Skills

Institutional Resistance

Systems Thinking Skills

Figure 9.I. Depiction of an educational system infused with system dynamics

Each of the systems skills (thinking and acting) reinforces the other; directly affects the cultivation of systems citizen attributes (Lyneis et al. 2002, 9) and influences school context. As well, these systems-thinking and acting skills are themselves supported by the realized attributes. The group embraced Richmond's progressive schema of essential systems-thinking skills that he had developed previously (Richmond 2000). Integrating systems-thinking concepts and dynamic modeling with much of the traditional content already present in K–12 education, Richmond suggested a progression of higher-thinking skills that encompasses three broad areas of learning:

- Filtering skills, that focus on identifying "what to include" in one's exploration (including defining big picture, spatial and temporal boundaries and seeking self-generating behaviors).
- Representation skills, that involve expressing one's understanding of nonlinear relationships in terms of closed feedback loops.
- Simulation skills, involving precise and objective computer modeling to test and revise mental models for purposes of managing systems.

These skills, the group observed, do not emerge out of any prescribed curriculum, but rather naturally grow out of recurring exposures and exploration of ever more complex systems. Over the course of their careers, using all of the tools of system dynamics as appropriate, student capacity to think, test, and ultimately manage complex systems grows.

The group's experience bore out a second and equally powerful learning component. In the course of learning and practicing the principles of system dynamics within the curriculum, the group observed that a corresponding set of systems-thinking attitudes and behaviors were also emerging. Fundamentally, these attitudes and behaviors, comprising systems acting skills, underscored a set of metacognitive processes that reflected deeper thinking about one's individual perceptions, one's capacity to work with others, and the ability and motivation to address meaningful real world problems. Significant traits associated with these attitudes and behaviors are highlighted here (Lyneis et al. 2002).

Individual Attitudes

- Patience and persistence in problem solving. Using systems-thinking skills to dig deeper and keep learning.
- The willingness to be wrong and learn from mistakes. An ability to take considered risks.
- The willingness to examine and change one's own assumptions and conclusions, metacognition.
- An acceptance that often there is no one right answer.

Collaboration

- Openness to the mental models of others. A tolerance for productive disagreement.
- An expanded sense of self. Seeing oneself as an integral part of a larger system with a shared responsibility for the common good.
- Empowerment: Using an understanding of a system to act on its problems with courage, confidence, and hope.

Engaging the Real World

- An extended time horizon. A suspicion of the short-term easy solution based on an understanding that short-term policies are detrimental in the long run, and vice versa.
- An ability to relate the past to the present and the present to the future. An ability to recognize patterns.
- An internalization of all these principles that informs actions and interactions with others.
- A final component involved the school context and visualizing a school environment that could nurture both the individual and a larger learning community. Built around the principles of system dynamics and learner directed learning, crucial organizational features of a supportive school environment included both curricular and organizational attributes (Lyneis et al. 2002).

Curricular Attributes

- System dynamics tools provide a framework to integrate and energize the current curriculum rather than supplant or add-on to existing coursework.

- Lessons will allow students to actively construct their own knowledge and understanding, with the teacher as a guide and coach.
- Problems are placed first. Instead of presenting students with a problem only after they have learned everything necessary to solve it, students will face the problem first and seek to learn what they need to solve it—as in real life.
- Students will work on interdisciplinary projects with real world relevance to their own lives, issues in their communities, or larger current events.
- Students will work on projects in multi-age groups, learning from one another.
- Students will be involved in their communities, contributing to the solution of problems.

Organizational Attributes

- Teachers, students, and administrators will have sufficient time (without conflicting assignments) available for learning, collaboration, and lesson refinement.
- Classrooms will be openly accessible to parents, other teachers, and students.
- Community members will be involved in their schools.
- Students will have access to system dynamics and subject experts.
- School governance will be shared.
- Administrators will facilitate collaboration, risk taking, open communication and continuous improvement—the school will be a learning organization.
- Administrators will encourage and support innovation (6–7).

The key to this system rests in the self-reinforcing interrelationships identified in figure 9.1. Rather than function independently, developments within each of the three areas trigger productive change in the others. This leads, over time, to the development and graduation of students who were systems citizens. In the language of the Essex report (Lyneis et al. 2002):

Systems citizens see themselves as an integral part of a larger whole with a shared responsibility for the common good. They have the skill, understanding, courage, empathy, hope and commitment to get involved and tackle big problems together. They have an expanded time horizon and sense of self. These represent the highest, most cherished goals of system dynamics in education. They reside at the core of our efforts. (9)

A vision is useful only to the degree that it includes a strategy for realizing it. Recognizing the enormity of the challenge, the Essex group interpreted their own experiences within a classic system dynamics process known as "the infection model," a word of mouth or grassroots process for diffusion. As early adopters, these teachers recognized that they had been drawn to the approach because they saw it could benefit their students. As these teachers experienced success in their classrooms, they had begun to attract the attention of colleagues who, in turn, were often willing to try it. Slowly but steadily, the idea had begun to spread.

The power of the infection process is evidenced in the fact that, if an "infected" person passes that "infection" to more than one other individual, the disease will continue to grow at an accelerating rate (or exponentially) over time. What begins slowly and remains under the radar of most people's perception has, over the long term, the potential for explosive growth and acceptance as more and more teachers actively use these tools of system dynamics.

In contemplating how to effectively manage and sustain the strategy, the group again benefited from a concept map, based on their discussions and drawn by Jim Lyneis,[3] identifying powerful feedback loops that could contribute to or undermine the group's goals. A simplified modification of that stock/flow feedback map (Lyneis et al. 2002, 27) is presented as figure 9.2.

Note in figure 9.2 that the change over time is expressed as the dynamics of the three "stocks" or accumulations of teachers in the system (shown as boxes); next, observe that changes in the overall numbers within each group occur through "flows" that move people in or out of each the stocks.

The important drivers of these changes in the system are feedback loops, illustrated in the connections that link the system together. Two key "reinforcing loops" capture the hopes expressed by the group. The first is the infection process, in which growing numbers of teachers using system dynamics materials will strengthen their collective capacity

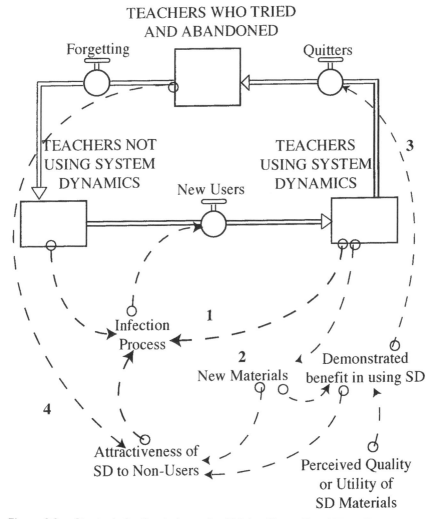

Figure 9.2.   Strategic feedback dynamics (driving "hopes" and "fears")

to infect others (#1 in figure 9.2). A second involves the likelihood that the larger the number of teachers using materials, the greater will be the probability that new materials will be generated, in turn enhancing a greater attractiveness of system dynamics to non users to try these materials in their classroom (#2 in figure 9.2). But there are fears that two additional reinforcing feedback structures could progressively undermine progress:

- If the perceived quality or utility of the materials were to diminish, the probability that those using or exposed to those materials would not be receptive to using them (#3 in figure 9.2);
- In addition, individuals who have rejected system dynamics may actively work to affect the willingness of others to try SD (#4 in figure 9.2).

Recognition of these feedbacks and their potential impact on hopes and fears clarified for the group important strategies to pursue in the future to bolster the desired reinforcing feedback loops. As described in the Essex Report as "The Strategy to Realize the Vision" (Lyneis et al. 2002), these included:

- To develop extensive curriculum materials of demonstrated benefit that are ready for teachers to use. Until now, teachers have had to create their own classroom materials. It is important to learn from the most effective lessons and develop more materials across the range of grade levels and disciplines. Because a shortage of good materials is a constraint, this is an early priority.
- To focus on teacher training and support. Teachers need training in system dynamics and ongoing support as they use it with their students. To this end, it is necessary to develop effective teacher training materials and train the teachers who will then be using the materials to train and support others. We need to build on our past system dynamics training experience and broaden the cadre of teacher-trainers because this is another bottleneck. Our goal must extend beyond simply transmitting computer modeling skills, however. In the process, we must help teachers become systems thinkers too. Training and support are equally crucial for school administrators.
- To assess student progress continually to demonstrate that a systems education can deliver its claimed benefits. Assessment will also be important for the ongoing evaluation and refinement of curriculum materials and teacher training. It will be necessary to engage experts in assessment because we do not currently have that expertise and because we can benefit from their feedback.

- To let students be our ambassadors. Students who have studied system dynamics can eloquently and enthusiastically express what they have learned. They always impress adults with their poise and depth of understanding of complex issues. Keeping students out front not only wins converts but also reminds all of us that students are the reason we pursue this.
- To value the vital role of administrators in effecting school change. A supportive administrator can encourage and facilitate the spread of system dynamics within a school. This is especially true if the administration embraces the principles of organizational learning, creating a climate of continuous improvement, collaboration, and creative risk taking.
- To engage local communities in their schools. Everyone benefits when schools, community members, businesses and other institutions work together to improve K–12 education. Outside initiative, feedback and support are vital needs.
- To work with the growing number of educators around the world who are also introducing system dynamics into their schools. We can learn from one another. (10–11)

At the same time, it is crucial to avoid pitfalls that may bolster undesirable balancing feedbacks:

- To recognize that system dynamics does not stick if it is mandated from above or pushed too fast. Teachers, administrators and communities need time and patient support to digest and accept these ideas at their own pace.
- To acknowledge that any effort to change K–12 education will naturally engender resistance. It is necessary to use the tools of system dynamics to look for leverage points and work within the system rather than against it.
- To maintain high standards of quality for curriculum materials and training because an erosion of standards will undermine credibility and sustainability. It will be important to enlist the help of system dynamics professionals throughout the process for help with quality control.

- To acknowledge that system dynamics can be difficult to learn at first because it requires looking at things through a new frame of reference. It will be up to skilled teachers to devise ways to make system dynamics accessible to a broad audience. Meanwhile, we all need support and patience (10–11).

SYSTEMS-THINKING IN ACTION AFTER ESSEX: REALIZING THE VISION

The concept maps contained in the Essex Report provide three dynamic frameworks with which to measure and evaluate successful change: One (figure 9.1) focuses on student benefits and connects students' curricular exposure to and growing mastery of the tools and concepts of system dynamics with their larger motivation for and capacity to be active citizens and problem solvers; another, not independent of the first (figure 9.2), involves the active number of "teachers using system dynamics" (and recognizes the crucial importance of two potentially active flows: an inflow of "new exposures" and the potential outflow of "disenchanted" or unconvinced educators). Accompanying these changes is a third focus, a dynamic organizational structure where institutional resistances are progressively replaced by structures and attitudes supportive of change. In assessing the efforts of the system dynamics community in the five years after the Essex meeting, it is important to consider the shape of change in each of these three areas, beginning with the key "agents" of change, teachers.

GROWING THE COMMUNITY OF "TEACHERS WHO USE SYSTEM DYNAMICS": BUILDING MATERIALS AND ENTHUSIASM

All who participated in the Essex meeting clearly understood the crucial need to develop "exemplary" curricular materials to assist teachers in doing better at what they need to do. It is, then, not coincidental that several Essex participants have emerged as leaders in vital area of creating and publishing such materials.

Carlisle (Massachussets) teachers Rob Quaden and Al Ticotsky collaborated with Debra Lyneis on *The Shape of Change* (2004), targeting an elementary and middle school audience. The book contains eleven lessons intended to provide students with a deepened capacity for both recognizing and understanding causal factors that contribute to different patterns of change. Familiar conceptual system dynamics tools, including behavior-over-time graphs and causal loop diagrams, provide the means to decipher patterns of change within a variety of contexts and a diversity of time frames, for example, mammoth extinction, the friendship game, infections, and issues of environmental sustainability. Each lesson poses a clear yet open-ended question and a "fun" challenge to students to participate in a game, experiment or other hands-on activity that permits them to experience a variety of "what ifs" and to describe (using system dynamics tools) their experience to others. Finally and most importantly, each lesson seeks to build a capacity to transfer a powerful conceptual discovery into a deeper appreciation for the way things in general work (e.g., "How does an epidemic spread, whether it is smallpox in the New World, this year's flu, a computer virus, or a rumor?"). Interesting feedback received by the authors indicates, that while the book was written for Grades 3 – 8, the "In and Out Game" and "Making Friends" have been played by children as young as kindergarten. Many of the games in the book can effectively played by students in high school and college and on into adulthood.

A noteworthy component of the book involves the presentation of a relatively new tool, connection circles. Connection circles have been developed to assist students in beginning to think explicitly about cause-effect relationships contained in stories. Here, the authors used a relatively simple template:

(1) selecting a limited number of elements that satisfy three criteria (they are important to the changes in the story; they are nouns or noun phrases; and they increase or decrease in the story),
(2) placing them around a circle,
(3) and then drawing arrows to show direct connections from "cause" to "effect."

Connection circles are a powerful tool for engaging younger students in constructing feedback thinking and eventually closed feedback loops.

This is a crucial step in the evolution of more rigorous systems-thinking tools (involving more complex stock/flow feedback maps and simulatable computer models).

An illustration (figure 9.3) developed in the book's *"Do You Want Fries with That?"* lesson (Quaden, Ticotsky, and Lyneis 2004, 110) helps students to construct "closed" feedback loops by moving from one variable to another, and eventually tracking changes back to the original variable. The illustration presents two feedback loops:

1) a self-reinforcing loop, in which increasing sales of fries lead to higher profits, the opening of new restaurants, and back to increase sales of fries, figure 9.4 (Quaden, Ticotsky, and Lyneis 2004, 111).

2) a balancing loop where fries sold cause more fries to be eaten, more fat to be consumed, more health concerns to be developed

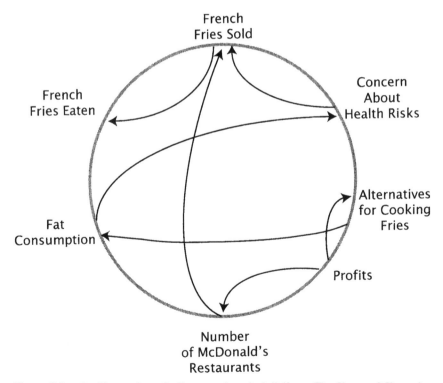

Figure 9.3.   An illustration of a "connection circle" (from *The Shape of Change*)

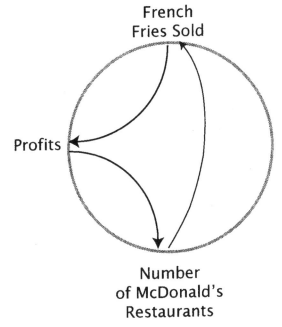

French
Fries Sold

Profits

Number
of McDonald's
Restaurants

Figure 9.4.   A self-reinforcing loop

which then reduces the fries sold, figure 9.5 (Quaden, Ticotsky, and Lyneis, 2004, 111).[4]

The Shape of Change (and its soon to be released successor *Shape of Change: Stocks and Flows*)[5] is an exemplary resource whose actually greater power may rest in its value for inspiring further innovation. Many of its lessons have already been adapted (some times with modified lesson plans) and subsequently shared through the Waters Foundation consortium of schools. Furthermore, the infection from the exuberance within Rob Quaden's math classroom inspired other colleagues to create curricula. Carolyn Platt developed a sixth grade literature lesson that allows students to use system dynamics tools to explore themes in the novel, *Tuck Everlasting* (Platt, Quaden, and Lyneis 2002). During these lessons students actually built computer models to simulate the demographic implications of longer (or, in the case of "Treetop," eternal) life in its residents and on students' own communities. In another example, Gene Stamel developed lessons to help third grade students draw behavior-over-time graphs from everyday life. The

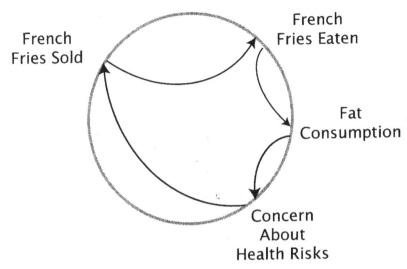

Figure 9.5.   A balancing loop

examples include daily temperature, friendship over time, science observations and news articles about lobster fishing and scooter injuries
(Stamel and Lyneis 2002).

Others, in addition to Stamel have made contributions at the elementary level. Author Linda Booth Sweeney has contributed to the
growing literature aimed at introducing system dynamics concepts to
young children (and their parents!). In her book, *When a Butterfly
Sneezes*, she uses common children's stories to explore the interconnectedness of the world with the principles of systems-thinking. She illustrates in a powerful way some of the beginning techniques for introducing systems-thinking in literature. Many teachers have used the
same techniques and the more precise tools of system dynamics to help
give students deeper insight into the books and stories they are reading
(Sweeney 2001).

Sweeney is also involved in an exciting collaboration with the distin-
guished system dynamicist Dennis Meadows, a coauthor of the 1972
bestseller *Limits to Growth*, in creating a series of new games and exer-
cises to build systems-thinking capabilities. Meadows' belief that gaming was a powerful vehicle to engage children (and adults of all ages) in
experiencing systems in connecting structure with behavior began in the
1980s with his development of two computer-model-based games: Fish-

banks, Ltd. (Meadows, Fiddaman, and Shannon 1987), allowing students and teachers an opportunity to experience the tragedy of the commons, where a common resource (fish) is depleted as a consequence of rational individual efforts to maximize their own personal gain (a debriefing using system dynamics principles was written by the system dynamics education project under the supervision of Jay Forrester [System Dynamics Education Project 2001a]; and Strategem, a dynamic simulation addressing global issues such as economic and population growth in a decision-making environment (Meadows 1985). Meadows and Linda Booth Sweeney's *systems-thinking Playbook* (1995; 1998; 2001; 2004) uses components of constructivist learning, kinesthetic learning, and active involvement to create systems understanding. Many teachers have used these games to reinforce the principles of system dynamics with their students.

In high schools where experimentation with system dynamics began in the 1980s (Mandinach and Cline 1994), the spirit of innovation continues. Essex participant, Diana Fisher, who, with colleagues in Portland, Oregon, spearheaded the innovative NSF-sponsored CC-STADUS and CC-SUSTAIN[6] interdisciplinary modeling workshops for high school teachers in the 1990s, has authored two guidebooks that focus on the powerful opportunities to improve high school student learning with and about system dynamics modeling. *Lessons in Mathematics: A Dynamic Approach* (Fisher 2001), employs the visual computer language of STELLA to engage students in "real world" dynamic problem solving, overcoming the difficulty many students have with the abstract language of mathematics and enhancing and expanding their capacity to solve complex and dynamic nonlinear mathematical problems typically accessible only to a small contingent of high achievers. A more recent book, the second edition of *Modeling Dynamic Systems: Lessons for a First Course* (Fisher 2004), offers an even more powerful and compelling case for expanding students' capacity to work with a broader interdisciplinary range of current topics including population dynamics, epidemics, and urban dynamics (see figure 9.6).

In addition to Fisher's work in the area of mathematics and modeling, there continues to be significant efforts to develop applications in science as well. The Maryland Virtual High School web site (www.mvhs1.mbhs .edu/mvhsproj/project2) also offers extensive curricula online, focusing

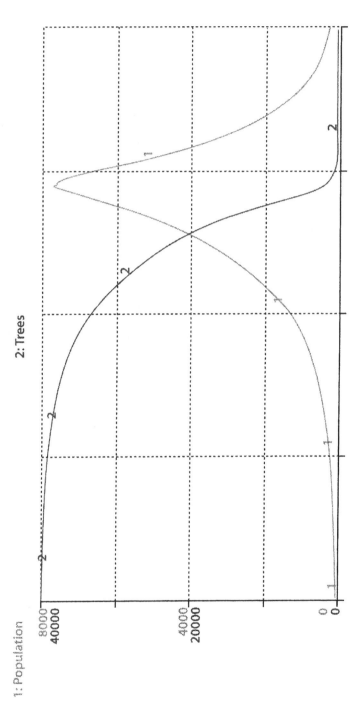

1: Population   2: Trees

Figure 9.6. An illustration from modeling dynamic systems illustrating the overshoot and collapse behavior of output generated through the demands of an exponentially growing population on a less quickly regenerating resource (trees, in this case), draws attention to issues of sustainability.

exclusively on science topics, including chemistry, biology, earth science, and physics for high school.

Strong advocacy for modeling in areas outside of math and science also exists. Tim Joy, a leader with Diana Fisher in the Portland, Oregon community for more than a decade, has continued to advocate for system dynamics as a bridge between the sciences and the humanities. A piece written in 2003, titled *Writing and Modeling: Using a Notebook to Learn about System Dynamics*, describes the benefits in integrating the writing process with system dynamics instruction. Moving seamlessly between powerful "generic" system dynamics models and the powerful art of writing, Joy powerfully communicates that the "writing process offers not only a good metaphor for model building; it also offers a means to composing the models themselves—a clearly told story that will help the model building, and a well-built model will help the story teller" (Joy 2003).

Although the previous examples constitute the most ambitious efforts to demonstrate the value-added possibilities for incorporating system dynamics into particular curricula, a growing engagement among a variety of educators building on the system dynamic tools and approaches is evidenced elsewhere as well. Perhaps the most significant inventory of materials can be found in the Creative Learning Exchange (CLE) library (www.clexchange.org). This site offers a broad diversity of curricula for K–12 that, in addition to math and science, includes literature, personal health, and social studies applications. The CLE web site includes curricula focusing on the application of systems-thinking and dynamic modeling to explore such "soft" variables as trust, anger, and power that represent important classroom dynamics. The work of MIT's System Dynamics Project with its self-paced system dynamics curriculum also resides at the CLE web site (System Dynamics in Education Project 2001b).

Another diverse collection is maintained at the Waters Foundation web site (www.watersfoundation.org). Through its networking of schools around the country, the Waters Foundation plays a leadership role in developing introductory systems-thinking training materials and programs with which to engage teachers in this country and others across the world. In addition to its collection of materials, developed over more than a decade's experimentation in more than a dozen schools, the Waters Foundation site explicitly frames its materials within the context of current educational, pedagogic, and learning theories. Systems-thinking tools, for instance, are explicitly linked with "habits of mind." Yet another interesting facet of the Waters Foundation focuses on their structured "action research" projects. These communicate both successes and failures; the latter—as Jay Forrester has taught—is at least as useful, in that they prevent continued repetition of the same mistakes.

Recognizing that there are other vehicles for connecting experience, overcoming resistance, and inspiring newcomers to join the community, the CLE continues to develop other avenues of national outreach to bolster person-to-person infection. Its quarterly newsletter (*The Exchange*) highlights networking opportunities and innovative practices in the development of new curricula. In addition, the CLE maintains an engaging K-12 listserv that encourages and supports regular exchanges of ideas, questions, and concerns among educators from around the world. And with its recently launched educational modeling exchange, the CLE has expanded both its capabilities to support and catalyze curricular innovation and publication and its training capacity for school systems interested in expanding their systems capabilities in the classroom, the school administration, and the community.

Last but not least, the CLE continues to hold well-attended biennial networking conferences that bring together a dedicated corps of world-class professional system dynamicists and educators from around the world to share experiences and to contemplate strategies and opportunities to promote the cause of systems-thinking and dynamic modeling" within kindergarten through twelfth grade education. This conference offers unparalleled training opportunities for neophytes and experienced educators. As has been noted previously, in no other discipline are the world-class practitioners so willing and available for contact with K–12 educators with a common goal to increase the systems learning capacity of students.

BUILDING SYSTEMS CITIZENS

Evidence of growing teacher interest and expanding curricular applications addresses one facet of positive change raised at the Essex meeting. In the second and more ambitious vision, that of producing systems citizens, there is a growing body of research indicating students are developing skills and habits of mind that are consistent with those identified at Essex as systems-thinking and acting. Working with two groups of fifth graders and a visual representation of a dynamically changing system using system blocks, researchers in the MIT Media Laboratory (Zuckerman and Resnick 2005) recorded that students were able to select and simulate a particular theory of personal belief and importance, identify misconceptions or false theories about dynamic behaviors associated with that belief, and subsequently revise, test, and develop-new-theories for guiding future behavior. By developing a powerful stock-and-flow modeling framework in a supportive environment with which students were able and willing to articulate and change mental models, the research offers encouraging evidence of deeper learning that challenges preconceptions, builds new and more powerful conceptual frameworks, and encourages a metacognitive transfer of real world learning and problem solving to other areas of personal interest (Donovan and Bransford 2005).

A second and more substantive piece of research was undertaken by Linda Booth Sweeney in doctoral research at Harvard University School of Education. This research focused on students' learning that Sweeney described as "homologous reasoning," or the capacity to develop a mental library of recurring patterns of behavior and recognize these generic structures in widely different domains (Sweeney 2005). Sweeney's research with middle school students bore out students' abilities to transfer behavioral knowledge across curricula and in the process, generate other deeper learning benefits beyond that building of coherence across the curriculum; these included increased engagement, improved transfer and problem-solving skills, increased retention, and most importantly for the purpose of systems citizenship, increased student empowerment. "The ability to recognize patterns of behavior within what may appear to be what Russ Ackoff has called a "wicked mess" is empowering. Armed with this understanding, young people have a greater ability to analyze and act in informed ways without jumping to blame a single cause for the challenges they will encounter" (Sweeney 2005, 7).

One of the most exciting and unique facets of the system dynamics community's cultivation of systems citizenship involves the manner in which professionals, educators, and students interact. Nowhere, perhaps, is this more impressive than in student presentations of their work. An important precedent in the mid-1990s was the creation of "SymBowl," a showcase for original student modeling projects, sponsored by Ed Gallaher (from the Oregon Health Sciences University), in collaboration with members of the CC-SUSTAIN team, including Diana Fisher, Ron Zaraza, Tim Joy, and Scott Guthrie. In addition to engaging students from across the country, SymBowl reached out to include notable system dynamics professionals as judges, to interact with, challenge, and ultimately encourage student performance. The breadth and depth of topics modeled by students, ranging from traffic projections (Andrews and Roth 1999) to issues of ecological stability (Brummer, Lennox, and Yellesetty 1999) to the implications of raising the minimum wage (Green and Martin 1999) to the evolution of galaxies (Anderson and Cottingham 1999) underscores their extraordinary capacity and motivation for addressing current crucial problems of interest to them (see the CLE web site for a description of these and other 1999 SymBowl papers).

The spirit of systems citizenship continues with another annual gathering, DynamiQUEST, sponsored in New England by the CLE, begun in 2000. Designed to recognize and mentor rather than judge student projects and to involve students from across the elementary, middle, and high school levels sharing original work using all of the tools of system dynamics, DynamiQUEST assembles a virtual "who's who" of East Coast system dynamicists who perform as coaches in listening to, learning from, and in turn providing guidance for, student presenters. The sincerity of their interest and the value of their feedback are not lost on student attendees. A noteworthy outgrowth of DynamiQUEST has been the development of the *Rubrics for Understanding: Using System Dynamics Tools* (Lyneis 2001), which presents standards for each of the major system dynamics tools (behavior over time graphs, causal loop diagrams, stock/flow diagrams, and computer models). These rubrics provide guidelines for helping students as they work on their projects to help articulate their goals and objectives.

A strength of DynamiQUEST is presented in a story of Omar Aboulezz that appeared recently in the CLE newsletter (Aboulezz and Lyneis 2005), a fifth grader who attended the 2005 DynamiQUEST gathering held at Worcester Polytechnic Institute. Drawing on his own recent experiences to explore the dynamics of childhood obesity, he began by developing a concept map, describing the reinforcing feedbacks between video gaming, obesity, and inactivity; then modifying it to incorporate policy options, then finally developing a computer model with which to simulate the impact of different choices. When finished, he proudly shared the work with his classmates. At first, he reported, they were confused by his concept map, but after he explained how the stocks and flows worked, what the connections meant, and what caused the behavior in the graphs, they understood. Omar was pleased by their reactions and concluded that, "system dynamics is a great way to solve problems" (Aboulezz and Lyneis 2005). Perhaps that is the strongest testimonial of systems citizenship to date.

ORGANIZATIONAL INNOVATION—POLICY

Although the Essex group, comprised primarily of teachers among the educators present, highlighted the importance of curricular innovation a direct connection to student learning and growth, their recognition of the importance of a supportive school environment underscored a need to engage the larger education community, including building and district administrators, school board members, and the public. To that end, a group of administrators and citizen advocates from the Society for Organizational Learning (SoL) joined the group in Essex.[7] Senge's book, *Schools that Learn* (Senge 2000), is a compendium of stories about the administrative and curricular uses of systems-thinking and the other four disciplines presented in his book *The Fifth Discipline* (Senge 1990). These efforts in schools across the country dovetail with those encouraged by the core group gathered in Essex.

Senge, in an effort to enhance systemic change and realize the vision of the future, is part of an embryonic movement to encourage schools and communities that learn. He, the Sol, the CLE, the Cloud Institute for Sustainability, and other systems-thinking organizations and individuals such as Linda Booth Sweeney are joining together to encourage the use of systems education in K–12 schools. The group is concentrating on nurturing all three sectors necessary in any given community for real systemic change: community, schools, and the classroom. They are currently working to provide a framework and methodology for deep transformational change in the way that our children think and act.

Their vision coincides with the vision of systems citizens put forth by the Essex group.

Another project in the organizational realm with encouraging results came from an effort to use the power of system dynamics modeling to shed light on some of the enormous practical problems facing school systems today. Ralph Brauer, director of the Transforming Schools Consortium in Minnesota, has, in his innovative MinSim project, inspired the most ambitious experiment to date in modeling school dynamics in relation to student achievement. The goal of this "data-driven decision-making" project was to "capture the key school system feedbacks of student achievement and model their interrelationships in a way that the model could be useful to any school or district" (Brauer 2004, 11). Focusing initially on diverse stakeholders' perceptions of student performance, Brauer engaged a pair of system dynamics modelers to join in the construction of a computer flight simulator, using district data that ran the gamut from finances and facilities to people (students, faculty, and administration) to standards and performance, designed to allow users to incorporate their own data to help simulate a variety of "what if" explorations of possible policies and strategies (Brauer, Heinbokel, and Potash 2004).

With substantial buy-in from teachers, administrators and others in the educational community, the model that evolved focused on the concept of "time" as the "common currency" through which student performance could best be understood. Time was both a "resource" generated by the various elements of the educational community and a "demand" generated by students with dynamically varying levels of behavioral and learning "needs." The model contrasted the two distinct variations on time, in a system with multiple and often complex feedbacks. Resources (e.g., teaching and administrative staff), demands (e.g., from students potentially falling academically further and further behind, behavioral problems intensifying, if not immediately addressed), and delays all dynamically changed to generate long-term patterns of student achievement that were often counterintuitive. The successful use of a preliminary model in several Minnesota settings, as described in Brauer's articles, opens yet another pathway through which both innovation and infection are expected to take hold.

CONCLUSION

A powerful message delivered to attendees at the close of the Essex meetings by Jay Forrester was this: Be patient. Recognize, even where a small and dedicated group of educators is successful in its quest to infect others and initiate a positive or reinforcing feedback loop, the dynamics still initially appear almost static or unchanging to the casual observer; in the long term, that growth, if sustained, can and will generate exponential and explosive consequences.

Visualizing the challenge of integrating the power of system dynamics into K–12 education as a long-term, feedback-based process provides a realistic and sustainable framework within which current innovators feel comfortable and confident in pursuing their efforts. Focus remains on doing a limited number of things (for a limited number of people) well. Quality is far more important than quantity, and humility and persistence are far preferable to a sudden but transitory burst of faddish exposure. The growth in numbers of those who use available materials and who participate in opportunities to network offers tangible proof that the community continues to grow in size and capacity over time.

It is safe to say that the group's vision for implementing "systems citizenry," initially articulated at Essex and subsequently developed further in the CLE's biennial conferences, though not yet realized, is achievable. We know, as we continue to learn about both how to manage systems and assess their performance over time, that achievability inspires us to continue.

RESOURCES

Brauer's paper in the "School Administrator" journal can be obtained at www.aasa.org/publications/.
Creative Learning Exchange library, available at www.clexchange.org.
Maryland Virtual High School, available at http://mvhs1.mbhs.edu/mvhsproj/project2.html.
Meadow's games, Fishbanks Ltd., and Strategem are available from The Sustainability Institute, Hartland, Vermont, available at www.sustainer.org.
Pegasus Communications, available at www.pegasuscom.com.
The Waters Foundation, available at www.watersfoundation.org.

REFERENCES

Aboulezz, O., and D. Lyneis. 2005. Get moving! Solutions to the epidemic of childhood obesity. *Creative Learning Exchange Newsletter* 14 (4): 1–5.

Andrews, B., and D. Roth. 1999. *How bad will Portland's traffic be in 2040?* Retrieved from www.clexchange.org, January 15, 2006.

Anderson, C., and S. Cottingham. 1999. *How does a galaxy evolve?* Retrieved from www.clexchange.org, January 15, 2006.

Brauer, R. 2004. Testing "what if" scenarios, *The School Administrator* (November): 10–14.

Brauer, R., J. F. Heinbokel, and P. J. Potash. 2004. Systemic planning. Creative learning. *Exchange Newsletter* 13 (1): 1–14.

Brummer, C., A. Lennox, and L. Yellesetty. 1999. *If a tree falls in the woods, will another replace it?* Retrieved from www.clexchange.org, January 15, 2006.

Donovan, M.S., and J. D. Bransford, eds. 2005. *How students learn.* Washington, DC: The National Academies Press.

Fisher, D. 2001. *Lessons in mathematics: A dynamic approach.* Lebanon, NH: isee systems.

———. (2004). *Modeling dynamic systems: Lessons for a first course.* Lebanon, NH: isee systems.

Joy, T. 2003 *Writing and modeling: Using a notebook to learn about system dynamics.* Retrieved from www.clexchange.org, January 15, 2006.

Lyneis, D. A. 2001. *Rubrics for understanding: Using system dynamics tools.* Retrieved from www.clexchange.org, January 15, 2006.

Lyneis, D. A., D. Barcan, W. Costello, D. Fisher, J. Forrester, S. Guthrie, J. Heinbokel, et al. 2002. *The future of system dynamics and learner-centered learning in K–12 education: A report from a planning meeting.* Essex, Massachusetts, 2001. Retrieved www.clexchange.org, January 15, 2006.

Mandinach, E., and H. Cline. 1994 *Classroom dynamics: Implementing a technology-based learning environment.* Mahwah, NJ: Lawrence Erlbaum Associates.

Meadows, D. 1985. *User's manual for STRATEGEM-1. A microcomputer based management training game on energy-environment interactions.* Hanover, NH: Resource Policy Center.

Meadows, D., T. Fiddaman, and D. Shannon. 1987. *Fish Banks, Ltd. A microcomputer-assisted simulation teaching the principles for sustainable management of renewable resources.* Durham, NH: Institute for Policy and Social Science Research.

Platt, C., R. Quaden, and D. Lyneis. 2002. Tuck everlasting—system dynamics, literature, and living forever. *Creative Learning Exchange Newsletter* 11 (1): 1–14.

Quaden, R., A. Ticotsky, and D. A. Lyneis. 2004. *The shape of change*. Acton, MA: Creative Learning Exchange.

Richmond, B. 2000. *The "thinking" in systems-thinking: Seven essential skills*. Waltham, MA: Pegasus Communications.

Senge, P. 1990. *The fifth discipline*. New York: Doubleday.

Senge, P., N. H. Cambron-McCabe, T. Lucas, B. Smith, J. Dutton, and A. Kleiner. 2000. *Schools that learn*. New York: Doubleday.

Stamel, G., and D. Lyneis. 2002 *Everyday behavior over time graphs*, Retrieved from www.clexchange.org, January 15, 2006.

Sweeney, L. B. 2001. *When a butterfly sneezes: A guide for helping kids explore interconnections in our world through favorite stories*. Waltham, MA: Pegasus Communications.

———. 2005. How is this similar to that? The skill of recognizing parallel dynamic structures on center stage. *Creative Learning Exchange Newsletter* 14 (3): 1–8.

Sweeney, L. B., and D. Meadows. 1995. *The systems-thinking playbook*, vol. xxx. Durham, NH: Institute for Policy & Social Science.

Sweeney, Linda B., and Dennis Meadows. 1998. *The systems-thinking playbook*, vol. I. Durham, NH: Institute for Policy & Social Science.

Sweeney, Linda B., and Dennis Meadows. 2001. *The systems-thinking playbook*, vol. II. Durham, NH: Institute for Policy & Social Science.

Sweeney, Linda B., and Dennis Meadows. 2004. *The systems-thinking playbook*, vol. III. Durham, NH: Institute for Policy & Social Science.

System Dynamics Education Project. 2001a. *Fish Banks Packet*, Retrieved from www.clexchange.org, January 15, 2006.

System Dynamics Education Project. 2001b. *Road maps 1–10*, Retrieved from www.sysdyn.clexchange.org, January 15, 2006.

Zuckerman, O., and M. Resnick. 2005. Children's misconceptions as barriers to learning stock-and-flow modeling. *Creative Learning Exchange Newsletter* 14 (2): 1–9.

NOTES

1. Jay Forrester is founder of the field of system dynamics, inventor of magnetic core memory for the computer, Professor Emeritus at Massachusetts Institute of Technology, and author of *Industrial Dynamics* (1961), *Urban Dynamics* (1969), and *World Dynamics* (1971).

2. Barry Richmond was a former professor of system dynamics at Dartmouth College and inventor of STELLA, the first user-friendly system dynamics software.

3. Jim Lyneis is an experienced system dynamics management consultant, Professor of Practice at Worcester Polytechnic Institute, and Senior Lecturer at MIT.

4. There is actually another reinforcing loop not mentioned in the text: This involves the possibility, as new alternatives for cooking fries lead to lower fat consumption and lower health concerns, there will be more sales of fries and higher profits with which to continue to explore still more alternatives.

5. The first four lessons of this new book are available now through the CLE. They take the first four games one step further by showing teachers and students the concepts inherent in stock flow mapping, a key element in the system dynamics tool set.

6. The Cross-Curricular systems-thinking and Dynamics Using STELLA (CC-STADUS) and Cross-Curricular Systems Using STELLA: Training and In-service (CC-SUSTAIN) NSF projects ran from 1993 to 2000 under the principal investigators, Diana Fisher and Ron Zaraza.

7. Peter Senge, one of the original founders of SoL, has been an active supporter of the use of systems-thinking and system dynamics in K–12 education.

10

CULTURE, CHAOS, AND COMPLEXITY: CATALYSTS FOR CHANGE IN INDIGENOUS EDUCATION

Ray Barnhardt and Anagayuqaq Oscar Kawagley

The principles of self-organization associated with the study of complex adaptive systems are being brought to bear on education in rural Alaska through the educational reform strategy of the Alaska Rural Systemic Initiative (AKRSI). Indigenous education in Alaska provides a fertile testing ground for the emerging sciences of chaos and complexity. These newly established sciences have derived from the study of complex physical (e.g., weather), biological (e.g., animal behavior), and economic (e.g., the stock market) systems whose dynamics exhibit adaptive patterns of self-organization under conditions that on the surface appear chaotic (Gleick 1987; Gribbin 2004; Sahtouris 2000; Waldrop 1994).

The constructs, principles, and theories emerging under the banners of chaos and complexity have also been extended to the study of human social systems (Epstein and Axtell 1996; Shulman 1997), and to the management of formal organizations as complex adaptive systems (Battram 2001; Wheatley 1992). The latter applications of complexity theory are being brought to bear on education in rural Alaska through the AKRSI educational reform strategy.

The AKRSI was established in 1994, bringing together more than fifty stakeholder organizations involved in education in rural Alaska (see figure 10.1). The institutional home base and support structure for the

AKRSI was provided through the Alaska Federation of Natives in cooperation with the University of Alaska, and with funding from the National Science Foundation and the Annenberg Rural Challenge (now Rural School and Community Trust). Statewide leadership for the AKRSI was provided by a director based at the Alaska Federation of Natives and two codirectors (the authors) employed by the University of Alaska Fairbanks. In addition, a regional coordinator was employed in each of the five major cultural regions of Alaska. As such, the AKRSI was the first major statewide educational endeavor initiated by and implemented under Alaska Native leadership and control.

The purpose of the AKRSI was to implement a set of initiatives that systematically documented the indigenous knowledge systems of Alaska Native peoples and developed pedagogical practices that appropriately integrated indigenous knowledge and ways of knowing into all aspects of the education system. In practical terms, the most important intended outcome was an increased recognition of the complementary nature of Native and Western knowledge, so both can be more effectively used as a foundation for the school curriculum and integrated into the way educators think about learning and teaching.

The central focus of the AKRSI reform strategy was the fostering of interconnectivity and symbiosis between two functionally interdependent but largely disconnected complex systems—the indigenous knowledge systems rooted in the Native cultures that inhabit rural Alaska, and the formal education systems that have been imported to serve the educational needs of rural Native communities. Within each of these evolving systems is a rich body of complementary knowledge and skills that, if properly explicated and leveraged, can serve to strengthen the quality of educational experiences for students throughout Alaska and perhaps elsewhere.

INDIGENOUS KNOWLEDGE, SCHOOLS, AND SYSTEMS THINKING

The sixteen distinct indigenous cultural and language systems that continue to survive in rural communities throughout Alaska have a rich cultural history that still governs much of everyday life in those communities. For more than six generations, however, Alaska Native people have

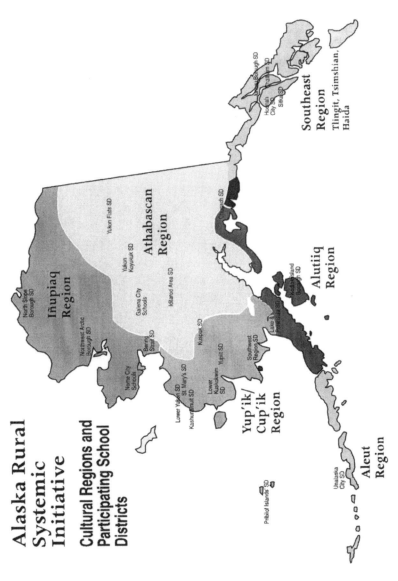

Alaska Rural
Systemic
Initiative

Cultural Regions and
Participating School
Districts

North Slope
Borough SD

Iñupiaq
Region

Northwest Arctic
Borough SD

Bering
Strait SD

Nome City
Schools

Lower Yukon SD
St. Mary's SD

Kashunamiut SD

Lower
Kuskokwim
SD

Yupiit SD

Yup'ik/
Cup'ik
Region

Pribilof Islands SD

Unalaska
City SD

Aleut
Region

Yukon Flats SD

Athabascan
Region

Yukon
Koyukuk SD

Galena City
Schools

Iditarod Area SD

Kuspuk SD

Southwest
Region SD

Lake &
Peninsula SD

Alutiiq
Region

Kodiak Island
Borough SD

Borough SD

Hoonah
City SD
Sitka SD

Southeast
Region

Tlingit, Tsimshian,
Haida

Figure 10.1.

been experiencing recurring negative feedback in their relationships with the external systems that have been brought to bear on them, the consequences of which have been extensive marginalization of their knowledge systems and continuing dissolution of their cultural integrity. Though diminished and often in the background, much of the Native knowledge systems, ways of knowing and worldviews remain intact and in practice, and there is a growing appreciation of the contributions that indigenous knowledge can make to our contemporary understanding in areas such as medicine, resource management, meteorology, biology, and in basic human behavior and educational practices (Helander-Renvall 2005).

Indigenous societies, as a matter of survival, have long sought to understand the irregularities in the world around them, recognizing that nature is underlain with many unseen patterns of order. For example, out of necessity, Alaska Native people have had to learn to decipher and adapt to the constantly changing patterns of weather and seasonal cycles. The Native elders have long been able to predict weather based on observations of subtle signs that presage what subsequent conditions are likely to be. The wind, for example, has irregularities of constantly varying velocity, humidity, temperature, and direction as a result of topography and other factors. There are nonlinear dimensions to clouds, irregularities of cloud formations, anomalous cloud luminosity, and different forms of precipitation at different elevations. Behind these variables, however, there are patterns, such as prevailing winds or predictable cycles of weather phenomena that can be discerned through long observation. Over time, Native people have observed that the weather's dynamic is not unlike fractals, in which the part of a part is part of another part, which is a part of still another part, and so on.

For indigenous people there is a recognition that many unseen forces are in action in the elements of the universe and that little is naturally linear or occurs in a two-dimensional grid or a three-dimensional cube. They are familiar with the notions of irregularities and anomalies of form and force (i.e., chaos). Through long observation they have become specialists in understanding the interconnectedness and holism of all things in the universe (Kawagley 1995).

The sciences of chaos and complexity and the study of nonlinear, dynamic systems have helped Western scientists to also recognize order in phenomena that were previously considered chaotic and random (Eglash

2002). These patterns reveal new sets of relationships that point to the essential balances and diversity that help nature to thrive. Indigenous people have long recognized these interdependencies and strive for harmony with all of life. Western scientists have constructed the holographic image, which lends itself to the native concept of everything being connected. Just as the whole contains each part of the image so too does each part contain the makeup of the whole. The relationship of each part to everything else must be understood to produce the whole image (Wilber 1985).

With fractal geometry, holographic images and the sciences of chaos and complexity, the Western thought-world has begun to focus more attention on relationships, as its proponents recognize the interconnectedness in all elements of the world around us (Capra 1996). Thus, there is a growing appreciation of the complementarity and symbiosis that exists between what were previously considered two disparate and irreconcilable systems of thought (Barnhardt and Kawagley 1999).

Among the qualities that are often identified as inherent strengths of indigenous knowledge systems are those that have been described as the focal constructs in the study of the dynamics of complex adaptive systems: "Complexity theory is about identity, relationships, communication, mutual interactions" (Stamps 1997, 36). These are qualities that focus on the processes of interaction between the parts of a system, rather than the parts in isolation, and it is to those interactive processes that the AKRSI reform strategy is directed. In so doing, however, attention must extend beyond the relationships of the parts within an indigenous knowledge system and take into account the relationships between the system as a whole and the other external systems with which it interacts, the most crucial and pervasive being the formal education systems which now impact the lives of every native child, family, and community in Alaska.

THE FORMAL EDUCATION SYSTEM

Formal education is still an evolving, emergent system that is far from equilibrium in rural Alaska, thus leaving it vulnerable and malleable in response to a well-crafted strategy of systemic reform. The advantage of working with systems that are operating "at the edge of chaos" is that they are more receptive and susceptible to innovation and change as they seek equilibrium and order in their functioning (Waldrop 1994). Such is the case for many of the educational systems in rural Alaska, for historical and unique contextual reasons. From the time of the arrival of the Russian fur traders in the late 1700s up to the early 1900s, the relationship between most of the native people of Alaska and education in the form of schooling (which was reserved primarily for the immigrant population at that time) may be characterized as two mutually independent systems with little if any contact, as illustrated by figure 10.2:

Figure 10.2.

Before the epidemics that wiped out over 60 percent of the Alaska Native population in the early part of the twentieth century, most native people continued to live a traditional self-sufficient lifestyle with only limited contact with fur traders and missionaries (Napoleon 1991). The oldest of the Native elders today grew up in that traditional cultural environment and still retain the deep knowledge and high language that they acquired during their early childhood years. They are also the first generation to have experienced significant exposure to schooling, many of them having been orphaned as a result of the epidemics. Schooling, however, was strictly a one-way process at that time, mostly in distant boarding schools with the main purpose being to assimilate Native people into Western society, as practiced by the missionaries and school teachers (who were often one and the same). Given the total disregard and often condescending attitude toward the indigenous knowledge and belief systems in the Native communities, the relationship between the two systems was limited to a one-way flow of communication and interaction up through the 1950s, and thus can be characterized in figure 10.3:

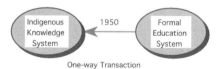

Figure 10.3.

By the early 1960s, elementary schools had been established in most Native communities, and by the late 1970s a class action lawsuit had forced the state to develop high school programs in the villages throughout rural Alaska. At the same time (in 1976), the federal and state-operated education systems were dismantled, and in their place over twenty new school districts were created to operate the schools in rural communities. That placed the rural school systems serving Native communities under local control for the first time, and concurrently a new system of secondary education was established that students could access in their home community. These two steps, along with the development of bilingual and bicultural education programs under state and federal funding and the influx of a limited number of Native teachers, opened the doors for the beginning of two-way interaction between the schools and the Native communities they served, as illustrated by figure 10.4 depicting rural education by 1995 (when the AKRSI was initiated):

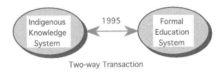

Figure 10.4.

Despite the structural and political reforms that took place in the 1970s and 1980s, rural schools have continued to produce a dismal performance record by most any measure, and Native communities continue to experience significant social, cultural, and educational problems, with most indicators placing communities and schools in rural Alaska at the bottom of the scale nationally. Although there has been some limited representation of local cultural elements in the schools (e.g., basket making, sled building, songs and dances), it has been at a fairly superficial level with only token consideration given to the significance of those elements as integral parts of a larger complex adaptive cultural system that continues to imbue peoples lives with purpose and meaning outside the school setting. Although there is some minimum level of interaction between the two systems, functionally they remain worlds apart, with the professional staff overwhelmingly non-Native (95 percent statewide) and with a turnover rate averaging 30 to 40 percent annually.

With these considerations in mind, the Alaska Rural Systemic Initiative has sought to serve as a catalyst to promulgate reforms focusing on increasing the level of interconnectivity and synergism between the formal education systems and the indigenous knowledge systems of the communities in which they are situated. In so doing, the AKRSI seeks to bring the two systems together in a manner that promotes a symbiotic relationship such that the two previously separate systems join to form a more comprehensive holistic system that can better serve all students, not just Alaska Natives, while at the same time preserving the essential integrity of each component of the larger overlapping system. The new interconnected, interdependent, integrated system we are seeking to achieve may be depicted in figure 10.5:

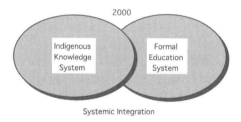

Figure 10-5

FORGING AN EMERGENT SYSTEM OF EDUCATION FOR RURAL ALASKA

In May 1994, the Alaska Natives Commission, a federal and state task force that had been established two years previously to conduct a comprehensive review of programs and policies impacting Native people, released a report articulating the need for all future efforts addressing Alaska Native issues to be initiated and implemented from within the Native community (Alaska Natives Commission 1994). The long history of failure of external efforts to manage the lives and needs of Native people made it clear that outside interventions were not the solution to the problems, and that Native communities themselves would have to shoulder a major share of the responsibility for carving out a new future. At the same time, existing government policies and programs would need to relinquish control and provide latitude and support for Native people to address the issues in their own way, including the opportunity to learn from their mistakes. It is this two-pronged approach that is at the heart of the AKRSI educational reform strategy—Native community initiative coupled with a supportive, adaptive, and collaborative education system.

Manuel Gomez, in his analysis of the notion of systemic change in education has indicated that, "Educational reform is essentially a cultural transformation process that requires organizational learning to occur: changing teachers is necessary, but not sufficient. Changing the organizational culture of the school or district is also necessary" (1997). This statement applies to both the formal education system and the indigenous knowledge systems in rural Alaska. The culture of the education system as reflected in rural schools must undergo radical change, with the main catalyst being standards-based and place-based curriculum grounded in the local culture. In addition, the indigenous knowledge systems need to be documented, articulated, and validated again with the main catalyst being place-based curriculum grounded in the local culture.

The standards referred to here, however, are not only the usual subject-matter standards established by the state, but also include a set of "cultural standards" that have been developed by Alaska Native educators and elders to provide explicit guidelines for how students, teachers, schools, and communities can integrate the local culture and environment into the formal education process so that students are able to achieve cultural well-being as a result of their schooling experience (Assembly of Native Educators 1998). The focus of these cultural standards is on shifting the emphasis in education from teaching about culture to teaching through the local culture as a foundation for all learning, including the usual subject matter.

If educational advocates are to abide by the principles of complexity theory and seek to foster the emergent properties of self-organization that can produce the systemic integration indicated previously, then it is essential that they work through and within the existing systems. The challenge is to identify the units of change that will produce the most results. In the terms of complexity theory, that means targeting the elements of the system that serve as the "attractors" around which the emergent order of the system can coalesce (Peck and Carr 1997). Once these crucial agents of change have been appropriately identified, a "gentle nudge" in the right places can produce powerful changes throughout the system (Jones 1994).

There are three key agents of change around which the AKRSI educational reform strategy have been constructed. In this case these are the Alaska Native educators working in the formal education system coupled with the Native elders who are the culture bearers for the indigenous knowledge system, along with the Native-initiated cultural standards adopted by the Alaska Department of Education. Together, these agents of change constitute a considerable set of "attractors" that are serving to reconstitute the way people think about and do education in rural schools throughout Alaska. The role of the Alaska Rural Systemic Initiative has been to guide these agents through an ongoing array of locally generated, self-organizing activities that produce the "organizational learning" needed to move toward a new form of emergent and convergent system of education for rural Alaska (Marshall 1996). The overall configuration of this emergent system may be characterized as two interdependent though previously separate systems being nudged together through a series of initiatives maintained by a larger system of which they are constituent parts, as illustrated in figure 10.6.

The components of the emergent system representing the indigenous knowledge subsystem and the formal education subsystem are depicted in figure 10.6 as they appear ten years into the systemic reform initiative. Over a period of ten years, the two subsystems have been brought in contact with one another with an increasing level of two-way interaction occurring daily that is slowly building the interconnectivity and integration of functions that is the goal of the reform strategy. Each of the initiatives in the field surrounding the two subsystems serve as a catalyst to energize the attractors within the subsystems in ways that reinforce the efforts of the agents of change identified previously.

For example, the Alaska Native Knowledge Network (ANKN) assembles and provides easy access to curriculum resources that support the work underway on behalf of both the indigenous knowledge system and the formal education system. In addition, the ANKN newsletter, *Sharing Our Pathways*, provides an avenue for on-going communication between all elements of the constituent systems. Concurrently, the AKRSI has been collaborating with the Alaska Department of Education and

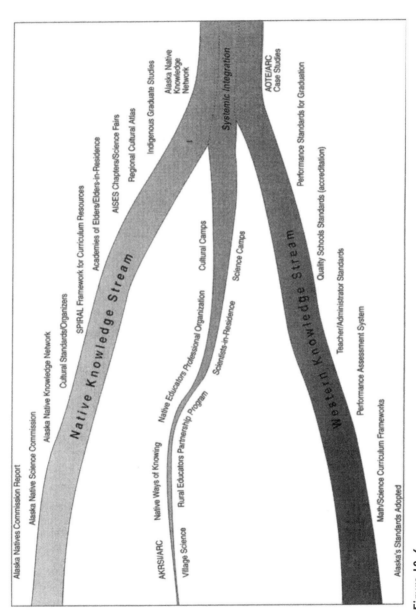

Figure 10-.6.

school districts in bringing Native educators from the margins to the center of educational decision making to shape policy development in ways that take into consideration the cultural context in which students acquire and demonstrate their knowledge, using the cultural standards as a guide.

CULTURAL INTERVENTION STRATEGIES

As the AKRSI component emphases are shifted from one region to the next, continuity is provided through the efforts and guidance of an AKRSI regional coordinator in each cultural region, who ensures that the activities from each initiative are adapted to the cultural makeup of their respective region. Along with the regional adaptation of each of the initiatives, there are also a series of cross-cutting themes that integrate the initiatives within and across regions each year. Although the regional initiatives focus on particular domains of activity through which special-ized resources are brought to bear in each region each year (culturally aligned curriculum, indigenous science knowledge base, etc.), the fol-lowing themes cut across all initiatives and regions each year:

1. Documenting cultural or scientific knowledge.
2. Indigenous teaching practices.
3. Standards or culturally based curriculum.
4. Teacher support systems.
5. Culturally appropriate assessment practices.

As schools adopt the emphasis that these initiatives bring to engaging students in the study of culture, community, and place, they are engaged in common endeavors that unite them, at the same time that they are concentrating on particular initiatives in ways that are especially adapted to the indigenous knowledge base in their respective cultural region. Each set of initiatives and themes have built on each other from year to year and region to region through a series of statewide events that bring participants together from across the regions. These include working groups around various curriculum themes, academies of elders, statewide conferences, the AKRSI staff meetings and the ANKN. Fol-

lowing is a brief description of some of the key AKRSI-sponsored initiatives to illustrate the kind of activities that have been implemented, as
they relate to the overall educational reform strategy outlined previously.

Alaska Native Knowledge Network

A bimonthly newsletter, web site, and a culturally based curriculum
resources database have been established to disseminate the information and materials that have been developed and accumulated throughout Alaska (www.ankn.uaf.edu).

SPIRAL Curriculum Framework

The ANKN curriculum clearinghouse has been identifying and cata-
loging curriculum resources applicable to teaching activities revolving
around twelve broad cultural themes organized on a chart that provides
a Spiral Pathway for Integrating Rural Alaska Learning (SPIRAL). The
themes that make up the SPIRAL framework are family, language or
communication, cultural expression, tribe or community, health or wellness, living in place, outdoor survival, subsistence, ANCSA (Alaska Native Claims Settlement Act), applied technology, energy or ecology, and
exploring horizons. These themes have also been used to formulate
whole new curriculum frameworks that have been implemented in several schools and districts. The curriculum resources associated with
each of these themes can be accessed through the ANKN web site.

Cultural Documentation and Atlas

Students in rural schools are interviewing elders in their communities and researching available documents related to the indigenous
knowledge systems associated with their place and then assembling
the information they have gathered into a multimedia format for publication as a "cultural atlas." These initiatives have focused on themes
such as weather prediction, edible and medicinal plants, geographic
place names, flora and fauna, moon and tides, celestial navigation,
fisheries, subsistence practices, food preservation, outdoor survival,
and the aurora.

Native Educator Associations

Associations of Native educators have been formed in each cultural region to provide an avenue for sustaining the initiatives that are being implemented in the schools by the AKRSI. The regional associations sponsor curriculum development work, organize academies of elders, and host regional and statewide conferences as vehicles for disseminating the information that is accumulated. In addition, a statewide Alaska Native Education Association has been formed to represent the regional associations at a statewide level.

Native Ways of Knowing

Each cultural region has been engaged in an effort to distill core teaching or learning practices from the traditional forms of cultural transmission and to develop pedagogical practices in the schools that incorporate these practices (e.g., learning by doing/experiential learning, guided practice, detailed observation, intuitive analysis, cooperative/ group learning, listening skills, and trial and error).

Academies of Elders

Native educators have been meeting with Native elders around a local theme and a deliberative process through which the elders share their traditional knowledge and the Native educators seek ways to apply that knowledge to teaching various components of the curriculum. The teachers then field test the curriculum ideas they have developed, bring that experience back to the elders for verification, and then prepare a final set of curriculum units that are pulled together and shared with other educators.

Cultural Standards

Alaska Native educators have developed a set of "Alaska Standards for Culturally Responsive Schools" that provide explicit guidelines for how students, teachers, curriculum, schools, and communities can integrate the local culture and environment into the formal education process so that students are able to achieve cultural well-being as a result of their schooling experience. In addition, a series of six additional sets of guidelines have been prepared around various issues to offer more explicit guidance in defining what educators and communities need to know and be able to do to effectively implement the cultural standards.

Village Science Curriculum Applications

Several volumes of village oriented science and math curriculum resources, including a *Handbook for Culturally Responsive Science Curriculum* (Stephens 2000), have been developed in collaboration with rural teachers for use in schools throughout Alaska. They serve as a supplement to existing curriculum materials to provide teachers with ideas on how to relate the teaching of basic science and math concepts to the surrounding environment.

All tasks associated with implementing the various initiatives outlined previously were subcontracted out to the appropriate state or regional entities with responsibility or expertise in the respective action area. In this way, the expertise for implementing the various initiatives is cultivated within the respective regions, and the capacity to carry on the activities beyond the life of AKRSI is imbedded in the schools and communities for which they are intended. Responsibility for the statewide support system (newsletter, web site, curriculum resources, etc.) for the regional initiatives has been taken up by the University of Alaska Fairbanks, and the regional Native educator associations have taken on the task of sustaining the impact of the initiatives within and between regions.

Together, these initiatives constitute the work of the Alaska Rural Systemic Initiative and are intended to generate a strengthened complex adaptive system of education for rural Alaska that can effectively integrate the strengths of the two constituent emergent systems. The exact form this new integrated system will take remains to be seen as its properties emerge from the work that is underway. Accepting the open-endedness and unpredictability associated with complexity theory and relying on the emergent properties associated with the adage, "think globally, act locally," we are confident that we will know where we are going when we get there. It is the actions associated with "thinking systemically, acting categorically" that have guided us along the way, so we continue to move in the direction established by the AKRSI educational reform strategy outlined previously.

IMPACT OF THE SCHOOL REFORM STRATEGY

The Alaska Rural Systemic Initiative has completed its ten-year cycle with a full complement of ongoing rural school reform initiatives in place stimulating a reconstruction of the role and substance of schooling in rural Alaska. The educational reform strategy we chose—to foster interconnectivity and symbiosis between the formal education system and the indigenous communities being served in rural Alaska based on current concepts, principles and theories associated with the study of complex adaptive systems—has produced an increase in student-achievement scores, a decrease in the dropout rate, an increase in the number of rural students attending college, and an increase in the number of Native students choosing to pursue studies in fields of science, math, and engineering.

The beneficial academic effects of putting students in touch with their own physical environment and cultural traditions through guided experiences have not gone unnoticed by school districts and other Native organizations around the state. One AKRSI school district has urged all of its schools to start the school year with a minimum of one week in a camp setting, combining cultural and academic learning with parents, elders, and teachers all serving in instructional roles. One school in the district has built in to their program a series of camp experiences for the middle school students, with a well-crafted curriculum addressing the state content standards as well as the cultural standards. Given the accountability demands of No Child Left Behind (NCLB), a central question throughout all these educational innovations has been, what impact do they have on student academic achievement.

With the advent of the state standards-based benchmark tests and the high school graduation qualifying exam (HSGQE) in 2000, we now have four years of data on student performance in the eighth and tenth grade math exams, from which we can make comparisons between AKRSI-affiliated schools and non-AKRSI schools for those two grade levels (AKRSI 2005). Figures 10.7 and 10.8 show the percentage of students performing at the advanced or proficient levels on those exams.

The most notable features of these data are the significant increases in AKRSI student performance for both grade levels each year between 2000 and 2003. However, whereas the eighth grade AKRSI students showed significant progress in closing the achievement (figure 10.7) gap with their

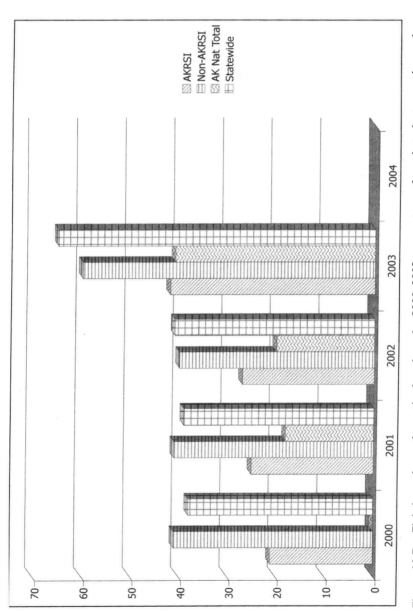

Figure 10.7. Eighth grade mathematics benchmarks, 2000–2003, percentage of rural students as advanced or proficient

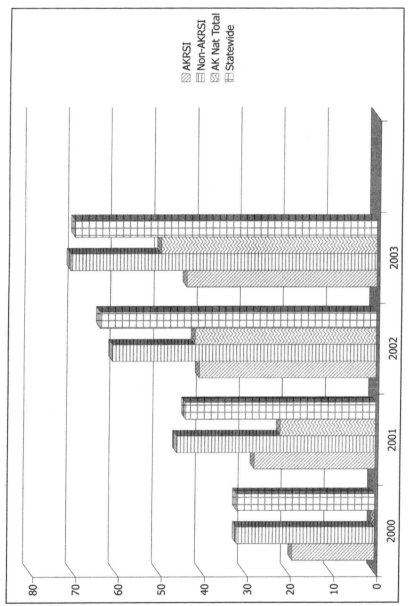

Figure 10.8. Tenth grade mathematics HSGQE, 2000–2003, percentage of rural students as advanced or proficient

non-AKRSI counterparts from 20 to 17 percentage points, the tenth grade students in both groups showed a substantial gain from 2000 to 2003 (figure 10.8), leaving the achievement gap largely intact at that grade level.

In addition to the state benchmark data, we also have norm-referenced test results for ninth grade students who have been taking the Terra Nova/CAT-6 since 2002 (figure 10.9).

Although the differentials for each group between 2002 and 2004 remain small, the AKRSI students do show a slight increase in performance, whereas the non-AKRSI students reflect a small decrease in their performance over the two years.

The consistent improvement in academic performance of students in AKRSI-affiliated schools over each of the past four years leads us to conclude that the cumulative effect of using the school reform strategies outlined in this chapter to increase the connections between what students experience in school and what they experience outside school appears to have a significant impact on their academic performance.

The AKRSI initiatives outlined here have demonstrated the viability of introducing strategically placed innovations that can serve as attractors around which a new, self-organizing, more integrated educational system can emerge, which in turn shows signs of producing the quality of learning opportunities that have eluded schools in Native communities for over a century. The substantial realignments already evident in the increased interest and involvement of Native people in education in rural communities throughout Alaska point to the applicability of complexity theory in shaping reform in educational systems.

Although the NSF (National Science Foundation) funding of the AKRSI initiative has been the catalyst for the core reform strategy as it applied to the areas of math and science, we have been fortunate to acquire substantial supplementary funding from the Annenberg Rural Challenge and other sources to implement comparable initiatives in the areas of social studies, fine arts and language arts. All of these funds combined provide an opportunity to address the issues facing schools in Native communities throughout rural Alaska in a truly comprehensive and systemic fashion.

As a means to help document the process of systemic reform in rural schools, we joined in a project that resulted in seven comprehensive case studies of educational practices and reform efforts in nine rural communities or schools in Alaska. The case studies are funded through

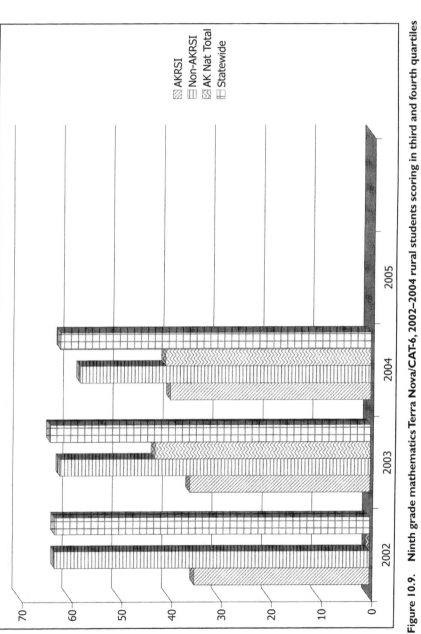

Figure 10.9. Ninth grade mathematics Terra Nova/CAT-6, 2002–2004 rural students scoring in third and fourth quartiles

the Northwest Regional Educational Laboratory by a field-initiated grant from the National Institute for At-Risk Youth under the U.S. Department of Education. Because all of the communities were in school districts associated with the AKRSI, we were able to obtain a good cross-section of in-depth data on the impact of the AKRSI reform effort over a period three years (Kushman Barnhardt 1999).

We are mindful of the responsibilities associated with taking on long-standing, intractable problems that have plagued schools in indigenous settings throughout the world for most of this century, and we have made an effort to be cautious about raising community expectations beyond what we can realistically expect to accomplish. Our experience is such that we are confident in the route we chose to initiate substantive reform in rural schools serving Alaska's Native communities, and although we expected to encounter plenty of problems and challenges along the way, we were able to capitalize on a broadly supportive climate to introduce changes that over time, will benefit not only rural schools serving Native students, but will also be instructive for all schools and all students. We are grateful for the opportunity to explore these ideas and find ways to strengthen and renew the educational systems serving people and communities throughout our society.

REFERENCES

Alaska Natives Commission. 1994. *Alaska Natives Commission: Final report.* Anchorage: Alaska Federation of Natives.

Alaska Rural Systemic Initiative. 2005. *2005 Final report.* Fairbanks: Alaska Native Knowledge Network.

Assembly of Native Educators. 1998. *Alaska standards for culturally responsive schools.* Fairbanks: Alaska Native Knowledge Network.

Barnhardt, R., and O. Kawagley. 1999. Education indigenous to place: Western science meets indigenous reality. In *Ecological education in action*, ed. G. Smith and D. Williams. New York: SUNY Press.

Battram, A. 2001. *Navigating complexity: The essential guide to complexity theory in business and management.* Dover, NH: Industrial Society Business Books Network.

Capra, F. 1996. *The web of life: A new scientific understanding of living systems.* New York: Doubleday.

Eglash, R. 2002. Computation, complexity and coding in Native American knowledge systems. In *Changing the faces of mathematics: perspectives on indigenous people of North America*, ed. J. E. Hankes and G. R. Fast, 251–62. Reston, VA: National Council of Teachers of Mathematics.

Epstein, J., and R. Axtell. 1996. *Growing artificial societies*. Cambridge: Massachusetts Institute of Technology Press.

Gleick, J. 1987. *Chaos: Making a new science*. New York: Penguin.

Gomez, M. 1997. *Science and mathematics for all*. National Science Foundation, Washington, DC.

Gribbin, J. 2004. *Deep simplicity: Chaos, complexity and the emergence of life*. New York: Penguin Books.

Helander-Renvall, E. 2005. *Composite report on status and trends regarding the knowledge, innovations and practices of Indigenous and local communities: Arctic region*. Geneva: United Nations Environment Programme.

Jones, R. 1994. Chaos theory. *The Executive Educator* (October): 20–23.

Kawagley, O. 1995. *A Yupiaq world view: A pathway to ecology and spirit*. Prospect Heights, IL: Waveland Press.

Kushman, J., and R. Barnhardt. 1999. *Study of Alaska rural systemic reform*. Portland, OR: Northwest Regional Educational Laboratory.

Marshall, S. P. 1996. Chaos, complexity and flocking behavior: Metaphors for learning. *Wingspread Journal* 18 (3): 13–15.

Napoleon, H. 1991. *Yuuyaraq: The way of the human being*. Fairbanks: Center for Cross-Cultural Studies, University of Alaska Fairbanks.

Peck, K., and A. A. Carr. 1997. Restoring public confidence in schools through systems thinking. *International Journal of Educational Reform* 6 (3): 316–23.

Sahtouris, E. 2000. The Indigenous way. In E. Sahtouris, ed., *EarthDance: Living systems in evolution*, 323–43. New York: University Press.

Shulman, H. 1997. *Living at the edge of chaos: Complex systems in culture and psyche*. Wilmette, IL: Daimon/Chiron Publications.

Stamps, D. 1997. The self-organizing system. *Training* (April): 30–36.

Stephens, S. 2000. *Handbook for culturally responsive science curriculum*. Fairbanks: Alaska Native Knowledge Network.

Waldrop, M. M. 1994. *Complexity: The emerging science at the edge of chaos*. New York: Doubleday.

Wheatley, M. J. 1992. *Leadership and the new science: Learning about organizations from an orderly universe*. San Francisco: Berrett-Koehler Publishers.

Wilber, K., ed. 1985. *The holographic paradigm and other paradoxes: Exploring the leading edge of science*. Boston: New Science Library.

⦿

EXPANDING THE SPACE OF THE POSSIBLE: UNDERSTANDING KNOWLEDGE, LEARNING, AND TEACHING AS NESTED AND RECURSIVELY ELABORATIVE PROCESSES

Brent Davis

One of the more provocative conclusions of the past half-century of research in the cognitive sciences is that humans are not principally logical creatures. Rather, our capacity for logical argumentation rides atop what might be called "analogical thinking." Our preferred ways of making sense of the world have to do with making associations, drawing analogies, and using metaphors, not deducing rational truths (Lakoff and Johnson 1999).

This issue emerges as one of the central importance when seeking to understand the relevance of complexity thinking for educational practice. Compared with classical science, complexity theories are developed around different sorts of images and associations, particularly with regard to descriptions of the structures and dynamics of living and learning forms. This chapter explores some of these images in this writing, endeavoring to foreground and explore alternatives to some troublesome figurative notion that have become commonsensical in contemporary discussions of schooling.

SOME TROUBLING LINES OF THOUGHT

Perhaps the most ubiquitous image in contemporary discussions of education is the line. It underlies popular stage-based conceptions of psychological and social development; it defines the shape of sequenced curricula and lesson plans; it is manifest in desires to get to the point, to make progress, and to see things through to the end. More subtly, for over a century, the holy grails of much of educational research have been straight lines that indicate direct relationships between such quantified phenomena as student achievement, teacher age, time-on-task, and classroom wall color.

Formal education is not alone in its broad embrace of the line as a defining image. This form is actually pervasive in the academic establishment, having been embraced within the physical sciences several hundred years ago. As it turns out, however, the preference for linear relations and other line-based interpretations within the sciences is not actually rooted in any deep-seated belief about an implicit linearity in the universe. Rather, line-based interpretations of phenomena rose to prominence for a pragmatic reason: Calculations based on many dynamic phenomena are enormously labor-intensive. Founding luminaries like René Descartes and Isaac Newton were well aware that many phenomena and relationships are decidedly nonlinear. However, because the mathematics associated with nonlinear events can be extensive and tedious, if not utterly intractable, when Enlightenment thinkers encountered such situations, they usually substituted more manageable linear approximations. By way of familiar examples, such phenomena as climate, heart rhythm, and insect population dynamics have tended to be discussed in terms of equibria (read: as definable in terms of linear trajectories or horizontal lines on graphs). Closer analyses have revealed that not only are there no equilibrium states for such cases, in fact the appearance of steady rhythms is often an indication of imminent disaster (such as an ice age, a heart attack, or a population collapse).

As the sciences grew, the tactic of inserting lines to characterize nonlinearities was extended from mechanical systems to more organic forms. As mathematician Ian Stewart (1998) explains, this

> habit became so engrained that many equations were linearized while they were being set up, so that the science textbooks did not even include the full non-linear versions. Consequently most scientists and engineers came to believe that virtually all phenomena could be described by linear

equations. As the world was a clockwork for the 18th century, it was a linear world for the 19th and 20th century. (83)

The timing of this emergent sensibility is crucial to studies of formal education. As a domain of inquiry, educational research arose at the moment that the "linear world," mentioned by Stewart, held sway. Originally oriented mainly by the more established fields of psychology and sociology, educational research not only adopted an already developed set of line-based interpretations and research methods but elaborated them into policies and practices that were—and that continue to be— rigidly direct (i.e., linear).

This point can be illustrated in a number of ways and through a range of subject matters. As a mathematics educator, in this writing I develop the issue around a few topics in arithmetic and teachers' subject matter knowledge, but I would underscore that similar sorts of analyses could be undertaken for other disciplines and structures that define the educational project.

Mathematics curricula and lesson plans are good places to start because of the deeply entrenched assumption that mathematics itself is a profoundly linear subject matter. The common belief is that, to do mathematics, one begins with one's premises and proceeds by knitting those starting points together into more sophisticated principles through carefully sequenced, impeccably logical processes. Certainly, this is the imagery endorsed by the founders of rationalist thought, which served as the philosophical frame through which virtually all curricula were defined for the modern public school. That is, programs of study in mathematics (and most other domains) are rooted in a line-based family of assumptions: Start by establishing the basics; build on those to develop more sophisticated competencies; progress from start to finish by taking incremental, lesson-sized steps. The underlying image is a simple, steady ascent up the slope of knowledge toward some model of complete understanding.

By the 1950s, learning theorists had begun to offer substantive critiques of this steady, accumulative sense of learning. Jerome Bruner (1960) had one of the loudest voices in this crowd, and he and his contemporaries were able to convince the educational establishment that the notion of steady linear development should be rejected in favor of a more spiral image. Learning does not proceed along a direct trajectory, they argued. As such, curricula should be structured in ways that enable learners to encounter topics in developmentally appropriate ways—and to revisit those topics when they were capable of more sophisticated understandings. His arguments supported a major restructuring of programs of study into "spiral curricula," by which, for example, fractions might be introduced on a physical-tactile level in the early grades, elaborated in terms of symbolic representations in upper elementary, and engaged in more abstract terms at secondary school levels.

In fact, the spiral curriculum did represent an important evolution in educational practice. Unfortunately, it preserved many of the deep-seated, line-based assumptions of previous educational theory and practice, including for example the notion that learning is some sort of forward progress or vertical ascent (i.e., descriptions persisted of moving "onward," "ahead," or "upward") and that the underlying subject matter is itself rigidly linear.

It is here that I believe complexity thinking has much to offer educational thought—not just by presenting critiques of implicit linearities, but by providing a means to interrogate the more subtle line-based assumptions that infuse popular beliefs about collective knowledge, curriculum, and pedagogy.

WHAT IS KNOWLEDGE?

The backdrop of most formal educational practice is established knowledge—that is, claims, conclusions, beliefs, and so on that are, for the moment, held to be true. Of course, the notion of "truth" is subject to a wide range of interpretations depending on philosophical frame, ranging from the realist faith in free-standing and objective facts to the pragmatist's more contingent attitude of "what works." Nevertheless, in the day-to-day worlds of curriculum development and classroom practice, established knowledge is most often treated as though it were "out there," embedded in the universe, waiting to be picked up by learners.

Overwhelmingly learning is understood as a process of internalizing something beyond the knower. Phrases, such as acquiring insight, grasping ideas, exchanging information, food for thought, solid foundations,

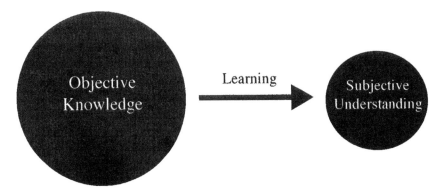

Figure 11.1. Popular metaphors of knowledge and knowing
In common figurative language, objective knowledge and subjective understanding are often framed in terms of two isolated domains that must somehow be bridged.

building understanding, and constructing meaning, help to hold this assumption firmly in place. Graphically, these turns of phrase seem to be organized around the sort of image presented in figure 11.1, in which knowledge and understanding are taken to be two discrete regions.

Critiques of this visual metaphor abound, dating back at least several centuries to John Locke, who argued that, clearly, no thing moves from the outside to the inside during moments of learning. What must be happening, he reasoned, is that individuals are constructing internal representations of the world, based on their experiences. They are constantly revising and updating these models to fit with new events. In other words, Locke suggested that personal knowledge is a reflection or mirror of reality, thus erasing the arrow that was thought to connect objective knowledge to subjective understanding (as depicted in figure 11.1) and replacing it with a few additional intervening processes that involve experience and interpretation (see figure 11.2).

Although troubling commonsense beliefs about learning, Locke's model preserves the assumed distinction between objective knowledge and subjective interpretation. In the process, this conception offers little challenge to linearized (or spiral-based) curricula. For this reason, Locke's theory of learning, and ones like it, have been dubbed "trivial" or "naïve constructivisms." They challenge images of taking things in, but they do not challenge assumptions of a radical separation of knowledge (that is still believed to be out there) and knowing (that is thought to be in here).

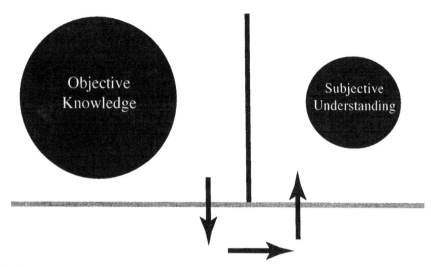

Figure 11.2. Locke's image of knowledge and knowing
John Locke elaborated popular understandings of the relationship between objective knowledge and subjective knowing (as depicted in figure 11.1) by suggesting that subjective understanding is rooted in one's physical experiences in the physical world.

It was not until that late twentieth century that dramatically different conceptions of the relationship between objective knowledge and subjective understandings began to gain broad acceptance. These structuralist theories (also referred to as constructivist, constructionist, and sociocultural, depending on which level of phenomena one focuses on) offer different, nonlinear, and complexified accounts of relationships between established knowledge and emergent knowing. In visual terms, the defining image of these theories is more toward that presented in figure 11.3, in which personal understanding is suggested to be nested in collective knowledge.

Of course, this sort of re-imag(in)ing calls for a different conception of knowledge. It cannot be seen as something independent of knowers but something that arises in their joint activities. Knowledge in this sense still transcends knowers (i.e., each of us contributes to the pool, but none of us has access to more than a small portion of the collective possibility), but it is anchored in the actions and interactions of knowers. Effectively, knowledge here is understood as a system's established but mutable patterns of acting. Correspondingly, learning is

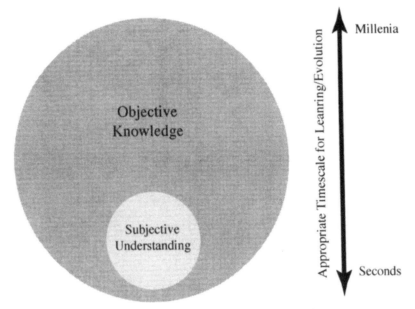

Figure 11.3.   A complexivist image of knowledge and knowing
Complexity theories of collective knowledge and individual knowing not only recast these phenomena as enfolded in and unfolding from one another but posit that they obey similar evolutionary dynamics (albeit on different time scales).

understood to refer to the dynamic processes by which a system transforms its knowledge.

Among the implications of this complexification of the notion of knowledge is that any complex system can be described as having knowledge and as being capable of learning. In other words, in complexity terms, it is not at all inappropriate to say that "mathematics learns" or "societies know" or "groups think" or "immune systems remember." Discussions of knowledge and learning, then, compel us to attend to the appropriate level of complex organization, which in turn requires that we consider the appropriate time scales for learning. For example, as a system of knowledge, mathematics learns or develops over years, centuries, and millennia—in contrast to individuals, whose understandings unfold over hours, minutes, and seconds. But complexivists argue, both phenomena obey the same sort of dynamics: They are subject to constant revision in response to experiential and contextual cues; such revisions are not matters of accumulation, but of redefinition in which both previous interpretations and future possibilities are reconfigured. Learning, that is, is a recursively elaborative process.

RECURSIVE ELABORATION, CURRICULUM, AND CLASSROOMS

A recursive process is a repetitive one that continuously transforms the object or form to which it is applied. As might be illustrated with the simple example of a fractal tree (see figure 11.4), every stage in a recursive process is an elaboration of sorts that transforms-while-preserving a "memory" of previous stages. (In fact, the illustrated example is a deterministic fractal in which the outcome is readily foreseen and the memory is never altered. A better visual metaphor for complex recursive processes is a probabilistic fractal in which random elements are introduced throughout the process, giving rise to much more organic appearing forms.)

To illustrate the educational relevance of recursive elaboration for matters of knowing and knowledge, one might consider the familiar example of number systems and operations on number systems—topics that currently serve as the core of most grade school mathematics programs. The following development of this topic is based on an ongoing longitudinal study of teachers' mathematical knowledge (see Davis and Simmt, in press).

The relationships among different systems of numbers can be discussed in terms of recursive elaborations, in which the iterative process has to do with "closure" or set-completion. For instance, starting with a set that includes only the numbers 0 and 1, the whole numbers arise when one seeks closure under addition (e.g., a larger set of numbers is needed to accommodate operations like "1 + 1 = 2"). Similarly, the in-

Figure 11.4.   An illustration of a recursively elaborative process
A recursive process is a continuously elaborative one in which the starting point at a given stage is the outcome of a preceding stage.

tegers (i.e., positives and negatives) arise as one attempts to close the set of whole numbers under subtraction—that is, the inverse of addition (e.g., "0 – 1 = –1"). Further, rational numbers (i.e., fractions) become necessary when considering closure of the integers under division—the inverse of repeated addition (e.g., "1 ÷ 2 = 0.5"). Still further, the set of real numbers arise when attempting to close the rationals under logarithms—which can be defined in terms of the inverse of repeated-repeated addition (e.g., "20.5 = 1.414...").[1]

Notably, these sorts of elaborations had profound, even revolutionary, impacts within mathematics when they were first proposed. For example, at various points in the history of the discipline, zero, negatives, and irrationals were considered impossibilities or abominations—mostly because they could not be readily assimilated into existing conceptions of disciplinary knowledge. Phrased differently as a system, mathematics had to learn to accommodate these new elements, in the process fundamentally redefining its own structure (its history; its core objects, etc.) and its possibilities (its future; the questions that could be asked and answered, etc.).

Even more interesting, perhaps, were the adaptations to number operations (i.e., +, –, ?, and ÷) to accommodate new number systems. As Mazur (2003) develops, the conceptions and definitions of operations that work within one set of numbers do not always work in another—a realization that is frequently encountered in middle school mathematics when students are faced with having, for example, to multiply two negatives or divide two fractions.

Why does a negative multiplied by a negative generate a positive? Mazur (2003) answers this question in terms of recursive elaborations of the metaphors and imagery associated with multiplication that occurred over the past millennium. Specifically, within the set of whole numbers, multiplication can be unproblematically defined in terms of stretching a number line, but this image is inadequate when signed values are introduced. To cope, mathematicians debated and eventually embraced an elaboration, whereby multiplication by –1 was interpreted in terms of rotating the number line by 180 degrees about the 0-point (so that +1 maps onto –1, +2 onto –2, etc.). By simple extension, a product of two negatives involves two 180-degree spins (i.e., 360 degrees, so that +1 maps onto +1 again, etc.). Blended with the already accepted image of whole number multiplication as stretching a number line, the resulting elaborated image not only served as a sufficient basis for characterizing integer multiplication, but also actually set the stage for the emergence of imaginary and complex number systems (see Mazur 2003).

Many similar evolutions or learnings have occurred within other operations across other number systems—and indeed, continue to occur as mathematics continues to grow. The significance of these developments for understanding the nature of mathematical knowledge cannot be overstated. Contrary to the popular image based on the line (of sequential, logical unfoldings), mathematical evolution is better described in terms of an image that is more reminiscent of the fractal tree in figure 11.4. Its future possibilities arise from decisions that are made now, as conditioned by applications, images, metaphors, definitions, and cultural obsessions. In other words, collective mathematical knowledge obeys the same sort of dynamic as individual mathematical understanding, which is also better characterized in terms of a recursively elaborated fractal image than in terms of a straight line. In the cases of both collective knowledge and individual knowing, learning is a matter of expanding the space of the possible by exploring and elaborating the current space of possibility.

In would follow, then, that curricula and classrooms, along with other educational structures that are intended to support the professional development of teachers, might be organized around similar sensibilities. This suggestion raises a series of immediate pragmatic concerns. Can programs of study and classroom spaces be framed in terms of nested complex phenomena? Can teachers' disciplinary knowledge be considered in emergent, collective terms, rather than the prevailing static and individualistic terms? How might the notion of recursive elaboration apply in these sorts of contexts?

Colleagues Elaine Simmt, Dennis Sumara, and I have been exploring these sorts of questions for several years now and have proposed an elaboration of the nested subjective/objective (or knowing/knowledge) image presented in figure 11.5. Based on our work with practicing teachers and oriented by complexity thinking, it has become apparent to us that there are intermediary levels of complex emergence between cultural knowledge and individual knowing. In particular, we focus on the articulation of subsets of knowledge domains that shape and are shaped by particular areas of education and the collective settings in

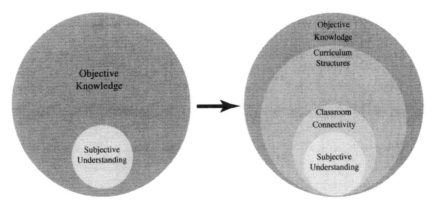

Figure 11.5.   Intermediary levels of complex emergence
Complexity thinking prompts attention toward possible intermediary levels of complex coherence that occur between subjective understanding and objective knowledge.

which understandings are interactively developed. Along with personal knowing and collective knowledge, we (Davis and Simmt in press; Davis and Sumara 2006) have argued that these levels of complex coherence are also learning, evolutionary forms. More provocatively, like the other layers, they are cognitive. None is a matter of representing some part of the real world at a different scale; rather, each has to do with ongoing, recursively elaborative adaptations that enable a knowing system to maintain coherence with its dynamic circumstances.

That last sentence was dense. In the next section, I attempt to unpack it—first, by explicating how recursive elaboration might be taken as a practical device for educators, and not merely a useful descriptive tool for researchers; and, second, by exploring some of the implications of reframing curricula, classrooms, and other educational structures in complex terms.

NESTEDNESS AND RECURSIVE ELABORATION AS EDUCATIONAL DEVICES

Complex unities are not things, but coherences—that is, patterns in the stream of matter or the flow of activity. Unfortunately, it is difficult to offer a one-size-fits-all definition of such forms and events. As a result, complexivists tend to resort to lists of descriptors. For a phenomenon to be classified as complex, it must manifest certain qualities. In addition to those already mentioned (i.e., nestedness and transcendence), the current list of necessary traits includes:

- Bottom-up emergent—complex unities cohere without the need for central organizers or governing structures; they arise as the actions of autonomous agents come to be interlinked and codependent.
- Short-range relationships—most of the information within a complex unity is exchanged among close neighbors, meaning that the system's emergent capacities often depend mainly on localized and specialized subsystems rather than systemwide capacities or communications.
- Ambiguous boundaries—complex forms are open in the sense that they continuously exchange matter, energy, and information with their surroundings (and so judgments about their edges are often quite arbitrary)
- Organizational closure—complex forms are closed in the sense that their patterns of internal relationships endure, even as they exchange elements with their contexts.
- Structure determinism—the changes that a complex unity undergoes as it adapts to its dynamic circumstances are determined by the unity itself.
- Complex systems embody their histories—they learn—and are thus better described in terms of Darwinian evolution than Newtonian mechanics.
- Far from equilibrium—complex systems do not operate in balance; indeed, a stable equilibrium implies death for a complex unity.

This list is hardly exhaustive, but it suffices to develop the suggestion that classroom collectives, teaching staffs, school districts, and so on can be understood in terms of complex coherences.

I illustrate this point by recounting an episode in which a cohort of twenty-four practicing teachers were asked to explore a mathematical topic. Colleague Elaine Simmt and I began by posing the question, "What is multiplication?" to the diverse group of K–12 teachers (see Davis and Simmt, in press, for a fuller account of the event). Their collective response, generated over the course of a few hours of discussion and argumentation was that, in fact, there is no singular answer to the question. Rather, multiplication seems to arise from a complex blending of experiences, metaphors, images, applications, and associations, including:

- Repeated addition: for example,, $2 \times 3 = 3 + 3$ or $2 + 2 + 2$.
- Equal grouping: for example, 2×3 can mean "2 groups of 3".
- Number-line hopping: for example, 2×3 can mean "make 2 hops of length 3", or "3 hops of length 2".
- Sequential folding: for example, 2×3 can refer to the action of folding a page in two and then folding the result into 3.
- Many-layered (literal meaning of 'multiply'): for example, 2×3 means "2 layers, each of which contains 3 layers".
- Ratios and rates: for example, 3 L at $2/L costs $6.
- Array generating: for example, 2×3 gives you 2 rows of 3 or 2 columns of 3.
- Area producing: for example, a 2 unit by 3 unit rectangle has an area of 6 units 2.
- Dimension changing: for example, an area multiplied by a height gives a volume.
- Number-line stretching or compressing: for example, $2 \times 3 = 6$ can mean that "3 corresponds to 6 when a number-line is stretched by a factor of 2".
- Number-line rotation: for exampled, multiplication by -1 can be interpreted as "rotate the number-line by 180 degrees."

This list has since been used by this cohort (which meets every few months for daylong sessions) as a starting place for conversations about how one might teach the topic. The notions of nestedness and recursive elaboration have been prominent across these discussions, as teachers explore and interrogate how the concept of multiplication is extended and transformed through, for example, the introduction of new number systems and contexts.

An issue that has been a topic of engaged discussion is the manner in which one's understanding of a concept like multiplication changes when a new metaphor (e.g., multiplication by a signed number as a rotation of the number line) is introduced. It is not simply an addition, nor merely an elaboration, but a recursive elaboration in which interpretations are transformed. Returning to the previous discussion of a pervasive linearity across educational structures, this in-service example foregrounds some of the issues that arise when educational processes are framed in terms of lines and directed movements.

As for the issue of nestedness, there is a striking similarity between these teachers' account of how the topic of multiplication unfolds through school grades and Mazur's (2003) description of the broader evolution of the concept over centuries and millennia. Clearly, and not surprisingly, the teaching of multiplication recapitulates the history of the concept within mathematics. Or, in other words, the teachers' collective work obeyed the same basic dynamic as the cultural production of knowledge and the personal production of meaning. Across all of these phenomena, the patterns of connection (i.e., the metaphors, images, and other interpretations) that are most successful in making sense of the world survive and serve as the starting place for subsequent events of sense making.

More subtle, and perhaps more significant in a discussion of education, are the influences across these levels of organization. It would seem that the emergence of the concept of multiplication (at the cultural level) has likely been profoundly affected by the way it has been taught (at the level of social collectivity)—that is, the metaphors and images that teachers have selected and emphasized in their efforts to render multiplication meaningful to new generations of learners has contributed to the shape of the concept. In other words, there are no clear and direct lines of influence here. To understand the relationship between formal knowledge and formal education, we need to think in terms of *embeddedness* and *mutual affect*, not in terms of *discontinuities* and *causality*.

None of this is to say that line-based representations and accounts are wrong (nor that, by implication, nested images and recursive descriptions are correct). In fact, it isn't a "right-or-wrong" issue at all. Rather, what matters here is usefulness; I'm arguing that, when dealing with complex learning systems like students, classrooms, and knowledge domains, lines are not as useful as images that involve nestedness and recursion. And the relevance of this issue extends beyond more appropriate descriptions of educational settings and events. Notions of nestedness and recursion can also provide some practical advice to teachers and educational leaders.

So, what might all of this mean for change leaders in the school system and for in-service experiences? Invoking another image from complexity thinking, specifically one from the subdiscipline of network theory (Barabasi 2002), I would suggest that bodies of knowledge, programs of study, and personal understandings might be productively recast as highly connect networks rather than pristine edifices or linear trajectories. As network theorists develop, all complex unities are structured in a particular way, namely as scale-free networks. A much-simplified image of such a network is presented in figure 11.6, in which, briefly, nodes[2] cluster into larger nodes, and so on. (A better depiction of an actual network would more closely resemble a hairball.) Departing from notions of "basics" and "logical progressions," there are no

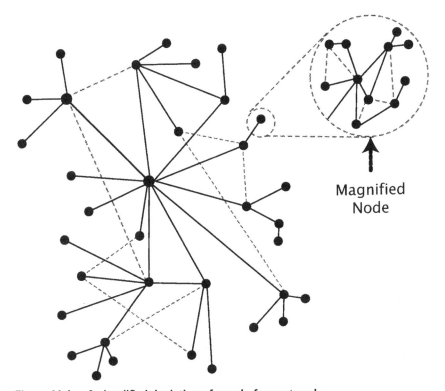

Figure 11.6.   A simplified depiction of a scale-free network
All complex systems are organized in scale-free patterns of nodes "noding" into grander nodes.

"simplest" or "fundamental" parts in a scale-free network. Every node, when examined more closely, will comprise a similarly structured network of associations.

This conception of knowledge, curriculum, and knowing supports what might be called a "pedagogy of dwelling," in which educators are not principally concerned with parsing and sequencing concepts, but with interrogating and untangling the structures that render ideas coherent. As illustrated through the multiplication example, such dwelling might serve to highlight the ways that educators contribute to the shape of collective knowledge. Significantly, such interrogation does not require a reworking of existing knowledge domains or programs of study, merely a concerted effort to rethink how these are interpreted and represented.

EDUCATIONAL STRUCTURES AND A PRAGMATICS OF TRANSFORMATION

So far in this writing, I have been organizing the discussion around an unspoken assumption: I believe that the learner that should occupy most of the teacher's attentions is not the individual student but the classroom collective. In making this assertion, I do not mean to suggest some sort of tradeoff—whereby the privileging of one aspect is assumed to entail an ignorance of another. Complexity thinking does not subscribe to this sort of win–lose (or zero-sum) logic, opting instead for a win–win way of thinking. This point was powerfully demonstrated during the multiplication exercise with the teachers, in which every individual emerged with an enhanced and more robust understanding of multiplication, even though the emphasis was on the collective production of knowledge. And so the suggestion to focus on the collective is not about ignoring individuals, but about recognizing the personal limitations can be exceeded within group settings. A lone teacher (or administrator) simply cannot track the idiosyncratic interpretations, interests, and potentials of thirty or more students (or staff members), let alone hope to affect or draw on those divergent aspects in effective ways. However, a leader advocating change can be acutely attentive to the movement of the collective. Moreover, because the leader is always part of such a collective, he or she can directly affect its movement.

Complexity thinking provides some eminently practical and explicit advice on how a teacher might contribute to the shape of classroom possibility or how an administrator might contribute to the shape of an organization's possibility. In particular, a teacher or other sort of educational leader should attend to conditions of complex emergence that are common to all self-organizing, self-maintaining, and adaptive forms.

To elaborate, over the past decade, an emergent emphasis in studies of complex systems has been the particular conditions that must be present for complex coactivity to arise in the first place. Those conditions include, for example,

- Means to preserve information—complex systems require some sort of memory—that is, some means to maintain relevant adaptations and to forget irrelevant ones.
- Reproductive instability—there must be room for error or deviation to adapt in the first place.
- Feedback mechanisms—systems require some means to keep their dynamics in check, so that they neither spiral out of control nor peter out.

So far, none of these conditions is of a sort that one can (or one would want to) tinker with in a knowledge-producing system, such as a student, a classroom, a teaching community, or a disciplinary realm—mostly because each of these systems comes preequipped with the aforementioned conditions. Other entries on the list, however, fall into a different category—that is, conditions that can be more readily and effectively manipulated, especially in social contexts like classrooms. Among these are the following:

- Internal redundancy—duplications and excesses must be represented among the agents comprising a complex collective; such redundancy contributes to the robustness of a system, enabling agents to interact and, when necessary, fill in for one another.
- Internal diversity—variations among agents are the source of a system's intelligence; how a system responds to novel contingencies

depends on the diversity represented among agents, so means must
be incorporated to allow the expression of difference.

- Decentralized control—a highly centralized system is usually no
  more effective than the agent at the center; by contrast, there is
  nothing (or no one) at the center of a complex unity.
- Neighbor interactions—for complex possibilities to arise, neighbors must be able to affect one another's activities, recalling that
  most of the information in a complex system is exchanged among
  near neighbors. (This list was developed in considerably more detail, along with illustrative examples, in Davis and Simmt 2003 and
  in Davis and Sumara, 2006).

Space prohibits an extended discussion of how a teacher or other educational leader might go about tinkering with these sorts of conditions,
but I will mention some ways that such tinkering played into the research
example, previously introduced. To address the issue of internal redundancy, for instance, we asked the teacher-participants to focus on the
same question ("What is multiplication?"), to think in terms of metaphors
and images invoked when teaching, and so on. More profoundly, everyone present had highly compatible cultural experiences and so were, in
effect, already highly redundant in terms of knowledge of the subject
matter, beliefs about schooling, and related matters. That is, in most social groupings, extensive redundancy is always already present.

In fact, redundancy was so great that most of our research efforts
were focused on developing means for the expression of diversity. To do
this, we asked teachers to represent their grade-level expertise by, for
example, highlighting how the concept is developed at their particular
levels and providing grade-specific examples of how multiplication is
used. As the outcome demonstrates, it was through the representation
of these diverse elements that a novel and elaborated "definition" of
multiplication was generated, accompanied by complexified insights
into the structures of mathematics and collectivity.

Such developments simply could not have been prescribed. Rather,
their emergence was a matter of decentralized control, in which the in-
service leaders took responsibility for ensuring the necessary structures
and resources were in place but did not attempt to reach a rigidly predetermined outcome.

Finally, the emergent result arose in the blending of ideas—a point that foregrounds a crucial feature of knowledge-producing systems. In a sense, the neighbors that had to be made to interact here were not people but were ideas, images, metaphors, and so on. It was not just that participants could talk, but that what they were talking about was sufficiently focused, yet sufficiently flexible, to allow for interesting new possibilities to arise.

I doubt that any of these points will come as much of a surprise to experienced educators. The fact of the matter is that we have all witnessed the emergence of collective possibilities that exceed the capacities of any individual present. But such happenings seem to be rare in formal educational settings, not in the least because of the way schools are framed by lines. When the ends are prespecified, it makes little sense to think in terms of expanding the space of the possible; the goal is simply to maintain the current space of possibility.

The issue, then, is not whether such events are possible, but why they seem to be so out of the ordinary in the context of classrooms and other levels of school organization. To address this issue presses the discussion into the domains of educational philosophy, sociology, history, and administration—among a host of other topics and discourses. A complexity mindset would anticipate that such a chorus of voices would be invoked: If complex forms are enfolded in and unfold from other complex forms in the educational world, then it hardly makes sense to attempt to isolate matters of theory and practice, individuality and collectivity, the established from the possible, top-down from bottom-up, or educator from learner. When we erase the lines that have separated these forms, we are left with embedded and iterative phenomena that are rich in possibility and, as far as we can tell, limitless in their potential (Kurzweil 2005).

REFERENCES

Barabási, A.-L. 2002. *Linked: How everything is connected to everything else and what it means for business, science, and everyday life.* New York, Penguin, 2002.

Bruner, J. 1960. *The process of education.* Cambridge, MA: Cambridge University Press.

Davis, B., and E. Simmt. 2003. Understanding learning systems: Mathematics education and complexity science. *Journal for Research in Mathematics Education* 34: 137–67.

———. (in press). Mathematics-for-teaching: An ongoing investigation of the mathematics teachers (need to) know. *Educational Studies in Mathematics*.

Davis, B., and D. Sumara. 2006. *Complexity and education: Inquiries into learning, teaching, and research*. Mahwah, NJ: Lawrence Erlbaum.

Kurzweil, R. 2005. *The singularity is near: When humans transcend biology*. New York: Viking.

Lakoff, G., and M. Johnson. 1999. *Philosophy in the flesh: The embodied mind and its challenge to Western thought*. New York: Basic Books.

Mazur, B. 2003. *Imagining numbers (particularly the square root of minus fifteen)*. New York: Farrar, Straus and Giroux.

Stewart, I. 1998. *Life's other secret: The new mathematics of the living world*. Cambridge: Cambridge University Press.

NOTES

1. Other recursively elaborative ways can define the relationships among these sets, including, for example, the incorporation of new metaphors or the development of definitions based on points on a number line.

2. A node in this sort of image is an agent or event that contributes to the emergence of a complex unity. For example, a person might be a node in a social collective, which in turn might be a node in a political systems, and so on.

CONCLUSIONS AND CONTINUED BEGINNINGS: APPLICATION OF THE SYSTEMIC FACTORS INVENTORY ANALYSIS MATRIX

Blane Després

The purpose of this final chapter is to present and apply the systemic factors inventory analysis (SyFIA) matrix (to maximize understanding of the matrix refer to figure 12.1). The SyFIA serves a dual purpose here. First, it affords the leader advocating change an opportunity to determine what are all the attending factors for any given organizational structure or event. By *factors*, I mean the pertinent and directly linked parts or variables of an event.[1] It is a tool that better enables diagnosis and analysis. For that reason, educational leaders advocating change will want to use the SyFIA to ensure that sustained improvements, policy decisions, best practices, or whatever the event are positioned within a truly systemic framework. Second, I use it here to demonstrate where the contributions in this book lie in relation to each other (see figure 12.2). To situate the SyFIA as an ideal, first tool for change leaders, some preparatory details are necessary in the form of the role of systemic thinking in education, background, and perceptions.

SYSTEMIC THINKING IN EDUCATION

Betts (1992) explains five key areas in education that thwart systemic change and the application of systemic thinking in education. He says systemic reform in education has been hampered because of "the piece-meal, or incremental, approach; failure to integrate solution ideas; a dis-cipline-by-discipline study of education; a reductionist orientation; [and] staying within the boundaries of the existing system (not thinking out of the box)" (38). As a partial response to the need for a more systemic ap-proach to education systems, Garmston and Wellman (1995) insisted that the developments in science, specifically "quantum mechanics, chaos theory, complexity theory, fractal geometry, and the new biology . . . can help educators rethink their approaches to school improvement and work in new ways within the principles suggested by these sciences" (6).

In a discussion about the application of systemic thinking in educa-tion, Peter Senge challenged schools—and school districts as a system—as learning organizations (in O'Neil 1995 20), an irony given the nature of what education systems stand for. Sanders and McCabe (2003) tell us that, "To be effective, an organization must learn to think and act as one coherent yet flexible system with a high degree of communication, co-operation and collaboration among its networks" (10). Similarly, accord-ing to Zemke (1999), a learning organization comprises "people [who] continually expand their capacity to create the results they truly desire, where new and expansive patterns of thinking are nurtured, where col-lective aspiration is set free, and where people are continually learning how to learn together" (49; see also Zmuda, Kuklis, and Kline 2004).

A crucial reason for the failure for schools to become learning organi-zations has to do with the structure and purposes of schools, such as the isolationism and the political nature of formal education. Marion (2002) claims that, "One often cannot change a system by pushing it to do better [e.g., accountability, government legislation]; rather, one changes a system by finding leverage points that remove barriers to growth and improve-ment." (325). Further Marion wrote, "'Learning disabled' organizations have difficulty thinking systemically. Such organizations focus on localized events rather than the systemic implications of behaviors" (323). That spirit of learning together in the complexity of education forms the impe-tus in large part for the work of the contributors in this book.

Perhaps a conundrum in formal education is not the individual factors that contribute to its problems or that inhibit systemwide reform, but how best to manage or understand the critical mass of factors that per-plex participants, leaders, and stakeholders in education. If a districtwide education system, or any organizational system, is to become a proactive learning organization (assuming that practitioners want that), then a means of recognizing and analyzing the systemic factors that contribute to or influence that system is crucial.

Systemic Thinking Background

The foundations of systemic thinking came into being in the 1930s and 1940s largely as a result of open-systems theory, which challenged the closed-systems view of things in biology and the sciences. Seeing organisms as interrelated and forming complex associations, a growing group of scientists led by scientist Ludwig von Bertalanffy, began to expand their scientific view of the world to include systemic factors. Their open-systems theory developed into what they called *general system theory*. Complexity theory developed from general system theory in the early part of the 1990s. Complexity theory, said Flood (1999), "appreciates the world as a whole, comprising many, many interrelationships expressed in endless occurrences of spontaneous self-organization" (2).

A differentiation must be made between systemic thinking and reductionistic thinking. The reductionistic approach to understanding the world by examining its parts is limited in the information that it provides. Breaking a system down into its constituent parts assumes better understanding of the whole but, one argument goes, only leads to a better understanding of the elements. Systemic thinking stands against reductionism by demanding not only that we examine an event itself, but also the contextual and relational environment of that event.

Flood (1999), in his study on organizations, described systemic thinking as follows:

> Systemic thinking explores things as whole and is highly relevant . . . because the world exhibits qualities of wholeness. These qualities of wholeness relate to every aspect of our lives—at work and at home. . . . Life events can be made sense of in a meaningful way only in the knowledge that our actions contribute to patterns of interrelated actions. . . . The world is whole and the whole is complex. It is increasingly complex with more and more information, intense interdependency, and relentless change. (13)

K–12 education comprises, among other systemic factors, a highly complex organization that necessitates a systems approach to its problems and operations. However, it also suffers from a paucity of systemic thinking applications in practice. Because K–12 education is a social system, I found Jackson's (2003) ideas an appropriate fit in this discussion. In his review of systems thinking, Jackson highlighted four common paradigms in use in social theory today. These are:

- The functionalist paradigm.
- The interpretive paradigm.
- The emancipatory paradigm.
- The postmodern paradigm (38).

The functionalist paradigm "wants to ensure that everything in the system is functioning well so as to promote efficiency, adaptation and survival (38). The interpretive paradigm "believes social systems, such as organizations, result from the purposes people have and that these, in turn, stem from the interpretations they make of the situations in which they find themselves" (38ff). The emancipatory paradigm "is concerned to 'emancipate' oppressed individuals and groups in organizations and society" (39). And the postmodern paradigm "opposes 'modernist' rationality that it sees as present in all the other three paradigms" (39). According to Jackson, these paradigms stand in an interpretive relation to nine metaphors or "images of organizations," in some cases mixing together depending on the particular paradigm:

- Organizations as machines.
- Organizations as organisms.
- Organizations as brains.
- Organizations as flux and transformation.
- Organizations as cultures.
- Organizations as political systems.
- Organizations as psychic prisons.
- Organizations as instruments of domination.
- Organizations as carnivals (34).

These are interesting metaphors and, in retorospect, I have seen all of those metaphors at one point or another in kindergarten through twelfth grade education and beyond throughout my experience. But unlike other social organizations K–12 education is rendered even more complex by the additional factors of adolescents, student-to-instructor and person-to-space ratios, the relationship of school architecture to learning, funding, timed schedules, curriculum development, parental involvement, the perceptions of the participants and stakeholders concerning education purposes, and the disparity between research and practice in the field. Given Jackson's (2003) metaphors and paradigms along with the added complex nature of education, perhaps it comes as no surprise when Garmston and Wellman (1995), for example, claim that the "high school . . . serves as a striking form of an adapted—not adaptive—organism. Designed in another time, for the purposes of that time, the typical high school often shows a remarkable lack of flexibility" (6). Why that might be so is perhaps better to be determined by a more comprehensive method of analysis and interpretation. Being adaptive in a highly complex environment—which K–12 education is—requires a certain buy-in by leaders and educators. Add to that the SyFIA as a means to locate the blockers to change.

Perceptions

A major problem set that besets formal education is that it suffers from divergent perceptions of its systemic purposes and form in society. Another major problem set is that education also suffers from limited or imperceptible change (e.g., Cuban 1984; Marshall and Tucker 1992). Contenta (1993) mentioned other factors regarding change and resistance in education:

> Our natural tendency to retreat in the face of change is reinforced by a nostalgia for a simpler time and a refusal to look beyond the mythologies that blind us. As our fear of change grows, we pressure schools to preserve a culture that's busy charting its own progress, or ruin. The economy becomes the main concern, not only because profits keep business happy and re-elect governments, but also because the economy has for centuries served as the litmus test for quality of life. And so, in looking forward and falling back, we bombard schools with mixed . . . messages while beefing up the hidden curriculum. In the end, the status quo and its blinding mythology of economic progress are reinforced. (191)

Pourdavood, Cowen, and Svec (1999) note, "Little is known about how educators experience and lead complex change in an organizational culture which has historically resisted and hindered major reform." Marion (2002) suggests that, "legislatures have a tough time making inroads into educational behavior because of the significant infrastructure that supports the current way of educating" (354). There are other problems of course, such as funding, international comparisons of achievements, and so on (Després 2003a; 2003b; Organization for Economic Cooperation and Development 1997), but I believe those problems are subfactors of the two major problem sets introduced previously.

In the case of the first problem set, there is a series of questions that need to be raised and answers sought, questions about the purposes of education in an information society, or education stakeholders' perceptions of the purposes of education, or the reasons for the purposes as they exist and how they are being achieved. At the same time, the factors of the system in question that give shape to the purposes along with the environment, or setting (physical, geographical, spatial), need to be examined followed by the infrastructure. Granted, the SyFIA consists of many questions (many more than shown in this chapter) and more questions arise as a result of the initial questioning. Resistance to adaptive change—which speaks to the second problem set mentioned—really results from alternative (personal desires running contrary to) or misperceptions of the systemic purposes. It is not the seeming infinity of questions and permutations of change possibilities that stymie systemic thinking. As answers are (re)formulated a clearer picture of the system and perceptions of it emerges. The acknowledgement that systems and life events are dynamic, and resist stasis is a beginning place allowing for a more adaptive environment in which learning and change are fostered and encouraged (see Emery 1999).

SYSTEMIC METACLUSTERS AND SYSTEMIC FACTORS INVENTORY ANALYSIS MATRIX

The SyFIA (Després 2003a, 2003b; 2004; 2005; 2006; see figure 12.1) is a tool designed to expose the congruity and discord or tensions between the metacategories, or systemic clusters (purposes, form and design, and

Systemic Clusters / Factors Categories	PURPOSES Conceptual-Ideal: Mission or goals, participants	FORM/DESIGN Creative-Explicit: Shape or form, site or setting	INFRASTRUCTURE Function-Practical: Governance, resources, timelines, actions
1 Philosophical Moral, epistemological, & metaphysical rationale	1.1.a Examine the foundations of the choice of purposes. 1.1.b Explore why those purposes are desired. 1.1.c Explore purposes as a function of desire.	1.2.a Explore the creative responses and what form/design ideas arise as a result of purposes. 1.2.b Explore why a particular form/design is desired.	1.3.a Examine the governance, actions, and timeframe articulation as logical outcomes of purposes and form/design. 1.3.b Explore how purposes are articulated practically. 1.3.c Examine the formal and informal steps that lead from purposes, to the particular shape of form/design and site, to practical actions. 1.3.d Examine resources to ensure achievement.

Figure 12.1. Systemic factors inventory analysis (SyFIA) matrix

Systemic Clusters **2** / Factors Categories	PURPOSES Conceptual–Ideal: Mission or goals, participants	FORM/DESIGN Creative–Explicit: Shape or form, site or setting	INFRASTRUCTURE Function–Practical: Governance, resources, timelines, actions
Personal cost or impact & well-being Emotional / Physical / Spiritual	2.1.a Explore personal cost of particular purposes and choices desired. What are the personal benefits? 2.1.b Examine the long-term physical/emotional/spiritual cost or impact on the individual and organization. 2.1.c Examine stakeholders' and participants' perceptions of, and responses to, the purposes. 2.1.d Examine how best to accommodate the variety of perceptions in the mission and goals at the personal level.	2.2.a Examine the physical/emotional/spiritual effects of the form/design on participants and the organization. 2.2.b Examine the form/design as a function of needs and perceptions of purposes on the individual level.	2.3.a Examine the real and perceived effects of the timeframes, actions and governance as functions of purposes and the form/design on the individual level. 2.3.b Explore what talents, gifts, or skills are necessary to achieve the purposes. 2.3.c Explore allocated resources as adequate response to all needs. 2.3.d (Post) Examine the proximity to or alignment between purposes practiced (actual state), originally conceived (initial state), and desired (ideal state).

Figure 12.1. (continued)

Systemic Clusters		PURPOSES	FORM/DESIGN	INFRASTRUCTURE
		Conceptual–Ideal: Mission or goals, participants	Creative–Explicit: Shape or form, site or setting	Function–Practical: Governance, resources, timelines, actions
3	**Factors Categories**	3.1.a (Smitherman & Stringer) 3.1.b (Smitherman & Stringer) 3.1.c	3.2.a (Duffy); Reigeluth; (Thornton & Perreault); Adelman & Taylor; (Bower); (Smitherman & Stringer); (Barnhardt & Kawagley) 3.2.b Thornton & Perreault; Adelman & Taylor; (Barnhardt & Kawagley) 3.2.c Duffy; Barnhardt & Kawagley	3.3.a Duffy; (Thornton & Perreault); (Adelman & Taylor); (Alsbury); (Smitherman & Stringer); (Stuntz, Potash & Heinbokel); (Barnhardt & Kawagley); (Davis)
	Community / Global	Socio-political cost or impact		

Figure 12.1. (continuted)

infrastructure[2]), and the principal factors categories. The factors categories comprise philosophical questions (moral, metaphysical, and epistemological rationale), emotional, physical, and spiritual questions (personal cost or impact and well-being), and community or global questions (sociopolitical cost or impact; Després 2004; 2005). Conducting a SyFIA will ensure that the factors and, vitally important, the participants' perceptions of those factors are exposed. This activity serves to initiate change dialogue, a far more productive beginning place than either reacting to symptoms (exposed as discordant systemic factors and subfactors) or attempting change in some of the factors as causal or relational links as if this would be appreciated or effective system wide.

The three systemic clusters, corral, so to speak, related crucial factors and elements of an organization or event. These systemic clusters are purposes, form and design, and infrastructure, which are comprised of factors and subfactors, which are further defined via the factors categories. The clusters provide us with an organized view of the crucial or driving factors in an event. That is, if an event were to be merely examined under these three metaclusters, leaders advocating change would be able to see, on a horizontal, linear plane, how the key factors align with each other. For example, the stated organizational purposes should logically lead to an appropriate form or design that, in turn, leads into a particular infrastructure that "animates" the purposes and the form and design.

The application of the SyFIA, which includes the metaclusters and the factors categories, helps to expose the philosophical, the personal, and the community or global factors and subfactors[3] pertinent or related to the event. Arguably, it would be beneficial to be able to seek patterns, or archetypes, which could afford comparative or more revealing qualities and characteristics of an event even to determine if that event is functioning optimally or whether change is necessary or even feasible. Also, as the term implies, these systemic clusters are conjoined and interactive, and therefore resist linear or piecemeal responses. The vertical orientation of the clusters indicates their permeating qualities throughout an event. In comparison, the factors categories extent horizontally across the clusters, which helps to refine nuances and subfactors. Keep in mind that despite its rigid appearance, the function of the matrix as a tool is more enabling of understanding the complexity of an event and, therefore, to better determine appropriate responses.

Procedure

The SyFIA is currently structured in two formats for use. As a change leader attempting, for example, to comprehend systemically an already-established event, I must work that event through the SyFIA leaders guide (figure 12.1) that presents the crucial questions and imperatives for each of the metaclusters and factors categories. A second format, the SyFIA response template (available through consultation), collects (corrals is a more suitable image) the elicited responses from the leaders guide.

The purposes cluster encompasses the factors of goals, or missions, objectives, and participants in a system. This cluster responds to questions of what the desired goals are and why those ones, who will be the participants that enjoy and instigate those goals or for whom or what the purposes are determined, and the participants' roles and status. It is helpful to revisit the purposes cluster regularly to ensure that what was originally espoused is still current and desired. And as the purposes are being formulated, one must keep in mind how those purposes might be articulated or their form and design. The form and design cluster comprises the factors of organizational image, protocol, regulative principles, dimensions, and site and place, or geographic setting. The infrastructure cluster is concerned with the factors of governance, resources, time frames and actions, or processes. This cluster articulates the means of, or steps to, achieving and sustaining the systemic purposes according to the particular form or design.

In turn, the factors categories of the SyFIA matrix (the left-hand column; refer to figure 12.1)—philosophical, emotional, physical, and spiritual, and social—provide further refinement of the questions needed to be asked to achieve as complete an understanding of an event.[4] The three systemic factors clusters provide a quick view of the interrelationship of the crucial factors of an event. Are the factors, the particular components beneath each of these clusters, compatible with one another vertically and horizontally? That is, are all the factors that pertain to an event congruent? Do they logically follow and continue to foster the necessary interrelationship that enables longevity, sustainable progress or success? Where there is a discrepancy between the clusters factors and factors categories, problems will arise or be highlighted. In a postanalysis, the SyFIA will expose those factors that thwart growth and sustainability. Applied in this field guide the SyFIA will help to determine the degree to which contributions are congruent with one another and with other systemic relationships as well as provide a perspective of what more is needed for educational change.

For each of the factors categories, a series of overarching questions further guides the analysis along with the imperatives found in each of the matrix cells. The "philosophical" category of factors seeks to understand:

1) What values are assumed or explicit?
2) Is bridging possible between contrary values or is compromise necessary? What compromises are suggested or implied? How are these contrary values or compromises accommodated for, and by, participants?
3) What are the worldviews expressed by the participants? What dialogue is necessary to ensure mutual respect and continuation?
4) What is the raison d'être for the choices of purposes, form and design and infrastructure?
5) What are the apparent or perceived ambiguities? How are these ambiguities accommodated for, and by, participants?

The "emotional/physical/spiritual" category of factors seeks to understand:

1) Why do this? What do I get, or what benefits accrue to me?
2) What is the personal cost to me and what is the impact on my well-being?
3) Are the explicit or implied worldview and values acceptable to me? Will compromise be necessary and are the conditions acceptable to me?
4) What is necessary to ensure mutual respect and continuation?
5) Are the apparent or perceived ambiguities acceptable, tolerable, or accommodated for, and by, me?

The "community/global" category of factors seeks to understand:

1) What benefits accrue to the community, organization, or beyond?
2) What are the sociopolitical, health, environmental, and economic impacts on, or cost to, the community, organization, and beyond?

3) What are the responsibilities of participants, stakeholders, and decision makers?

Set up as a three-by-three matrix,[5] each of the cells contains further guiding questions phrased as imperatives aimed at uncovering some of the
deeper-seated aspects of a system. In this way, we begin to see the immediate and long-term problem areas and draw attention to those problem areas in need of discussion toward creative responses and solutions.

Drawing from Flood (1999) and Emery's (1999) works, the metaclusters help to build "holistic pictures of social settings [and suggest] systemic ways of coping with them that challenge the very idea of problems,
solutions, and normal organizational life" (Flood, 6). Emery explains
open-systems thinking—from which the SyFIA has emergedi—as:

> Open-systems thinking is quite different from linear causal or relational
> thinking [which, by the way, seem to make such good sense when analyz-
> ing or responding to problems]. In causal thinking and research the task
> is to single out, from a multitude of data, pairs of acts between which
> there is a necessary connection. In systems thinking, the task is not to find
> direct relations between items but to find the super-ordinate system in
> which they are connected to define their positional value within such a
> system (ci8).
>
> The task then of an open-systems thinker becomes that of identifying
> the system principle, that which generates, organizes and gives meaning
> to the system, and also to the set of lawful relations which exist in the to-
> tality of the system-environment complex. *Until this total set of lawful re-
> lations is understood, methods and strategies for diffusion will be inade-
> quate.* (emphasis added, p. 8)

It is Emery's claim that needs to be emphasized and which expresses
well the rationale for the SyFIA.

CONTINUED BEGINNINGS

Figure 12.1 presents an overview of the SyFIA coupled with the overarching questions. Figure 12.2 depicts where the contributors' works in
this book could be situated. The intent is to stimulate further dialogue

about systemic thinking applications and missing points, how to complete a genuinely holistic and comprehensive view of a system so that needed change areas could be exposed. It also is meant to catalyze a community of change leaders and the new "systems thinkers in action" to continue the important work of applying systems thinking in education both to affect necessary changes and to educate the community about the complex nature of bringing adolescents and formal education together.

Figure 12.2 also sheds light where education leaders, practitioners and researchers could continue on with further explorations and directions especially from a crucial systems-thinking beginning point. Perhaps it is not so much a matter of filling in the holes in the matrix as it is an opportunity to work arm-in-arm to achieve the best possible education system. Complete the contributors' matrix yourself as you reflect through this book or as you contemplate other writings to expose the pertinent and critical factors, what the foci are as well as where the "holes" lay. Visually, figure 12.1 illuminates the complexity of K–12 education and the enormity of the task of any reform efforts. Figure 12.2 gives us a glimpse of current thinking and practices from just a few areas around North America and how, even in the context of thinking and acting systemically, ensuring as broad a perspective as possible is a tremendous challenge not for the faint at heart.

Outside organizational systems need to recognize that although education arguably is in great need of reform, there are a number of attending, systemic factors demanding consideration. Identifying the systemic clusters in education demands more than deliberate or official statements. Whose needs are being represented, for example? What should we do when "visions of a better, more democratic and egalitarian world" (Ornstein 1995) are contrary to the feelings and beliefs of others, or what if the visions are myopic? Whose "oughts" and "shoulds" deserve privileging and why? These questions and the research of their answers are part of the SyFIA work. Also, what Pai and Adler (1997) have raised is how the problem of establishing education purposes—as just one set of factors—is rendered more complex through people's perceptions of them, and how they are achieved or pursued in the social ethos and practices of the practitioners.[6] The diversity of perceptions, which can so easily lead to problems, demands a robust, systemic analysis. In

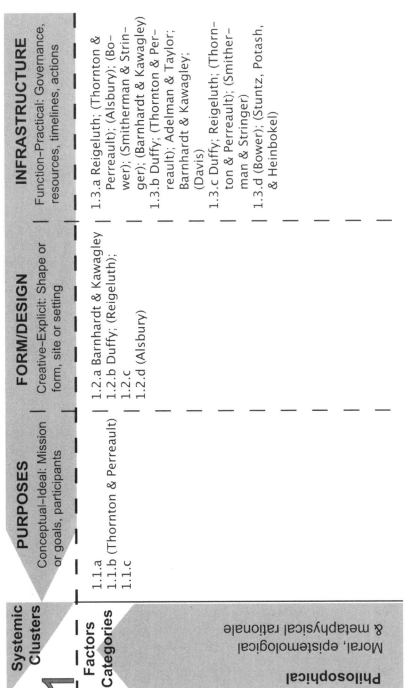

Figure 12.2. **SyFIA** populated with contributors' chapters

Systemic Clusters 2	PURPOSES Conceptual–Ideal: Mission or goals, participants	FORM/DESIGN Creative–Explicit: Shape or form, site or setting	INFRASTRUCTURE Function–Practical: Governance, resources, timelines, actions
Factors Categories Emotional / Physical / Spiritual Personal cost or impact & well-being	2.1.a 2.1.b Duffy; (Stuntz, Potash & Heinbokel); Barnhardt & Kawagley 2.1.c Duffy 2.1.d	2.2.a Barnhardt & Kawagley 2.2.b Thornton & Perreault; Adelman & Taylor; (Stuntz, Potash & Heinbokel)	2.3.a (Reigeluth); Thornton & Perreault; Adelman & Taylor; Alsbury; Bower; (Stuntz, Potash & Heinbokel); Barnhardt & Kawagley 2.3.b Duffy; Thornton & Perreault; Bower; (Smitherman & Stringer); (Stuntz, Potash & Heinbokel); (Davis) 2.3.c 2.3.d

Figure 12.2. (continued)

Systemic Clusters **3**	PURPOSES Conceptual-Ideal: Mission or goals, participants	FORM/DESIGN Creative-Explicit: Shape or form, site or setting	INFRASTRUCTURE Function-Practical: Governance, resources, timelines, actions
Factors Categories Socio-political cost or impact **Community / Global**	3.1.a (Smitherman & Stringer) 3.1.b (Smitherman & Stringer) 3.1.c	3.2.a (Duffy); Reigeluth; (Thornton & Perreault); Adelman & Taylor; (Bower); (Smitherman & Stringer); (Barnhardt & Kawagley) 3.2.b Thornton & Perreault; Adelman & Taylor; (Barnhardt & Kawagley) 3.2.c Duffy; Barnhardt & Kawagley	3.3.a Duffy; (Thornton & Perreault); (Adelman & Taylor); (Alsbury); (Smitherman & Stringer); (Stuntz, Potash & Heinbokel); (Barnhardt & Kawagley); (Davis)

Figure 12.2. (continued)

this way the diversity of perceptions can be mapped and reviewed. Indeed, until a SyFIA is undertaken, the participants and stakeholders risk hitting on the various factors without understanding their relationship to, or repercussions in, the whole system.

Although there have been developments in systemic-thinking applications over the past three decades (e.g., Allen and Cherrey 2000; Baker and Richards 2004; Checkland 1999; Collen 2003; Fullan 2005; Jackson 2003; Kay and Bawden 2006; Midgley 2000; von Bartalanffy 1981; Weinberg 1975), a means of determining and analyzing the crucial factors that comprise a problem in a cohesive and articulated framework is lacking. Certainly, adequate programs can be used to map out the range of factors contributing to or challenging an organization's life. Jackson's (2003) "creative holism" (274ff), for example—and toward which the SyFIA leans heavily—is an attempt to provide a far more penetrating understanding. Bringing into the light the diverse factors surrounding an event or organizational system is far more enabling both for better comprehension of the system or event and for prognosticating possible solutions, alternative responses, and affirmations.

REFERENCES

Allen, K. E., and C. Cherrey. 2000. *Systemic leadership: Enriching the meaning of our work*. Lanham, MD: University Press of America.

Baker, B. D., and C. E. Richards. 2004. *The ecology of educational systems: Data, models, and tools for improvisational leading and learning*. Columbus, OH: Pearson.

Betts, F. 1992. How systems thinking applies to education. *Educational Leadership* 50 (November): 38–41.

Checkland, P. 1999. *Systems thinking, systems practice*. West Sussex, UK: John Wiley & Sons.

Collen, A. 2003. *Systemic change through praxis and inquiry*. New Brunswick, NJ: Transaction.

Contenta, S. 1993. *Rituals of failure: What schools really teach*. Toronto: Between the Lines.

Cuban, L. 1984. *How teachers taught: Constancy and change in American classrooms, 1890–1980*. New York: Grove.

Després, B. 2003a. Cultures in tension: Perceptions of business and education in partnership. Paper presented at the UNESCO Conference on Intercultural Education: Teaching and Learning for Intercultural Understanding, Human Rights and a Culture of Peace, Jyväskylä, Finland.

———. 2003b. Systems in tension: Perceptions of business and education in partnership. Unpublished Ph.D. dissertation, University of British Columbia, Vancouver, Canada.

———. 2004. Systemic thinking and education leadership: Some considerations. *International Electronic Journal for Leadership in Learning*, 8 (7), www.ucalgary.ca/~iejll/

———. April 2005. Introduction to the SyFIA (Systemic Factors Inventory Analysis) matrix: A meta-analysis tool for understanding complexity. Paper presented at the American Education Research Association Annual Meeting, Montréal.

———. 2006. Toward a perfect university, part 1: Corporate reality or Descartian dilemma? Paper presented at the annual meeting of the American Education Research Association, San Francisco.

Emery, M. 1999. *Searching: The theory and practice of making cultural change.* Amsterdam: John Benjamins.

Flood, R. L. 1999. *Rethinking the fifth discipline: Learning within the unknowable.* London: Routledge.

Fullan, M. 2005. *Leadership and sustainability: System thinkers in action.* Thousand Oaks, CA: Corwin Press.

Garmston, R., and B. Wellman. 1995. Adaptive schools in a quantum universe. *Educational Leadership* 52 (April): 6–12.

Jackson, M. C. 2003. *Systems thinking: Creative holism for managers.* West Sussex: John Wiley & Sons.

Kay, R., and R. Bawden. 2006. Learning to be systemic: Some reflections from a learning organization. *The Learning Organization* 3 (5): 18–25.

Marion, R. 2002. *Leadership in education: Organizational theory for the practitioner.* Upper Saddle River, NJ: Pearson Education.

Marshall, R., and M. Tucker. 1992. *Thinking for a living: Work, skills, and the future of the American economy.* New York: BasicBooks.

Midgley, G. *Systemic intervention: Philosophy, methodology, and practice.* New York: Kluwer Academic/Plenum, 2000.

O'Neil, J. 1995. On schools as learning organizations: A conversation with Peter Senge. *Education Leadership*, 52(7), 20–23.

Organization for Economic Co-operation and Development. 1997. Sustainable flexibility: A prospective study on work, family and society in the information age, *OECD Working Papers* V (29), OECD, Paris.

Ornstein, A. C. (Ed.). 1995. *Teaching: Theory into practice.* Boston, MA: Allyn & Bacon.

Pai, Y., and S. Adler. 1997. *Cultural foundations of education*, 2nd ed. Upper Saddle River, NJ: Merrill/Prentice Hall.

Pourdavood, R. G., L. M. Cowen, and L. V. Svec. 1999. *Complexity of school reform: Order and chaos.* Paper presented at the annual meeting of the American Educational Research Association, Montreal.

Sanders, T. I. and McCabe, J. A. 2003. The Use of Complexity Science: A Survey of Federal Departments and Agencies, Private Foundations, Universities and Independent Education and Research Centers. A report prepared for the U.S. Department of Education. http://www.complexsys.org Accessed July 21, 2007.

von Bertalanffy, L. 1981. *A systems view of man,* ed. P. A. LaViolette. Boulder, CO: Westview Press.

Weinberg, G. M. 1975. *An introduction to general systems thinking.* New York: John Wiley & Sons.

Zemke, R. 1999. Why organizations still aren't learning. *Training* 36 (September): 40–49.

Zmuda, A., R. Kuklis, and E. Kline. 2004. *Transforming schools: Creating a culture of continuous improvement.* Alexandra, VA: ASCD.

NOTES

1. Event is being employed here to comprise a definable whole under scrutiny, be it an organizational structure (e.g., school district, business, department or group, governing body, etc.), organizing principles (e.g., legislation, bill, governance guidelines, curriculum, etc.), action (e.g., articulated principles, practices, etc.), or any combination of these three.

2. Betts (1992) explains systems in terms of openness and "characterized by three important concepts: hierarchy, homeostasis, and purposiveness" (39). I would argue that the SyFIA metaclusters accommodate these concepts, or characteristics, by broadening the scope of view which provides a genuinely systemic perspective.

3. Or variables or parts or elements. These designations are, for the purposes of the SyFIA, interchangeable because regardless, they will be exposed through the matrix.

4. I have employed the SyFIA response template even with students to help them as they critiqued literature articles to determine the focus and missing factors. By doing so, students were better prepared to discuss the limitations, for example, of research or ideas.

5. Three systemic clusters across by three factors categories down. The systemic clusters are further divided into declared and perceived columns (in the

SyFIA response template) to see the articulated factors or properties against those perceived by participants or stakeholders. The infrastructure cluster is also further divided into its four constituent parts: governance, timelines, resources, and actions.

6. In the full model of the SyFIA, I incorporate columns that indicate the "declared" and the "perceived" to show another layer of complexity that needs to be dealt with.

INDEX

ABOUT THE CONTRIBUTORS

Michael Fullan is the former dean of the Ontario Institute for Studies in Education of the University of Toronto. Recognized as an international authority on educational reform, Michael is engaged in training, consulting, and evaluating change projects around the world. His ideas for managing change are used in many countries, and his books have been published in many languages.

Fullan led the evaluation team which conducted the four-year assessment of the National Literacy and Numeracy Strategy in England from 1998 to 2003. In April 2004, he was appointed special advisor to the Premier and Minister of Education in Ontario.

His widely acclaimed books include: *What's Worth Fighting For* trilogy (with Andy Hargreaves); *Change Forces* trilogy; *The New Meaning of Educational Change*; *Leading in a Culture of Change*, which was awarded the 2002 Book of the Year Award by the National Staff Development Council; *The Moral Imperative of School Leadership*; and *Leadership and Sustainability: System Thinkers in Action*.

Francis Duffy is a professor of Change Leadership in Education at Gallaudet University. He is also the founding editor of Rowman and Littlefield's Leading Systemic School Improvement Series. He has published eight books on creating and leading systemic school improvement, the most recent being *Strategic Communication during Whole-System Change: Advice and Guidance for School District Leaders and PR Specialists*, which was coauthored with Dr. Patti Chance from the University of Nevada, Las Vegas. Frank was also a 2002–2003 Education Policy Fellow with the Institute for Educational Leadership in Washington, D.C., and he held an honorary faculty position in the Harvard Graduate School of Education that was sponsored by professor Chris Argyris.

Charlie Reigeluth has a B.A. in economics from Harvard University and a Ph.D. in instructional psychology from Brigham Young University. He taught high school science for three years. He has been a professor in the Instructional Systems Technology Department at Indiana University since 1988, and was chairman of the department for three years. He cofounded the Council for Systemic Change in the Association for Educational Communications and Technology and founded the Restructuring Support Service at Indiana University. He has worked with several school districts to facilitate their systemic change efforts. He served on the Indiana Department of Education Restructuring Task Force. He has been facilitating a systemic change effort in a small school district in Indianapolis since January 2001 and is using that as an opportunity to develop more knowledge about a guidance system for transforming public education.

Bill Thornton teaches in the Department of Educational Leadership at the University of Nevada and has served on the faculty of Idaho State University. He has worked as principal, director, superintendent, and county administrator in Nebraska, Colorado, and Washington. His research interests include organizational change, program evaluation, and systems thinking. He also serves on the editorial board of two national journals.

George Perreault teaches in the Department of Educational Leadership at the University of Nevada. He previously served as a principal and superintendent in Florida and New Mexico and on the faculty of New Mexico Highlands University, Gonzaga University, and East Carolina University. He has published numerous professional articles and has authored or coauthored seven books, including *The Changing World of School Administration*. In addition, he is associate editor of the *Journal of School Public Relations* and serves on the editorial board of two other national journals.

Howard Adelman is a professor of psychology and codirector of the School Mental Health Project and its Center for Mental Health in Schools at UCLA. His research and teaching focuses on youngsters in school settings who manifest learning, behavior, and emotional problems. In recent years, he has been involved in systemic reforms to enhance school and community efforts to address barriers to learning and enhance healthy development.

Linda Taylor is codirector of the School Mental Health Project and its Center for Mental Health in Schools at UCLA. Previously, she served for thirteen years as assistant director of the Fernald Laboratory School and Clinic at UCLA and then for fourteen years worked with the Los Angeles Unified School District. Throughout her career, she has focused on a wide range of psychosocial, mental health, and educational concerns. Currently, she is involved with systemic reform initiatives designed to weave school and community efforts together more effectively to address barriers to learning and enhance healthy development.

Tom Alsbury is currently assistant professor of Educational Administration in the Department of Educational Leadership and Policy Studies at North Carolina State University. Tom previously spent eighteen years as a high school biology and chemistry teacher and kindergarten through twelfth grade principal. His current line of research is in organizational theory, the superintendency, and school board governance and has also assisted in the development of university leadership programs in the United Arab Emirates and Berlin, Germany.

David F. Bower is an assistant professor of middle childhood teacher education in the College of Education at Ohio University. He completed his Doctor of Education in Educational Leadership at the University of New Mexico in May 2003. He received his M.A. degree in Educational Administration from University of New Mexico in 1996 and holds a B.A.

degree in English, Theater Arts, and Education from Grove City College in Pennsylvania. He was a high school English and drama teacher for twenty years and is a former principal of Roosevelt Middle School in Albuquerque. His professional affiliations include the National Middle School Association, the Coalition of Essential Schools, and the American Educational Research Association. Research interests include teacher preparation, quality, and leadership; chaos and complexity theory as applied to schools and organizations; learning community dynamics; and middle childhood education. His work with the Ohio University Appalachian Learning community may be found at: http://appalachia.citl.ohiou.edu/.

Sarah Smitherman Pratt just completed her Ph.D. in Curriculum and Instruction from Louisiana State University after receiving her B.S. in Interdisciplinary Studies from Texas A&M University and M.A. in Mathematics Education from Louisiana State University. She began work as an adjunct professor in the School of Education at University of North Carolina–Greensboro in 2006.

Angelle Stringer received her Ph.D. from Louisiana State University in Curriculum and Instruction through the College of Education after several years as an educator in the public school system in various roles. Stringer is a founding member of Louisiana Violence Prevention Task Force comprised of local and state agencies designed to promote a violence-free schools and communities. In 2002, she joined the staff of Louisiana Resource Center for Educators as Practitioner Teacher Program Director.

Carlos Antonio Torre is currently professor of Education at Southern Connecticut State University. He is an elected member of the Academy of Arts and Sciences of Puerto Rico and was awarded the Academy's *Medal of the Academician*. Through the use of Holter monitors and Recurrence Quantification Analysis (RQA), his research seeks to identify characteristic patterns in the autonomic nervous system associated with specific emotions. His work explores the emotions children experience as they learn and examines how different educational processes and activities mediate the experience of emotions and how these emotions encourage or restrain children's ability to learn.

Charlene Voyce is currently a research associate in the Department of Pediatrics at the Yale School of Medicine. She has a M.A. in public health from the University of North Carolina School of Public Health, Department of Health Behavior and Health Education. Areas of study and practice include school reform, adolescent risk-behavior prevention, and social and emotional learning and education.

Lees N. Stuntz has been the director of the Creative Learning Exchange for fifteen years. She has been a kindergarten through twelfth grade educator for all of her adult life in many volunteer and paid capacities. Her focus is building collaboration and sustainable use of systems thinking and system dynamics in education.

P. Jeffrey Potash is a U.S. religious historian by training, former college professor, and long-term educator with an interest in the use of system dynamics to support student learning. He currently codirects the Educational Modeling Exchange of the Creative Learning Exchange.

John F. Heinbokel is an aquatic ecologist and educator with a particular focus on the role of zooplankton within aquatic food webs and the use of system dynamics to support student learning. He currently codirects the Educational Modeling Exchange of the Creative Learning Exchange.

Ray Barnhardt is a professor of cross-cultural studies at the University of Alaska–Fairbanks, where he has been involved in teaching and research related to Native education issues since 1970. He has served as codirector of the Alaska Rural Systemic Initiative for the past ten years. Over the past thirty-five years, he has also served as the director of the Cross-Cultural Education Development (X-CED) Program, the Small High Schools Project, the Center for Cross-Cultural Studies, and the Alaska Native Knowledge Network. His research interests include indigenous knowledge systems, Native teacher education, distance/distributed/higher education, small school curriculum, and institutional adaptations to rural and cross-cultural settings. His experiences in education beyond Alaska range from teaching mathematics in Baltimore, Maryland, to research in Canada, Iceland, India, Malawi, and New Zealand.

Angayuqaq Oscar Kawagley was born at Mamterilleq, now known as Bethel, Alaska, where he was raised by a grandmother who encouraged him to obtain a Western education, along with the education he received as a Yupiaq child in the camps along the rivers of southwest Alaska. Although this created conflicting values and caused confusion for him for many years, he feels he has come full circle and is researching ways in which Yupiaq language and culture can be used in the classroom to meld the modern ways to the Yupiaq thought world. He has completed four university degrees, including a Ph.D. at the University of British Columbia. He is an associate professor of education at the University of Alaska–Fairbanks and is codirector of the Alaska Rural Systemic Initiative.

Brent Davis is professor and David Robitaille Chair in Mathematics Education at the University of British Columbia. His research is developed around the educational relevance of recent developments in the cognitive and complexity sciences. His most recent book, *Complexity and Education* (co-authored with Dennis Sumara) is an exploration of the emerging influence of complexity thinking on educational research and practice. He has published articles in the areas of mathematics learning and teaching, curriculum theory, teacher education, epistemology, and action research. Davis is currently coeditor of *Complicity: An International Journal of Complexity and Education* and associate editor of *For the Learning of Mathematics*.

Blane Després has a background in teaching French as a second language, gifted and experiential learning (the da Vinci Program) at the secondary level, and has taught many subjects in elementary and middle schools. He also dabbles in poetry writing, and house design and construction. He is currently assistant professor, Faculty of Education, Trades Technology Education at the University of British Columbia in Kelowna, British Columbia. He is actively pursuing research in the following areas: systemic-thinking applications (business–education partnerships, education, leadership), education versus schooling, homeschooling, experiential and alternative learning approaches, architecture, and learning.